574 . . .

T3-BSF-098

Introduction to

HUMAN GEOGRAPHY

D. C. Money, M.A., F.R.G.S.

LONDON
UNIVERSITY TUTORIAL PRESS LTD
9-10 GREAT SUTTON STREET, E.C.1

Published 1954, Reprinted 1955
Second Edition 1957
Third Edition 1960
Fourth Edition 1962
Reprinted (with minor alterations) 1964
Fifth Edition 1968
Reprinted (with minor alterations) 1970
Sixth Edition 1973

ISBN: 0 7231 0610 X

PRINTED IN GREAT BRITAIN BY UNIVERSITY TUTORIAL PRESS LTD
FOXTON, NEAR CAMBRIDGE

Preface

This book provides a necessary link between textbooks which serve the general courses of Geography up to the "O" Level Examinations and the more specialised books and papers which must be referred to in the course of more advanced studies. Emphasis is placed upon the human aspects of Geography, from simple patterns of settlement to the geographical background to modern world problems. Its breadth of coverage will be of particular value to those reading for the General Certificate Examinations at Advanced Level and those taking Diploma Courses in Geography.

The aim is to guide the student towards an appreciation of the many ways in which man and the elements of his natural surroundings affect each other, rather than to provide a mere compendium of geographical knowledge, which would tend to dampen rather than kindle a desire to read more widely and so make use of libraries and geographical journals.

Because the field of study is necessarily wide, and the results of human activities continually changing, particular care has been taken to avoid a dogmatic approach. To this end, each chapter includes, in some detail, a number of examples taken from different parts of the world, each helping to illustrate the theme of the chapter, providing case studies, for example, of various forms of agriculture, situation and layout of villages and towns, and types of boundary problem. There is never exactly the same balance between natural and human features in any two places, no matter how strong their superficial resemblances may be; therefore we cannot say, for instance, that certain conditions *will* produce such and such a type of agriculture—or *will* cause this or that form of settlement to thrive. Thus, while the examples chosen show the relations between men and their natural environment *in the particular cases described,* they are intended to lead to the recognition of similar human-physical relationships in other parts of the world without implying that such relationships *must* exist because of specific environmental circumstances.

There *are* certain patterns of settlement, and similarities in settlement patterns in different parts of the earth's surface, which may be recognised as responses to particular economic circumstances and physical conditions. To analyse complex patterns, geographers seek to acquire quantified data, from personal surveys or secondary sources, and use mathematical techniques to process them. They may well establish significant patterns and their causes, and be able to present these in the form of simple models and maps for geographical information and study.

Unfortunately, this laudable approach is sometimes regarded as being, in itself, "New Geography", and the techniques involved are apt to be seen as ends in themselves. Today, these are essential aids to the study of urban societies and rural-urban relationships, which are apt to be complex. But in Human Geography, which considers the nature and areal distribution of man's many activities, man must firmly be at the centre of our studies, whatever techniques are used to establish the facts.

Many of the problems of the modern world (such as those discussed in Part II) can only be seen in their true perspective if there is knowledge and appreciation of their geographical background. Such knowledge should be the property of anyone who seeks a better understanding of human relations in the world about him, and especially of the large number of students who nowadays travel widely and, at an early age, encounter many of these problems at first hand.

I would like to express my gratitude to Mr A. F. Martin, Mr C. D. Reeve, and Prof. R. W. Steel who kindly read portions of the original text during stages of preparation, and whose criticisms and suggestions were of such great value.

Many other individuals, Government and University Departments, Foreign Embassies, Business Firms, and Agencies provided diagrams and photographs for the illustrations, and due acknowledgement is made wherever such illustrations appear.

Special thanks are due to the Editors of *The Geographical Journal* and *The Geographical Magazine* for putting me in touch with sources of material for the text and illustrations; and to Prof. N. J. G. Pounds, Dr D. F. Thomson, Mr P. H. T. Beckett, and the West Midland Planning Group on Post-War Reconstruction, for placing papers and documents at my disposal, and for allowing me to reproduce tables, diagrams, and photographs.

D.C.M.

Contents

PART I

PART II

PART III

Plates

FRONT   The seas off south-western Sri Lanka teem with fish.   Here
JACKET lines of men laboriously haul in nets dropped off-shore by
PHOTO   local rowing boats.   The government's efforts to mechanise
        fishing will produce more food, but also affect the livelihood
        of these fishermen.

BACK   Beyond the relative sophistication of Paraguay's capital,
JACKET Asuncion, and the river Paraguay stretches the undeveloped
PHOTO   Chaco, with groups of Indians at a bare subsistence level.

                                        [*Photos: D. C. Money*]

PART I

CHAPTER I

MAN AND HIS ENVIRONMENT

In Human Geography we seek to examine those facts of geography which relate directly to Man and his activities, observing both their effects upon him and the results of his own impact on his surroundings. It soon becomes apparent that such geographical facts and their effects on man are virtually innumerable, and even in the smallest area occupied by man they are interwoven with his activities in a great variety of ways.

To understand the full relationship between man and the region in which he lives, we should properly take into account every single part of his environment; for if one single element is altered in any way it may set up a chain of events which will ultimately affect all the others.

Consider, for instance, the possible consequences of deforestation. An indiscriminate destruction of forest cover by get-rich-quick lumbering, without subsequent reafforestation, has taken place in many parts of the world, and has produced striking results (cf. Chapter X) and repercussions which have been far from local. The lack of protective vegetation means that the ground becomes exposed to wind and rain, and the soil cover may be removed. The rain now runs off the land more quickly, so that, with rapid evaporation, the result may be that not enough sinks into the ground to maintain the water-level. Plants, other than the deep-rooted, may perish, and the animals which feed on them migrate. The water-supply of settlements on the same strata, though far removed from the despoiled areas, may similarly suffer, with direct effect upon human occupation. Link by link the chain of effects may extend throughout the region.

Even in a small area, so many factors must be considered that only by making a piecemeal study of very many single environmental elements, or of groups of elements, is it possible, ultimately, to obtain a broad view of the overall effect of environment upon man, or to predict the possible consequences of certain actions on the part of man.

Man is the central figure in Human Geography, and therefore, perhaps, we should first observe the facts of his occupation of the earth's surface—how and where he lives. These are, however, considered in some detail in the chapters which follow, and it is convenient first to draw attention to the ways in which various natural phenomena affect mankind.   Such phenomena do not affect man singly but as part of his general environment, and although countless others have some influence, however remote, upon his activities, we cannot hope even to list, let alone appreciate, them all; many will come to light during

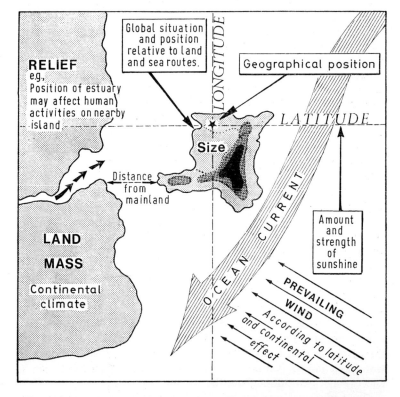

Fig. 1.   *Some elements of the natural environment which are closely connected with the geographical position of a place and with its situation relative to other land and sea areas.   In this case the area considered is a small island whose cross-section is shown in Fig. 2.*

further reading, and the effects of others must be left to the reader's own experience, observations, and perhaps, quantitative investigation, for the collection and analysis of relevant data may enable one to evaluate the significance of various influential factors.

Characteristics of a Natural Region

Consider first those facts which together give a natural region its particular characteristics; for, despite the modifications man may make, such is his background.   Three general facts have great bearing on the character of any region: (a) *Latitude;* (b) *Relief and Structure;* (c) *Situation relative to an ocean or land mass.*   Figs. 1 and 2 show that the individual elements connected with these three facts might combine to create small natural regions within the limits of an imaginary island.

On their interactions depend the types of climate and vegetation. The direction of the prevailing wind in any *latitude,* in conjunction

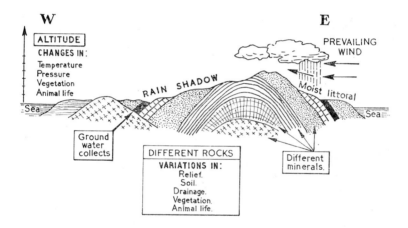

Fig. 2.   *Elements of the natural environment which closely depend on relief and structure, illustrated by a cross-section of the island shown in Fig. 1.*

with a *maritime or continental location,* for instance, affects the rainfall, temperature, and consequently the vegetation, of a region.

Relief, besides influencing the type and amount of rainfall, may be a prime factor in forming an isolated climatic region.   The "continental" nature of the extremes of climate occurring in the Po Valley and the Hungarian Plain, in contrast to their surrounding areas, is caused partly by the relief—in each case, an enclosed plain surrounded by mountains of sufficient height to diminish maritime influences.

The *structure* and nature of the underlying rocks affects the soil, the drainage, and, of course, the relief itself.   In these rocks may lie untapped minerals whose exploitation by man may alter considerably the appearance of the region itself. Clay, gravel, and limestone, for construction; coal, petroleum, and metal ores, for power and industrial development; these and much besides may lie passive, with little noticeable influence upon the region. Through man, the active agent, they become significant.

The mention of exploitation has brought man once more into the scene. His stage is the region, whose broad setting and individual characteristics deeply influence his . activities, often in surprisingly indirect ways. The influence of some of the natural features are examined below. Man himself brings about modifications, and uses the elements of his environment to his own advantage in accordance with his capabilities.

Some Natural Elements and How They Affect Man

Climate.—The climate as a whole plays the principal part in sustaining various types of vegetation, which adapt themselves to the prevailing conditions. Human groups cultivate crops suited climatically to their region: dates in the desert oases, wheat on the temperate grasslands, rice in the monsoon and equatorial lands. Here, however, man's selective powers may come into play, so that climate by no means entirely decides crop distribution, for the most important crops grown in a given region are not necessarily indigenous, nor those best suited climatically. Where many crops could thrive, economic considerations may cause one of them to predominate; witness the concentration on the growth of maize in the Corn Belt of the U.S.A.

Climate directly influences the type of house man builds, the clothes he wears, his mode of transport—whether it be sled, wheeled vehicle, or camel train. So many and so varied are the effects of climate that it will be clearer to outline the influences of its individual elements, leaving to later chapters the more specific examples of their effects upon soil, settlements, and communications.

Temperature. The balance of the natural vegetation is closely related to the temperature regime and individual plant species to precise upper and lower temperature limits. Extremes of temperature directly affect man. Within certain limits the body is able to adjust itself to such extremes; but, even though we create our own local climate, by living in a heated house, or by the use of fans and ice, the hottest and coldest regions of the earth remain distinctly unfavourable for permanent residence.

The physiological effect of air at varying temperatures depends on other weather conditions especially the humidity. Moist equatorial lowlands are more enervating than dry savannahs, though their absolute maximum temperatures and daily ranges are far lower; even a moderately high temperature can be uncomfortable if the humidity is high, and experienced over a long period is debilitating.

In the cooler parts of the middle latitudes, the outdoor temperatures seem to suit mankind well and to provide enough variation to act as a stimulus. But it is within man to respond to all types of climate by making suitable adjustments: with improved types of building and clothing, civilisation has steadily advanced into the colder lands, and this poleward movement of settlers is still continuing. In the extremes of heat, the Indian peasant responds by adjusting his hours of labour to the cooler parts of the day, and in the hot season is on his way to the fields before dawn, taking his rest as the sun climbs overhead.

Extremes of cold or of dry heat are often fatal to plants, particularly at the time of flowering. Frost is a major factor in the control of crop distribution, but like so many natural occurrences it is not wholly adverse in effect. It helps to break up the soil for spring sowing, and kills, or renders dormant, harmful bacteria at a time when human resistance to disease may be low.

Atmospheric Pressure. At altitudes where the pressure and oxygen supply for respiration are much lower than the average there are very noticeable physiological effects, particularly on those unaccustomed to living at heights. Sickness occurs at first, but in a matter of days adjustments take place within the body. With long residence, as in the high settlements of the Andes, human beings not only become accustomed to the conditions but develop increased lung capacity, and a high concentration of haemoglobin in the blood.

The lower density of the air at higher altitudes means that radiant heat is more readily received and lost, thus causing considerable diurnal range of temperature. For this reason, in settlements on the high Tibetan Plateau it may be pleasantly warm in the sunlight but literally freezing in the shade.

Changes in atmospheric pressure are responsible for air movement and we may consider wind separately.

Wind. The influence of wind is felt chiefly through its physical violence and by its promotion of rapid evaporation. Plant growth may be inhibited by a strong prevailing wind; while damage to crops and property is frequently caused by hurricanes at places in very different latitudes. Within a single year, 1951-2, Jamaica, the Orkney Islands, parts of the Philippines, and Arkansas, suffered devastating losses relative to the area affected; and in 1953 gale-force winds in conjunction with high tides caused disastrous flooding in England and the Netherlands.

Wind is a prime factor in causing soil erosion (Chapter X). The drying effect loosens the top soil into a dust which is borne away by the wind itself. Wind-borne particles can also be highly erosive; yet the deposition of wind-borne material, as loess, has produced some of the world's most fertile areas. On the other hand, shifting dunes have overwhelmed men's works in both desert and coastal regions.

The winds, which once strongly influenced the path of the shipping routes, and must still today be reckoned with by vessels large and small, have also a measurable influence upon air travel, and on the siting of airfields.

Humidity. The physiological effect has been briefly mentioned in connection with temperature. Thus a day is "raw", rather than merely cold, when the humidity is high and the temperature low; it is "muggy", rather than hot, when the humidity and temperature are both high.

Sweat evaporates rapidly in those hot regions where the air is very dry. If man sweats freely, he may lose a large quantity of salt, which, if not replaced, may cause heat cramps; although if man works in such conditions over a long period adjustments are made by the body, controlling to some degree the quantity of salt lost.

When the air is nearly saturated with water vapour, evaporation is greatly reduced, so that the body is not cooled by sweating. Men find it difficult to concentrate and, finally, if the air temperature is near body temperature, may suffer from heat stroke.

Many plants flourish in a warm humid atmosphere; so do minute organisms, and bacteria which act on plants and animals multiply rapidly. The humidity of the air controls the rate of evaporation, and so exerts a powerful influence upon plant distribution; for when the air is humid the soil can retain its moisture, whereas a dry wind soon dries out the top soil. A succession of drying winds can render vegetation, in such regions as south-east Australia, particularly liable to forest fires.

A high humidity is desirable in certain industries, for instance, in cotton spinning, where dry threads are apt to break. In some large-scale confectionery processes it is essential to know the exact humidity before allowing crystallisation to begin.

Precipitation. The pattern of the world's natural regions follows the rainfall distribution very closely, for the distribution of plants and animals is closely related to the regional regimes of precipitation and evaporation.

The seasonal distribution sets the rhythm of the agricultural year and brings many other responses from man, many of which are considered in subsequent chapters. In the Mediterranean and monsoon regions, for instance, and wherever long dry spells are followed by rain, the most stringent action is required to conserve water and to guard against soil erosion.

Erratic rainfall also brings problems which, because they are unpredictable, may cause distress to mankind. Over the greater part of the occupied territory of Australia a long drought occurs, on the average, more than once in every five years. This includes much of the agricultural land of the Murray-Darling Basin, where serious drought is frequently followed by flooding. Here is another of those phenomena

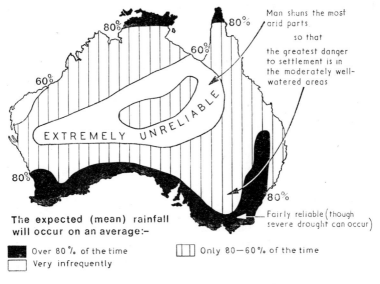

The expected (mean) rainfall will occur on an average:—

Over 80 % of the time Only 80—60% of the time
Very infrequently

Fig. 3. THE UNRELIABILITY OF RAINFALL IN AUSTRALIA.

The greatest dangers to human settlement, with the threat of large-scale destruction of crops or animals, are in those areas where sufficient rain falls to encourage agricultural development yet where absolute drought or excessive flooding occurs from time to time.

which produce contrary results, for while flood-waters may destroy standing crops, in the long term the reduction in the number of rabbits, by drowning, may well benefit future crops.

It is not in the exceptionally dry areas that man suffers most from unreliable rainfall, for there he is usually dependent on some form of irrigation. It is in closely-settled border zones between the dry and the well-watered lands where the dangers mostly exist, as in Western Bengal where disastrous famines may follow a few weeks' delay in the monsoon rains.

The effects of excessive rainfall or snowfall need little elaboration. Crops are affected according to their state of development, communications and power supply are hindered, and buildings damaged. In some areas, like the great deltas of south-east Asia, natural periodic flooding deposits alluvium, and thus renews the fertility of the land.

Hail, occurring chiefly as a result of intense convection, is likely to be most frequent in the summer months, so that the damage to standing crops is often considerable, and can take place in a short space of time. In Colorado, U.S.A., farmers are unwilling to risk all on wheat, which is especially vulnerable to hail, and often plant beet or maize as well; though the return from a good crop of wheat may be considerably higher.

"Hail can kill a county full of wheat in half-an-hour. If hail could be abolished, there would be no beets or corn (*i.e.* maize) in Colorado." (John Gunther, *Inside U.S.A.*)

The Climograph. In order to appreciate the relative influence of climatic factors in combination, a climograph may be used.

A climograph of relative humidity against temperature may be plotted representing these conditions for each of the months of the year; these points are joined by a line. The area enclosed by the plot then occupies a position on the graph which indicates, more clearly than a single temperature or rainfall chart, the physiological effects of climate.

Monthly rainfall and temperature figures are usually more readily available, and it is instructive to select and plot figures for representative towns in the major climatic regions. Strictly, such plots of rainfall and temperature are termed *hythergraphs*.

Structure and Relief.—So closely is man's occupation related to the geology of the region in which he lives that here we will simply note a few of the more obvious relations between the relief and structure of a region and its inhabitants; for, again, these and other relations are mentioned more spontaneously, and in greater detail, at intervals throughout the book.

Relief. The features of relief depend upon the parent rocks and their formation, upon earth movements, and subsequent modelling by the agents of weathering and erosion. Some instances of the effect of relief are:—

(i) Modifications imposed upon climatic elements by a relief barrier, such as a rain-shadow effect, or variations in altitude, where the decrease of temperature, pressure, and available oxygen with height is reflected in modified forms of plant and animal life.

(ii) The proportion of highland to lowland and the degree of slope have a strong influence on rural settlement, and the suitability of a region for certain types of agriculture may largely depend on these facts. Plains, in contrast to mountain areas, tend to be more densely settled, for physically they are easier to cultivate and their soils usually deeper and more fertile.

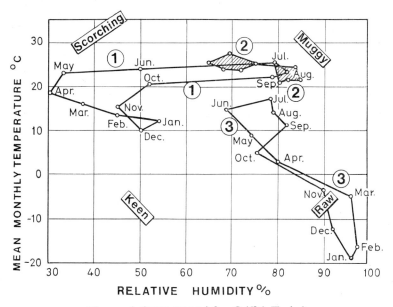

Fig. 4. A CLIMOGRAPH (after Griffith Taylor).

Plot (1). Jhansi, India. This shows the change from winter drought to the heavy, humid, monsoon period (June to October).

Plot (2). Madras. A high temperature is maintained in this city which lies at sea-level in a low latitude. Moisture is brought both by the south-west monsoon and by the north-east winds (from November to March).

Plot (3). Winnipeg. This plot shows the extremes of temperature in the interior of Canada, and also the high relative humidity of the cold air.

(iii) The creation of drainage and river systems, with all they mean to man.

(iv) Tactical relief features which may provide sites for defence or, conversely, give ease of access to an invader.

(v) The aspect, or lie of the land, in relation to sun and wind. In temperate latitudes, for instance, man usually chooses the sunny slopes for settlement or cultivation, or chooses to live leeward of a hill.

The Underlying Rocks. (i) Weathering produces the mineral particles of the soil, although, of course, the soil in a region may not necessarily be derived from local rocks, but from glacial or alluvial deposition.

(ii) The permeable or impermeable nature of rocks may largely determine the run-off, the character of the streams and their valleys, and the water-supply, all of which closely influence settlement.

(iii) They provide materials suitable for shelter, housing, and road construction, which may be used by even the most primitive communities.

(iv) The minerals present vary in their importance to man according to his state of development. For example, primitive men have no use for bauxite, but may well use small quantities of iron or copper ores. When minerals are exploited, they may have the most widespread material or political consequences. The materials connected with power production—water, coal, petroleum, and the raw materials for the release of atomic energy—have all in their turn stimulated interest in regions hitherto ignored by mankind.

This is in no sense a comprehensive summary, but is intended to stress the interrelations between man and the physical features surrounding him. A careful observation of the details of man's settlement should start a train of thought which will seek relationships between those facts which are observed and the natural environment. But beware from the start lest casual observations lead to false conclusions. Human beings and human groups do not always behave in a logical manner. Also, as societies become more complex there are likely to be many anomalies; buildings, factories even, may be situated in a position dictated by no more than the whims of the owner's wife!

Oceans and Large Lakes.—These may act either as barriers or routeways. These two functions operate in accordance with man's own desires and abilities, for they may either restrict movement, or open the way to travel, trade, or emigration. As with all natural features, they contain in themselves possibilities, which are partly embodied in the land masses which surround them. For the nations of Western Europe the expanse of the North Atlantic ceased to be an absolute barrier in 1492; with the realisation that here was an open path to a "New World", which had itself inestimable possibilities, men began to regard it as a great routeway.

The Channel "moat" has played a great part in preserving English freedom, yet to Western civilisation the function and importance of the ocean as a barrier has diminished with the years. A long enemy coastline has always given the invader some advantage of surprise, especially with a short crossing, for he can choose where he will attack. With the speed and range of the modern missile, bomber and troop transport, even an oceanic "moat" provides little security.

The climatic modifications caused by oceans applies also to the larger lakes; witness the relatively mild winters of the Ontario Peninsula. The mode of livelihood around the shores of Lake Victoria is strongly influenced by local climatic factors, and in Uganda the moisture brought by the south-east wind, and the prevalence of thunderstorms near the shore, help to make possible the intensive agriculture of the lake-side zone.

Among their attractions to man is the harvest to be obtained from the waters. Fishing, pearling, or the extraction of salts, sometimes from inland drainage areas or enclosed seas, have all stimulated settlement. Sea-water distillation can now provide fresh supplies for expanding settlements on arid coastlands.

Other Living Things.—The flora and fauna are active elements of the regional environment which may sometimes attract and sometimes repel the would-be settler. Local plants and animals may supply many of his needs, with little effort on his part; on the other hand, pests, such as the tsetse fly or mosquito, may endanger his existence, and in some cases prevent settlement. Some microscopically small organisms may produce disease, while others, such as the nitrifying bacteria, can act to restore fertility to an exhausted soil, thus allowing further harvest from the land.

All kinds of animals, large and small, horse, rat, rabbit, and Colorado beetle, bring their influence to bear upon mankind. In any particular area there is usually a very delicate balance, a biological control, between the numbers of each species present, and upsetting this control may well have dire consequences. For example, two members of the prickly pear family were introduced into Australia in 1839 and 1860. In America their spread had been checked by the insects which feed on them, but in Australia there were no such insects, so that, by 1925, over twenty million hectares had become infested with such a mass of cactus as to make the land quite unusable. Organisms which would feed on the plants were introduced, but some were unable to stand the climate, and others attacked not only the cactus but other plants as well. Finally, an imported insect caused the majority of the cactus to decay in the space of a few years.

The relations between man and other living creatures are so widespread and complex as to merit very special consideration. Man wages a perpetual war against pests and disease the world over. Pest control is closely connected with the most pressing problem of matching increasing population with increasing food production.

Technical achievements by man may sometimes leave more serious problems in their wake: modern hygiene has decreased the number of infant mortalities but caused a great increase in the number of mouths to be fed and the possibility of general under-nourishment. Again, the first successes of insecticides are in many cases followed by the development of an insecticide-resisting creature which, by processes of selection, may be hardier than the previous forms. The result of man's actions upon his environment is seldom straightforward for such actions are likely to cause not one but a whole chain of effects.

CHAPTER II

PRIMITIVE AND WANDERING GROUPS

The Pattern of Human Occupation

Suppose it were possible to take an air photograph of a natural region, showing its relief and original vegetation, and then, by some miraculous means, a second photograph from the same view point, showing the effects of occupation by several generations of human beings. What obvious differences would show up on the second print?

The apparent changes in the landscape would largely depend on the technological skills and cultural background of the occupants. Primitive peoples might leave few permanent traces, whereas settlers from some present-day technological society would most likely have altered its whole appearance. Consider, for instance, the changes caused in a few generations in parts of Kenya and Tanzania (and study Plate I).

Whatever the background of the peoples, the patterns man's occupation imposes upon the region are chiefly due to his attempts to satisfy certain basic needs.

His prime needs are *food, clothing, shelter,* and *simple aids to defence* (spears, axes, etc.).

As he emerges from the primitive state these are met by forms of *agriculture, settlement,* and *security measures* (stockades and fortifications).

With progress, the pattern of his occupation is complicated by schemes designed to improve the land, perhaps by irrigation or drainage; by routeways; by the spread of individual settlements; and by the growth of market centres. His food supply is augmented by barter or trade with his neighbours; his security strengthened by developing the border zones, by fortified towns in strategic positions, and by pacts, extending his influence over neighbouring regions.

Finally, there is the evolution of village, town, and city, to meet the varied functions of a more civilised society. With this goes the use of land for cultural, religious, and recreational purposes.

Not all human groups progress regularly from one state of development to another. Some retrogress, or are arrested at a particular stage, by harsh surroundings or lack of contact with foreign groups. Others are accelerated, perhaps from the semi-primitive to the "modern", by contacts with advanced cultures. Here the progress is too often material rather than intellectual, the peoples finding themselves called on to

13

make difficult mental and psychological adjustments in order to accept in a few decades social changes which others have evolved in centuries of steady progress.

Primitive Groups.—Early man obtained his food, clothing, and shelter, from the natural flora and fauna of his surroundings. Exhaustion of local resources, or movements of his prey, caused him to shift on, so that he led a migratory existence. Gradually he supplemented the food supplied by hunting and fishing with the fruit of plants cultivated from gathered seeds, and from gleaning and gathering he developed primitive agriculture. This did not happen at any given period of time, and never universally. The precariousness of this new occupation, and the exposure of sedentary folk to sudden attack, probably checked the rate at which human groups became primarily agriculturalists.

HUNTING COMMUNITIES. There are few primitive hunting groups remaining today. The Eskimos fish, and hunt bear and seal, living almost entirely on animal products; but the pure primitive Eskimo societies have dwindled and in their place have developed more sophisticated groups, such as the North American Eskimos, visited regularly by parties from patrol vessels, and travelling regularly to trading posts for manufactured articles, packed food, and mass-produced clothing.

Many of the Bushmen of the Kalahari Desert still live by hunting; but their very existence is threatened by the decreasing rainfall and the drying up of wide areas, which were once savannah, rich in game, although they use ingenious methods of obtaining and storing water. They are also threatened as pure communities by the encroachment of white and Bantu peoples.

The pigmy groups, commonest in the rain forest of the eastern Congo basin, have been more fortunate, for fish and game abound and there are many wild edible plants. With no agriculture or domestic animals, they have probably been the most truly representative of the pure hunters. The groups roamed freely, erecting only temporary light shelters, but mostly shunning contact with other peoples. In view of the virtual absence of history or religion, their relation to their environment is transitory and slight; their needs have been met with little or no permanent effects on their surroundings. Now they, too, are threatened as a group by contacts with modern settlement and the advent of tourism.

In South America, south-east Asia, New Guinea, and Australia, live other hunting communities, but for most of these folk closer

contact with more advanced forms of civilisation seems imminent, and
many are already suffering permanent changes in their mode of living.

SEMI-NOMADIC GROUPS.   In Australia many of the native black
population live and work in the areas of extensive farming and grazing.
But some tribes of the northern coastal lands and the interior carry on
the hunting, fishing, and gleaning, of their ancestors.

Dr D. F. Thomson* shows, in his papers noted on page 17,
that in Arnhem Land the natives are really wanderers, neither pure
hunter nor pure nomad.   They divide their year consciously and
systematically into seasons, to which are related their principal
occupations and their forms of habitation.   This is extremely interesting, for it shows that they sum up their environment in a critical and
scientific way, making a thorough appreciation of the resources available
season by season.   Thus in a relatively simple community there is
displayed a continuously changing series of interactions between man
and his environment.   Being only semi-nomadic, their "pattern" of
occupation is much more defined than that of the pigmy hunters.

The Arnhem natives respond to prevailing natural conditions in
ways which are shown in the table on page 16.   The form of shelter
which they construct varies with the seasons.   At certain times of the
year grass is burnt to start animals prior to hunting, to facilitate travel,
and to discourage reptile and insect pests.

NOMADS.   In some regions the early hunting peoples turned by
degrees to agriculture.   Elsewhere nomadic folk have continued
to graze their flocks or herds; though sometimes settlement followed
migration to favourable permanent pastures, where, unless over-
stocking took place, the population ceased to be nomadic.   But there
are still many groups of nomadic peoples in the semi-arid lands of
central Asia, and in the deserts of North Africa and the Middle East.
Even after many have settled, powerful grouping of Kazak clans and
of Bedouin tribes are major political factors in their respective areas.

In Spain, Provence, and elsewhere, there is considerable *transhumance*; a seasonal movement of men and animals between different
grazing grounds.   Men leave winter settlements and may travel
hundreds of kilometres as they shepherd the flocks to the high summer
pastures.   But the true nomad has no village to return to, and, as he
wanders, depends on his animals.

Their Environment.   The chief influences on the life and movements of the nomad are the continuous areas of grazing, which, though
often sparse, must be sufficient for feeding the herd or flock moving at

Arnhem Land Natives and their Seasonal Activities

SEASON	HOUSE TYPES	ACTIVITIES AND FOODS
Late March and April End of wet season. Hot and humid.	Chiefly for protection against mosquito.	Mostly sedentary and in big camps. Long grass, floods, and mosquito restrict nomadic activity. Goose hunting, fishing, yam collecting starts.
Late April to August	Permanent houses little used.	Nomadic; camps break into groups. Systematic burning of grasslands. Kangaroo and other game hunted. Fishing. Vegetable food plentiful.
September, October Hot dry season.	Camp in open. Open type house, for shade only.	Nomadic travel declining. Intense heat and scarcity of surface water restricts movement. Fish poisoning and spearing. Fruits and corms collected.
Late October-December Maximum heat and humidity. Thunder storms.	A few wet type houses appear.	Concentrations develop in camps on permanent water. Fruits and berries plentiful.
Late December-January N.W. wind. Wet season begins.	Wet season houses.	Almost sedentary life in wet season camps. Many fruits.
January-March Wet season.	Wet season houses.	As above, but most vegetables become soggy and unpalatable.

its maximum rate of travel; and the need for reliable, even if widely dispersed, water points.

Subsidiary Occupations. Some nomads are merchants as well as herdsmen, and their wanderings take them to centres convenient for barter and trade, where animals and animal products may be exchanged for grain, cloth, metals, and other desirable commodities. They may also undertake to transport goods from one people to another.

SEMI-NOMADS AND COMMERCIAL GRAZING. Nomadic herds and flocks may in some cases provide surplus raw materials for exchange, but, unlike the animals which form part of regular commercial grazing, this is not their main function.

In some of the world's extensive grasslands commercial grazing is restricted by periodic drought and by poor communications. On the African savannahs, animal produce, usually hides, comes from semi-nomadic herdsmen. In the long dry season the cattle must be moved

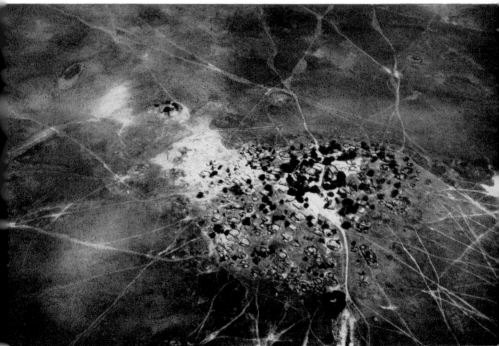

PLATE I

Above: A diamond mine on the savannah land of Tanzania (*Aerofilms*), and (*Below*) an African village on the savannah land of Zambia, showing the difference in land use by peoples of different cultural background and different technical knowledge. Contrast the cluster of native houses and the well-worn but often haphazard system of tracks with the regular planned layout of the mining camp. (*Aerofilms.*)

PLATE II

Above: Planting out rice seedlings. To the peasants of South-East Asia the water brings rich alluvium for cultivation, and is itself retained in the paddy fields to nourish the growing crops. (*KLM—Aerofilms.*)

Below: Terracing in Indonesia. The steps, while helping to retain the soil on the steep hill sides, enable the cultivators to make full use of its high fertility. (*KLM—Aerofilms.*)

over considerable distances, away from the herdsmens' village, situated in an area more favourable to agriculture. Under such conditions the stock of the African herdsmen is usually of poor quality, and a contributory factor is the practice of regarding head of cattle as wealth. Where cattle are used as units for barter, quantity counts for more than quality.

Once a degree of settlement occurs the problems of periodic drought and of pests may be more serious, threatening both herds and land. Should territorial limits be rigidly fixed, there is a danger of over-grazing, and consequent soil erosion (Chapter X). For example, the Swazi population of the East Transvaal once roamed their herds freely over the grasslands, practising also a shifting type of agriculture, until in 1909 a partition into European and Native areas brought fixed tribal boundaries. The Swazi people remained chiefly pastoral for a long time so that over-stocking, within the limits of their territory, caused serious deterioration of their land.

Summary

Primitive wanderers and nomads have little permanent contact with the soil. They may, however, modify their surroundings by causing the growth of forms of secondary vegetation. The traces of shifting agriculture are soon obliterated by natural growth, but the new vegetation may contain species which could not thrive among the original cover; for example, lower scrub forest may replace original tall stands.

Continuous grazing affects not only the nature of the grasslands but may expose the soil to the weather. This is more likely to occur amongst settled peoples than with the true nomads. The greater the degree of settlement the more man affects soil stability and fertility, and the greater therefore his responsibility towards the land.

---

* D. F. THOMSON, "Arnhem Land" (Pt. I) *Geogr. Journ.*, **112**, p. 146; (Pt. II) *Geogr. Journ.*, **113**, p. 1; (Pt. III) *Geogr. Journ.*, **114**, p. 54.

I. TO H. G. 2

CHAPTER III

WATER—ITS INFLUENCES ON SETTLEMENT

As soon as settlement occurs, man's pattern of occupation becomes more firmly imprinted upon the region. Early settlement was closely, though not absolutely, tied to agriculture; and soon, besides the changes caused by the various forms of agriculture, developing communications, habitations, and buildings with other specialised functions, such as church, mill, or barn, became part of the rural landscape.

The facts of settlement are examined in some detail in the following chapters, and if one single element more than any other is foremost in giving a recognisable, and often a characteristic, pattern to a region, it is water. Therefore, at the risk of placing emphasis on an environmental element rather than on man, the influences of water upon settlement are considered first. It would be impossible to make a separate study of each environmental element, even if one could identify them, but water in its many forms so pervades man's life and activities that it is convenient to make this an exception.

Some aspects of the close relationship between settlement and the availability and distribution of water fit more naturally into other sections of the book (*e.g.* waterways in Chapter IV); as a climatic element its influences have been already considered to some extent in Chapter I, and almost every Plate shows the influence of water upon a particular landscape.

Effects on Plant and Animal Associations

The type of plant and animal species in any area depend very much on the available water. The actual quantity which is eventually available for plant growth depends on the rainfall, the rate of evaporation, and on that which runs off the surface, or seeps through, to be drained away from the area by the rivers.

Water for agriculture need not necessarily be available in the form of precipitation, for, where rainfall is scarce, other sources are sometimes available for irrigation and to establish the plants or animals man introduces; in Australia, the successful development of the pastoral industries on the dry interior grasslands is largely due to the use of water from the artesian basins. Here the nature of the water is often more suitable for pastoral rather than agricultural development.

Salts dissolved in this underground water may make it unsuitable for irrigating crops, but an added benefit to sheep and cattle, who can thus replenish some of the salts lost by sweating.

Sources

Man's own need of water is equally fundamental, and the quality and quantity of his local supply of vital importance. Wherever he may settle, he is bound to use one of these sources of supply:—

> *Direct Precipitation*
> *Catchment Water*
> *Surface Water*—Streams, Lakes, or Seas
> *Ground Water*—Springs or Wells

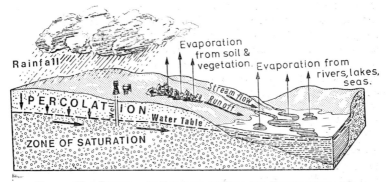

Fig. 5. THE DISPOSAL OF RAINFALL BY RUN-OFF, PERCOLATION, AND EVAPORATION.

Most of the rainfall is distributed by direct flow down the slope, by percolation to form ground water, and by evaporation; some is absorbed by the soil and vegetation, and subsequently evaporated, and some moves through the soil and sub-soil to the streams.

As in all his activities, man tends to free himself from some environmental controls by making technical improvements, and usually achieves some freedom from dependency on local supply. The nucleus of many a modern town was originally sited so as to have access to drinking water; though the original supplies may now be insufficient for the increased population, water can be piped from a considerable distance away. Thus Birmingham obtains its supply from central Wales, and Los Angeles from the Sierra Nevadas, more than three hundred kilometres away. Where the rainfall is slight, man turns to distant sources to water the parched land, as in north-west Pakistan. Here the rainfall and snow-melt from the Himalayan heights is delivered to fields from great canals which tap the upper reaches of the rivers, and brought through small, open, wooden channels which tap mountain streams.

Catchment Water. This form of supply has been used by man since the earliest times, wherever surface water is scarce and ground water deep. In Mediterranean lands both these reasons have caused many structures to be built to catch and hold the water; some of those constructed by the Romans in Libya are still in use today. If stored carefully, such water is usually of good drinking quality; Bermuda, for example, largely depends on catchment water.

Surface Water. The distribution of human settlements is often closely related to the pattern of streams, rivers, and lakes. As the run-off and absorption of water depend on the nature of the under-lying rocks, this distribution may change abruptly with the geological formation. If we compare population distribution on fissured lime-stone, and on impermeable rocks, we usually find that because the limestone has little surface water, except in deep valleys, people have tended to cluster in nucleated settlements close to a source of water. On impermeable rock water is at the surface and many streams form a veined pattern, so that dispersed farms may have their own water-supply; here small hamlets and villages tend to be more widely distributed over the entire area (Figs. 6 and 7). It must, however, be emphasised that water is only one of a number of factors which may affect the distribution of settlements. It may be that because of the need for concentration for defence purposes, or for organising tillage or harvest, rural settlements are large and compact, even though surface water is available over a wide area.

Both surface and ground water contain salts from minerals in the rocks and soil. These may be in sufficient quantity to affect the quality of drinking water, as in parts of the Red River basin, south of the Canadian border, where soluble salts make the water dangerous to drink. But their effects are not always adverse, and the presence of mineral salts of medicinal value have often attracted men to sample, and perhaps settle, in spa towns.

Chemicals which cause "hardness" in water, chiefly calcium and magnesium sulphates and bicarbonates, have had a widespread influence upon industries and therefore upon settlement. In certain industries, notably in the case of textiles, a supply of soft water is essential, and factories have been sited with this in mind—in Lancashire and York-shire, for example. But once again technology breaks down immediate environmental control by introducing water softeners. Sometimes it is an advantage to have certain salts present in water. The establishment of brewing and its rapid development at Burton-on-Trent was due to the fact that the local well water contained gypsum—although artificial hardening is now in common use.

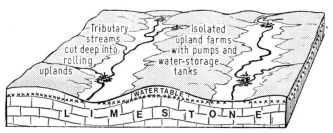

Fig. 6. *A Region of Pervious Limestone, Characterised by a Lack of Surface Water, except in the River Valleys and Deep-set Tributaries. Farms and hamlets are dispersed on the uplands with their own pumps and storage tanks, while the larger settlements lie close to the streams.*

Surface water may also have the effect of making certain areas unattractive to the would-be settler. Apart from temperature extremes the lakes and swamps formed among glacial drift and in rock hollows of the Canadian Shield make large areas unsuitable for settlement, though they may be used by aircraft serving the occasional mining or

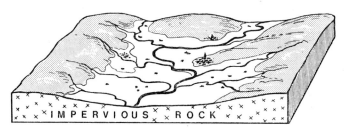

Fig. 7. *In this Region of Impervious Rock the Majority of the Rainfall remains as Surface Water, or Returns to the Rivers as Run-off. Small settlements can readily obtain water and are scattered throughout the region. Riverside sites are generally avoided, for rapid run-off can lead to sudden flooding, and, consequently, the larger villages are on higher ground.*

lumbering settlement, and in the south are used for recreation. Surface water may also limit agricultural possibilities; bogland makes much of central Ireland relatively inaccessible, so that stock rearing is a more suitable occupation than dairying, which needs good communications for collecting and marketing the milk.

Even such strong environmental influence can be overcome, however, where other factors provide an incentive to occupation. Papyrus swamps of Lake Huleh in Israel have been drained and developed under the stimulus of increasing pressure of population; and to meet the ever-growing need for cultivable land, the Dutch have

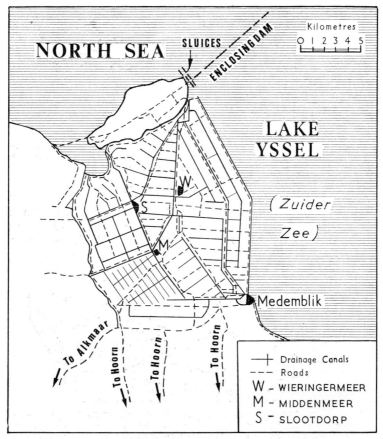

Fig. 8.   THE NORTH-WEST (WIERINGERMEER) POLDER OF HOLLAND.
Nine-tenths of this reclaimed land is cultivated.

long struggled to gain new fertile land by reclamation projects. Despite many setbacks, though not all as desperate as the terrible flooding of 1953, they have won great tracts of land from the sea, with a success that is illustrated by Figs. 8, 9, and Plate III.   Under the stimulus of the world-wide demand for steel, railways were constructed across forests and swamps of the Canadian Shield to tap vast reserves of iron ore in the hitherto remote district of Ungava. There, in the north-east, Schefferville has become a sizeable town.

Swamps may seem unlikely areas to have any commercial value in themselves, but papyrus, flax, and jute are among the fibres produced from such regions. Also, alluvial soil is usually very fertile and the flood-plains of the huge rivers of south-east Asia are the world's greatest rice producing areas, on whose productivity depends the very survival of millions of people (Plate II).

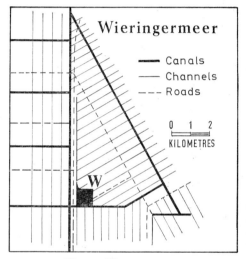

Fig. 9. WIERINGERMEER.

Plate III shows the carefully planned town on the reclaimed land of the North-West Polder. The regular pattern of roads, canals, and drainage emphasises the efforts made to create productive farmland.

Ground Water. We have already seen that water from under-lying strata is often highly mineralised, which may be advantageous or otherwise.

The influence of ground water on settlements depends on the extent of the water-bearing strata and on the accessibility of the water. Settlements frequently occur where springs issue at points along an exposed line of contact of permeable and impermeable rocks. The volume of water available is usually small, so that supply from another source may become necessary as the population increases.

Where water-bearing rocks are sufficiently near the surface, wells may be constructed; occasionally, as in some Saharan oases, ground water appears as natural surface pools.   The layer of clay, preventing the downward seepage of water below a certain level, which underlies the central portion of the Indo-Gangetic Plain, is sufficiently extensive to allow cultivation over a wide area, independent of the irrigation canals.   Further south, throughout the Deccan, there are innumerable wells; for the rivers, which in any case carry little water in the cool season, are often far below the level of the plateau.   Such wells allow widely dispersed village settlement; within the village the well acts as a social centre, particularly for the womenfolk.

Sea-water distillation has become a practicable, if expensive, source of supply for some coastal desert settlements, in Kuwait, for instance; here hydroponics (involving soil substitutes) is also used to grow vegetables and conserve water.

POLLUTION.

Both surface and ground water are liable to pollution from organic sources, such as sewage and agricultural manure, and from chemical fertilisers and pesticides.   In densely-populated China and south-east Asia, disease spread by impure water is a potent contributory factor to the high mortality rate.   Even in Western Europe the reservoirs and pumping stations must be carefully sited and the water chlorinated.   Here industrial waste is responsible for much pollution, destroying fish and plant life in the rivers, and pollution is critical in the Great Lakes of North America.

Water Projects

From the days of the early settlements in the Tigris and Euphrates valleys, man has devised structures to control the natural flow of the waters, altering the appearance of the landscape by methods of irrigation as varied in scale and technological achievement as the early canal systems, the shadoufs of Egypt, the water wheels of China, and such huge projects as the Grand Coulee and Aswan Dams.

Plate XXI shows how remarkable a change can be effected by means of irrigation.   Equally remarkable is an aerial view of a closely-settled irrigated area like the Punjab, which stresses the way the intricate patchwork of small intensively cultivated fields depend on the network of canals, cuts, and irrigation channels.   Most large projects change the whole aspect of a countryside, by the appearance of dams themselves, the reservoirs, the pipe-lines and canals, and, most completely, by the ploughing of land and the introduction of new crops.

The larger projects usually include, or are created for, the development of hydro-electricity, and consequently have far-reaching effects. Transmission lines carry the current to distant industrial centres, while other industries may be developed near the dams themselves, as in the case of aluminium production at Foyers in Scotland and in the Saguenay Valley in Canada, and the industrial growth near the Owen Falls Dam in Uganda. The light and power made available may become inducements to halt the rural depopulation which has taken place in so many outlying agricultural regions; by bringing additional amenities to the rural population, and also by stimulating local industries. Electric pumps help to extend settlement in dry lands, where a combination of irrigation and hydro-electric power can establish a well-balanced modern community upon new or reclaimed agricultural land. Examples of such development projects, broadly following the lines of the successful Tennessee Valley Scheme, are given in Chapter X.

Water as an Obstacle

Where man encounters water as an obstacle he is stimulated to find means of overcoming it. The development of water transport from coracle to modern ship presents a vast field of study in itself, and the changing form of the vessel has affected man in many ways. Because of the increasing bulk which ocean vessels have been able to carry, many ancient land trade routes and trading settlements have been rendered obsolescent; with the ability of ships regularly to transport a cargo equal to many caravan loads, the absolute importance of the camel routes from the Sudan and Mediterranean to the West African coast suffered a decline. The increase in the size of ships has necessitated a continual improvement in harbour facilities and an increase in the depth of entrance channels. Where these have not been practicable, other ports have taken the trade, or an outport has been constructed (*e.g.* Avonmouth for Bristol).

Other direct responses on the part of man include the construction of bridges, causeways, and, occasionally, tunnels.

Water has frequently been incorporated in defensive arrangements, Plate XXII (Durham) shows how a settlement may make tactical use of a river bend. With bigger stretches of water, strategic positions, such as narrows, may be guarded by specially constructed fortified towns and naval bases like Gibraltar and Singapore. In this way an existing island settlement may assume an importance out of all proportion to its apparent economic potential, as has Malta.

Fishing

On a small scale, the extent to which men engage upon fishing depends partly on the relative attractions of land and sea. Along the coasts of Norway, Scotland, and Ireland, fishing may be a full-time or a part-time occupation. Agriculture is limited by relief, soil, and climate, and becomes a seasonal occupation, so that summer crofting alternates with winter fishing. The same is true, with varied forms of agriculture or collecting economy, of small fishing settlements through-out the world; near the fishing port of Negombo, in south-west of Sri Lanka, coconuts and rice provide the land harvest; and along the middle reaches of the Zaire (Congo) fish traps are set regularly to supplement a subsistence agriculture.

But man reaps his biggest harvest from the sea through his fishing fleets. Some fishing ports may be multi-functional, with fishing only one of the important functions, as at Hull. Others have fishing as the principal occupation, as in Labrador and Newfoundland. All must, of course, be located within fair trawling distance of the great fishing grounds, although the use of refrigeration ships has enabled the fishing fleets to extend the area of their activities.

Other Activities Connected with Water

Water routes and navigation are separately considered in Chapter IV. There are also the recreational uses of water, and sailing, fishing, and especially bathing facilities have brought rapid growth and prosperity to many seaside and lakeside towns. An illustration of this is seen in the growth of such great resorts as Brighton (page 161).

There are, of course, innumerable other ways in which water, as solid, liquid, or vapour, is bound up with the life of man, and one may finally reflect that, in youth, 65 per cent. of the weight of a man's body is water.

CHAPTER IV

FEATURES OF SETTLEMENT—
HOUSES AND COMMUNICATIONS

The Facts of Settlement—Different Approaches

Water, which is connected with human activities so closely and in so many ways, is but *one* element of the environment; which emphasises the fact that it would be too large a task to attempt to trace similar interrelations between man and all the other natural components of his surroundings. Human settlement is affected by economic, historic, religious, and other social influences, as well as by purely physical ones, so that some other method of approach is essential.

The French geographer Brunhes approached Human Geography by observing and considering a great many facts related to man's occupation and subsequent transformation of the earth's surface. He studied the facts of unproductive occupation of the soil, such as dwellings and roads; the facts of plant and animal conquest by man namely, the distribution and type of crops and pastoral activities; and the facts of destructive exploitation of the world's resources, in the forms of mining and unrestricted trapping or lumbering; all of which profoundly affect the earth's surface.

He approached each selected example in its most elementary form. Therefore, as an approach to the study of village and town, he examined the house, and by observing and classifying types of houses in many different regions found that certain causes exerted a great influence on their design and their situation. Further observation enabled him to observe the effect of these same causes on the village and town.

Finally, in the light of the knowledge obtained by this approach, he selected certain small and well-defined regions of occupation in which to study as far as possible the results of the interplay between man, his natural surroundings, and all the existing topographical features "as a whole in all their natural complexity".

This method has the merit not only of being simpler than that of classifying separate environmental features, but also of placing man firmly and logically at the focus of such studies. The following chapters examine facts of human settlement in the light of present-day circumstances. Today, geographers concentrate more firmly on a search for order and recognisable patterns in all aspects of human settlement. This involves the collection of quantified data which may be appropriately processed and analysed.

27

Once a geographer assumes a measurable degree of order in spatial behaviour he may then express this by simplified models, of settlement location or urban structure for example. These are intended as frameworks to lead to a deeper understanding of the spatial organisation of human activities. Examples are shown on pages 80-84.

Here, like Brunhes, we turn first to elementary forms of man's occupation of the earth's surface, and view the physical, economic, and social factors influencing them: but as more complex forms of settlement are considered, we turn from time to time to examine models, whose simplified form enables us to see order in the complexities.

HOUSES

For human beings, who spend up to a third of their life in sleep, some form of shelter is a fundamental requirement. The form and function of the individual house vary with the climate, the available building material, and with a wide range of social influences. In simple societies the dictates of climate and the necessity of using local materials have resulted in some striking similarities in house types in corresponding climatic regions. But differences in social conditions, as well as different levels of culture, so influence the form of buildings that even classification on a regional basis becomes a difficult task.

The Simple Dwelling.—*Materials.* The form of simple buildings owes much to the climate and vegetation of a region. This is illustrated by such dwellings as the igloo of the Polar regions, the wooden house of the coniferous forests, those of sun-baked mud of the semi-arid countries, and the wattle and palm-thatch of the equatorial rain forests.

Sturdier buildings are generally of stone or brick, and consequently the nature of a local stone, or clay belt, tends to give nearby houses a typical appearance. In the British Isles, especially, the many different geological formations have associated with them a variety of house types, with characteristic architectural features. For not only the superficial appearance of the stone, but also the quality of the stone, Cotswold limestone, hard grits of the north, or soft sandstone of the Midlands, give rise to characteristic local styles, for each demands special architectural treatment. In the London Basin, the abundance of timber and the scarcity of stone were geographical facts which had a great bearing on the extent of damage caused in the Great Fire of 1666, which spread through a city still built largely of oak.

The Roof. The form of the roof is also closely related to the climate. A steep pitch is constructed in regions of heavy snowfall or rainfall, and can be seen in both the cool temperate lands and the equatorial forests. In hot dry lands the mud or stone dwellings are commonly flat roofed, thus saving timber, which is usually scarce, and acting as a storage place for fodder or fuel, as in southern Turkey and in Kashmir, where apricots are spread out to dry on the flat stone roofs. Variations include the low cupola, built both as a protection against the sun, and to ward off the infrequent but extremely heavy downpours which may occur (Plates XIV and XVI).

Roofing materials frequently differ from those of the main body of the house, according to resources and custom. Where suitable geological formations exist slate may replace the shingles of the northern forests or the straw thatch of the temperate zones.

Resemblances in Different Regions. Similar methods of construction can be observed in similar, though widely separated, natural regions. The Egyptian, flat-topped, single-storied, building of sun-dried brick has its counterpart in many a Mexican village, and the thatched house raised on piles is common to North Borneo and the Amazon Basin. These examples from arid and rain-forest regions show an obvious response to exacting conditions, where the environment leaves man with very little choice, either of materials or site.

In stone houses the different types of material give a much greater scope for variation in construction, but similarities do exist; although before attributing them to the result of original thought on the part of separate human groups, we should be quite sure that past contact has not allowed an exchange of ideas. Brunhes observed, in both Italy (Apulia) and in the Balearic Islands, circular stone houses, which narrowed vertically to an opening topped by a flat stone; and noted that each was built of a limestone which would readily split horizontally. He later found almost identical structures in Ireland and the Hebrides, and although the stone used in construction was different, it was capable of cleavage in exactly the same way as the Mediterranean limestone.

Other common elements of the environment can evoke similar responses in different regions. It is remarkable how many simple buildings incorporate mushroom-shaped pillars in the lower parts of their supports as a protection against rats. This device can be seen in the older buildings and barns in the Cotswolds, in the all-wooden buildings of the remote valleys of northern Norway, in village store-houses in Indonesia, and elsewhere (see Plate VII).

None of these facts is surprising in itself, for, after all, men the world over use ingenuity to solve their material problems, and in so doing employ a fundamental common sense. When needs are dire "necessity becomes the mother of invention", and it is, therefore, not to be wondered at that the influence of environmental features is reflected in man's works in a similar way in different localities.

Where separate natural regions are closely akin, a study of common features in houses, agriculture, or any form of settlement, can be a most useful form of comparative geography.

Other Forms of Dwelling.—Besides purely geographical facts and conditions, social and historical influences also act upon the style and form of the simple dwelling.   The social customs of human groups may give rise to characteristic forms of dwelling, as in the evolution of the "long-house" of Indo-China and elsewhere in South-East Asia. This has a variety of forms according to local customs.   For instance, the Kelabits of Borneo construct one or more continuous long-house, on stilts, to make up a "village".   Each house has a long verandah, and a long, undivided, common room to the rear, shared by all the families.

Pressure of population may lead to the adoption of make-shift houses, or the occupation of unlikely sites.   Thus, thousands of Chinese have their permanent dwellings on flat-bottomed, bamboo-roofed boats, moored to the banks of the great rivers.

Some houses differ from the simple form by having stables or granaries directly attached to them, while in others troubled times may have led to the incorporation of defensive features, strengthened walls, watch towers, or narrow windows.   Such features are, however, more likely to be part of a major stronghold, where protection can be sought when lesser buildings are abandoned.

Sometimes a conquering nation has introduced its own cultural and technical developments in new buildings and created a style which has been ultimately incorporated in native structures.   Also, after a while, local variations of the foreign style appear, as in the innumerable modifications and adaptations of Spanish colonial architecture in South and Central America.   Geographical influences may, however, remain prominent, as in Peru and Mexico, where later Spanish buildings have, in some cases, been built on top of earlier buildings because their foundations and first storeys were specially constructed to withstand the effect of earth tremors.

In Britain there is evidence that relief had a subtle influence upon the earlier distribution of house types.   In regions where features of relief and vegetation made access easy for invaders, foreign methods of construction were more readily adopted, or incorporated with local styles; but where Saxon or Scandinavian penetration failed, or was successfully resisted, there was little immediate effect upon the local form of construction.

The Effects of Social and Cultural Differences.—A direct comparison of house types between one region and another has little value unless the cultural background and social status of the occupants is known.

Owing to the protection afforded by its desert surroundings, the early civilisation of Ancient Egypt enjoyed a certain security, which gave the ruling classes time and leisure to make changes in the form and style of their architecture, according to their own taste. But the fellah had neither time nor wealth enough to improve his dwelling, even if he had the desire to do so. Other stable civilisations, have constructed great buildings in styles now considered typical of their period, especially during long peaceful reigns. Yet throughout the ages, particularly in the warmer lands, the house of the peasant has changed but little. In more northerly countries the climate has, perhaps, been responsible for more frequent structural alterations at all levels of society. This, however, is a generalisation, and must be qualified by admitting the effects of rapidly-changing social conditions and the relative abundance of suitable building materials in those lands.

Although characteristic period style tends to disguise local influences, closer examination often shows small revealing features. In Hertfordshire, for instance, the depletion of local forests is reflected in the wider spacing of the uprights in many Jacobean "half-timbered" houses.

With other buildings the intended function largely determines their form. The design of a religious building, castle, or municipal centre, is usually found to have been conditioned by historical associations or traditional pattern, *e.g.* the Gothic architecture of English cathedrals, and the neo-classical style of many municipal buildings.

The Modern House and Local Character.—Today, many lands have large urban populations, and, with rapidly increasing numbers of people, the habitations cluster together in still larger groups. In an urban society where houses are "made to order", can there be local character, and, if not, is there any value in studying the simple form of dwelling?

The effects of environmental influences are certainly shown most clearly in the form of rural dwellings; but most urban folk would claim that their town, however industrial, has a character of its own. Most towns do indeed possess distinct regional character, and towns, after all, are made up mostly of houses. The individual modern house, or group of houses, can, with intelligent design and careful choice of material, be made to conform to the character of the region, and here the geographer can give a hint to town or landscape planners.

To design modern houses to conform to a regional plan is not merely a matter of imparting local character by imitating the form of existing houses. A modern house can be given a form of its own which is in keeping with its surroundings simply because it functions as efficiently as possible in the natural conditions of that region. An example of this is seen in the work of the modern architect Le Corbusier, who planned the new Indian city of Chandigarh (page 159). Here he designed buildings provided with a large parasol, or umbrella, to shade them in the months of great heat, to shed the rain water in the monsoon months, and to allow air to circulate freely beneath. Because he acknowledged the direct influence of climate on the form of these modern buildings, Le Corbusier produced structures for northern India which are very different from the "glass sun-traps" which he, and others, designed for more northerly locations. Here in Chandigarh the architect had the great advantage of planning for the development of a virgin site, so that the modern buildings form a separate grouping apart from the older, and more slowly evolved, forms of buildings in the region. Time has revealed various drawbacks in the spatial layout of the city in relation to its functions, and internal arrangements of some of the administrative buildings have been found to be impracticable: but these facts do not invalidate the general concepts.

In modern urban developments economic considerations can strongly influence the form and location of dwellings. The high land-rents in and about the central parts of a town have caused much clearance of old two- and three-storied residences, and their replacement by multi-storied flats or business premises, which creates a large floor area on a relatively small ground space, and a correspondingly large return from individual rentals.

COMMUNICATIONS

In any occupied region there will be evidence of some form of intercommunication, even though the signs of habitation be few, for not only man but other members of the animal kingdom make use of tried and trusted routes to and from their water-points or resting places.

Man has adapted himself to travel by air as well as by land and water. Whereas tracks are evidence of his passage over the land, his sea and air routes are indicated by installations, which may be as prominent as Liverpool Docks or London Airport.

The Road and Land Transport.—When we examine forms of communication, we must study the *agency*—man, animals, or machines—as well as the *path* itself.

PLATE III

Above: A Maltese landscape. The natural vegetation and forms of settlement respond to the climatic conditions and to the type of rock. Here the outcrops, stony fields, terracing, and building material all blend into scenery typical of a dry limestone region. Cactus and low bushes reflect the length of the long dry summers. (*Central Office of Information. Crown Copyright Reserved.*)

Below: Wieringermeer. Here water is in excess. Contrast this polder scene with the environment of the Maltese peasant. (*KLM—Aerofilms.*)

PLATE IV

Above: A mule-driven scoop wheel, Malta. The farmer splashes water down the gulleys into fields banked-up by hand. Notice the large limestone blocks used in construction. (*Central Office of Information. Crown Copyright Reserved.*)

Below: Large-scale irrigation in Salinas Valley, California. The farmer clears machine-made irrigation ditches. (*USIS.*)

When early human groups were on the move porterage was usually the woman's task, while the man hunted for food or remained ready to act in defence. Means were soon evolved for supporting the load, such as the yoke and the shoulder basket (of the type employed today in tea plantations). A grass ring was devised to help distribute the load over the crown of the head. This method is still used by many people, from the tribesmen of East Africa, to wholesale fish porters, while the artisan in Sri Lanka frequently wears a semi-circular comb in the hair, publicly denying the practice of this kind of porterage.

The earliest trackways generally avoided, as far as possible, low and swampy territory, and probably followed existing animal tracks on the higher ground. But this was not always possible, so that, besides the track itself, felled trees and rope bridges soon became semi-permanent features of the landscape.

When man began to use animals for transport he could travel further afield and his tracks could be extended across more difficult terrain. Oxen, donkeys, and especially camels, helped man to open up many of the old-world trade routes, such as the ancient silk route to China, and that from Egypt through the Fertile Crescent to Mesopotamia. The llamas of Peru were probably responsible for the early development of well paved roads in that country; for, although well adapted to the altitude, and able to carry more than the average man-load, these beasts find it difficult to cross soft ground. But, outside the tropics, the horse, on account of its speed and adaptability, has been man's most important beast of burden.

It is not certain when wheeled vehicles were first used, but they were undoubtedly preceded by sleds and wooden, or stone, rollers. The use of wheeled vehicles meant that the routeways had to be more carefully sited, and acted as an incentive to the improvement of road surfaces, although, even in England, road surfaces remained very bad, by present standards, until the nineteenth century.

Routes

The economic and military value of a good road system has frequently been recognised by governments and monarchs, among them the Mogul Emperor Akbar, who was largely responsible for the excellent system of major roads covering northern India. It was an act of benefit to countless millions of travellers when trees, planted for shade, were spaced out along these long, straight roads.

Military requirements have always stimulated road construction, from the Roman roads to the German autobahnen. The Roman roads aided economic and cultural unification throughout the area of Roman domination, besides fulfilling the main purpose—military mobility;

and with their decline many regions again became insular in character and outlook.

As civilisation develops, the network of roads becomes more complex. Trade is a great incentive to road building, and the location of mineral or agricultural surpluses, or, conversely, the demand for goods not supplied locally, stimulates road construction. Networks are therefore developed, linking the primary producing areas with the collecting and distribution centres, such as the great ports.

In the British Isles, the roads often skirt the boundaries of agricultural holdings. Their devious paths respond to those geographical features which, long ago, led to the fixing of the shape and size of fields, according to soil, drainage, and so on; though by-passes and arterial roads now cut across this established pattern, and make more direct, speedier, and safer, channels for modern traffic.

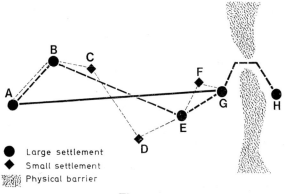

● Large settlement
◆ Small settlement
▨ Physical barrier

Fig. 10.

The actual route of any road must take account of relief features, which affect the alignment of even the most modern highways. In the "new" countries, however, an artificial pattern is frequently imposed on areas of low relief, with roads orientated to the major points of the compass—see page 103 and compare Plates XV and XIX.

Route Location

If we consider routes in general, we may use a series of simple models to demonstrate how, where, and why routes are likely to be located.

Fig. 10 shows three paths linking settlements *A* and *G*. The direct route *A-G* would save on the length of road to be constructed, while the route linking each settlement (the light, broken line) would ensure the maximum traffic, but greatly increase road length. The heavy broken line indicates a compromise, linking the larger settlements and being fairly close to the smaller ones, but requiring an intermediate length of road.

Here the route is making *positive* deviations to collect traffic, as opposed to *negative* deviations which might be necessary to avoid a barrier, as between *G* and *H*.

Route Networks

A somewhat similar approach may be made to the study of route networks.

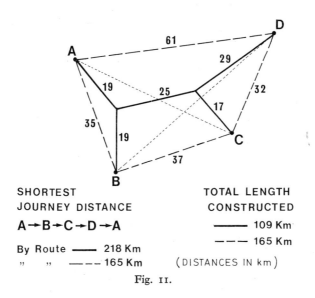

Fig. 11.

In Fig. 11 the four places *A*, *B*, *C*, *D*, are linked by the routes shown (full line). But to start from *A* and visit each in turn would mean retracing paths. If they were linked *instead* by the paths indicated by broken lines one could visit each in turn more conveniently and cover less ground. But a journey from *A* to *C* would be longer by this new route. Also, it would be more expensive to construct this new linkage, if expense depends solely on the cost per unit length of road.

To give complete connectivity, one might combine the routes shown by the dotted lines with those of the outer broken lines: this would be convenient for visits to any other settlement, or to each in turn, but very expensive to construct. Much, of course, depends on

the number of people, or freight, likely to use the routeways.   Completely linked networks may be desirable in urban areas with dense
population.   Away from urban clusters building costs are likely to be
the dominant factors.

In order to calculate the location of the shortest cyclic path connect-
ing a number of settlements, a high-speed computer is needed, for the
number of possible linkages is likely to be very great indeed.

Networks and Settlements

It is easy to assume that a place (such as *A* in Fig. 12) *is* where it is
because it is well-served by communications: whereas it is quite

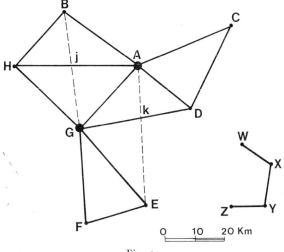

Fig. 12.

probable that the communications developed because there was need
of them; and as *A* grew so it acquired functions which were attractive
to folk in *B*, *C*, and *D*, so that inter-connections were essential.

However, once a close network is established, the most-connected
points of the network are the most likely to grow; also, as new routes
add to the complexity of the network, settlements may well become
established where the routes intersect.

Routes connect settlements *A-H*, forming a closed planar graph, or
route network, in which the main linking routes (*edges*) have no intersections except at the settlements (*vertices*).   Routes between *W*, *X*,
Y, *Z* form a separate open sub-graph.

Settlements A and G are well-connected and may prosper accordingly. Should routes be developed between B and G, A and E (broken lines) settlement may well occur at j and k, the new route intersections.

Network Density and Connectivity

High network densities are often closely related to high levels of economic development and for comparative purposes, to seek valid correlations, we should look for ways to express these quantitatively.

The density can be measured quite simply by dividing the total length of the network (L) by the area it covers (A). In the closed network in Fig. 12, for example, A_n is 4 900 km² and the total length L_n is 350 km, giving a density of 7·1 km/100 km².

This can, of course, be applied to all routes, or to roads of a certain class, or to railways—and on a regional or national basis.

One way of stating the degree of connectivity of a network is to divide the number of edges (E) by the number of vertices (V)—where "vertex" refers to the settlements so connected and to any intersection of two or more roads. This is expressed as the β index, where

$$\beta = \frac{E}{V}$$

In Fig. 12 the closed graph has a degree of connectivity expressed by
$$\beta_A = \tfrac{11}{8} = 1·38$$
(considering only major routeways) whereas the open network, including the place X, has a degree of connectivity expressed by
$$\beta_X = \tfrac{3}{4} = 0·75$$

Modern Road Transport.—Until 1830 the great majority of the roads in Europe and America were on undrained dirt foundation. Pioneers in modern road construction, such as Telford and McAdam, insisted on adequate drainage and properly prepared road surfaces.

The improved main roads were already in existence when the automobile came into general use, at the beginning of the twentieth century. The rate of construction of all-weather roads then increased rapidly. The ways they have helped to transform so much of the earth's surface are too numerous and complex to consider in detail. They have widened the scope for human intercourse; made possible the bulk transport of goods; and the increasing use of petroleum has resulted in a rise in economic and political importance of oil-producing countries. These are, of course, only a few of the many important consequences. Problems exist in countries where old road systems must be adapted to the needs of modern traffic. Here the planned alignment of motorways is an essential part of the communication system.

The Railways.—In some ways the consequences of railroad building have been even more startling. When first laid down in the new countries they became corridors along which passed streams of settlers and bulky goods, which it had hitherto been impossible to transport in quantity. In North America, for instance, townships sprang up along the railroads, and from these a network of communications spread out into the countryside. On the Canadian prairies grain elevators, about ten kilometres or so apart along the railroad, were nuclei near which small settlements developed (Figs. 37 and 38).

The rapidly developing communications within North America soon enveloped the few existing isolated settlements, which together with the newly-established communities became, in both Canada and the U.S.A., part of a large unified state. In many Latin American countries on the other hand, settlements had been established far inland long before the coming of the railways, and were for the most part geographically and politically segregated; which partly account for the lack of any overall political unity among the numerous states of Central and South America. In Brazil, however, there were lines of penetration from Rio de Janeiro and Sao Paulo and the growth of trading centres at the terminals, followed by the growth of feeder routes and lateral connections inland. Thus a network was created in south-eastern Brazil out of the systems focused on these two great cities.

In recently settled countries, railways have played, and still do play, a major part in development. The mineral areas of Haut Zaïre (Katanga) and Zambia are mainly dependent on railways for the distribution of the growing volume of metals produced. In northern Australia, the distance of suitable grazing lands from the existing railways is an important consideration for those contemplating an extension of the cattle industry. As in Canada, the Australian railways are the chief means of transporting freight overland between widely dispersed metropolitan areas with their relatively compact local networks of routeways.

In those parts of the older countries most affected by the Industrial Revolution, the canal systems rapidly became inadequate to carry raw materials and manufactures to and from the new industrial towns. The railways soon formed webs with such towns as the foci. This happened especially early in the north of England, where Manchester was soon connected to Liverpool, to the weaving districts of north Lancashire, and by a local network to the spinning towns.

Population and industries grew together at the terminals and crossing places of the main lines. Even before the invention of the steam engine, Cardiff owed much to its position at the focus of routes from the valleys, down which horse-drawn trucks, running on track-ways, were carrying coal from the coalfields. Crewe and Swindon, at which railway works and allied industries are still important functions, each developed about railway junctions.

But while railways have helped the development of big urban centres, they have also had the effect of distributing the people more evenly throughout the countryside. They have provided links between the more remote districts and the provincial centres, so that it has been possible for people to travel quickly to the large towns. One result

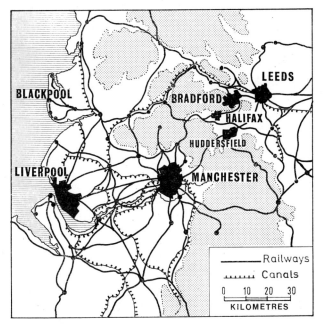

Fig. 13.   THE RAILWAYS AND CANALS OF MERSEYSIDE AND THE CROSS-PENNINE LINKS.
High network densities are closely related to high levels of economic development.

has been that many metropolitan workers commute from "dormitory towns", particularly around London and New York; business men travel daily to the city from distances of a hundred kilometres or so.

Inland Waterways.—*Rivers.* The significance of rivers and the degree to which they are used depend upon other human activities. Whether the full possibilities of a waterway are developed or not must be subject to the needs and capabilities of whoever controls the region through which it flows. Rivers may be very suitable for navigation by large vessels, and yet be relatively little used. Ocean-going vessels can berth at Manaus, fifteen hundred kilometres up the Amazon, where the depth is 20-25 fathoms; even at Iquitos, over three thousand kilometres from the mouth, it is still 10 fathoms deep. Yet despite the navigational advantages of the Amazon, the lack of a rich hinterland means that the volume of trade carried is only a fraction of that taken by the Mississippi.

Moreover, rivers, like the Congo and the Nile, may be interrupted by falls and cataracts and yet be navigable over thousands of kilometres of their course. Also, while a really effective river route needs deep water channels, with little fluctuation in the volume of water, if man is bent on employing water transport in a given region, the most unpromising water courses can be turned to his advantage by dredging, excavation, locks, or control of seasonal flow. Men overcame the inability of the Mississippi to take vessels of large draught, by using paddle steamers; now shallow-draught motor vessels push strings of barges.

Many a river has become significant as a trade route by acting as a link between other extensive waterways. Just as the Hudson River has become an important trade route by virtue of its link with the Great Lakes through the Erie Canal, so the St Lawrence Seaway acts as a through-route, and associated power stations supply hydro-electricity for industrial development near Lake Ontario and Montreal. The St Lawrence, however, suffers from the great disadvantage of becoming ice-bound in the winter months.

A waterway is generally of little use unless it runs in accordance with the desired direction of the flow of trade; but when it does so men will make every effort to overcome natural disadvantages, such as falls or swift currents. This is illustrated by the rivers of China. The Yangtse is well-aligned for trade between the rich basin of Szechwan and the delta; despite the narrow gorge near Ichang, through which craft are still manually hauled against the fast-flowing river, this is one of China's most important routeways. The less navigable Hwang-Ho and Si Kiang also flow in a general direction from west to east; but there is no natural waterway between north and south, so the Grand Canal was constructed to provide a route from Peking through the fertile lowlands to the Yangtse, a section of it being dug more than 2 500 years ago. This, too, is the main direction of the railway system, which still is less developed along the line of the rivers.

The use and importance of a river are closely connected with the surrounding relief. In mountainous country or dense forest the river may provide the only satisfactory means of communication. Yet with all the advantages and none of the disadvantages mentioned, a waterway may remain with only latent possibilities; if there is no trade incentive, or if a good alternative routeway exists, it may be little used by man.

Canals. These are known to have been used from very early times, certainly in China and, over seven thousand years ago, in prehistoric Egypt. Much later it is recorded that, about the year 600 B.C., Necho II began a great waterway from the Nile Delta to the Red Sea, "wide enough for two triremes to be rowed abreast", in order to improve the trade of lower Egypt; but unfortunately an adverse oracle changed his plans and instead he increased his existing merchant navy. A through route was later completed under the Persian, Darius.

Trade has always been the principal motive for canal construction, except where they form part of irrigation projects. The great era in canal construction in England was in the late eighteenth century. One of the first was the Sankey Canal in Lancashire, constructed in 1755 to act as an outlet for the Wigan coalfield; followed in 1761 by Brindley's canal from Worsley to Manchester, which really paved the way for the rapid growth of a canal network in that weirs, culverts, stop gates, and other devices were used in a canal for the first time. During the next half-century an extensive system developed, in order to serve the growing industrial areas, which lay chiefly in the Midlands and the North. The poor state of the roads, and the cheap canal freight rates, gave the latter a great advantage in the carriage of bulky goods. The importance of the part they played in hastening industrial development in the nineteenth century can scarcely be realised today. The Grand Trunk Canal, from the Trent to the Mersey, had a remarkably stimulating effect upon the pottery towns, and the Liverpool-Leeds Canal an equally great effect in fostering the progress of cotton weaving in mid-Lancashire and the trade of the woollen centres in the Aire Valley.

Improved roads and the rapid growth of the railways brought about a decline in their importance. Much of Britain's canal system is obsolescent; abandoned, or being reclaimed for amenity or recreational purposes. Those canals still in service are used for short hauls—of coal, fuel, bulk liquids and, non-perishable bulky merchandise. The craft are small compared with those on the continent.

The canal systems of Holland, Belgium, France, and Germany are very well-established. Canals not only join the great rivers which cross the North European Plain (see Fig. 56), but also form links between these rivers and the Rhône, Loire, and Danube, thus giving uninterrupted communication by water from the Black Sea to the Atlantic, and from the North Sea to the Mediterranean—political barriers excepted. The bulk of the transport (thousands of tons at a time) is handled by steam tugs and self-propelled barges pushing others. Further east the Russians have constructed waterways which connect the Black Sea with the Caspian and northwards through the Volga to the White and Baltic seas.

The industrial north-east of America has important canal transport links between the lakes, the eastward flowing rivers, and the east coast ports, and the construction of the deep-water channel between Lake Ontario and Montreal allows ocean-going vessels to serve the heart of the continent. Further implications of this are discussed on page 145.

Some of the canals do not really come under the category of "inland waterways"; for instance, those direct sea to sea connections, such as the Suez and Panama canals, which are of such great strategic and economic importance. Technical innovations and increasing traffic, with larger vessels of greater draught, make even these great waterways obsolescent. Alternative courses, deeper channels, and dual canals are proposed.

Enforced closures alter the routes of ocean shipping and accelerate the building of larger vessels, so that a large volume of freight may be carried on a single journey along the longer alternative routes.

Lakes. As with rivers, lakes allow the transport of bulky goods, but their importance to man varies with their location.

By far the most important, economically, are the Great Lakes of North America. To the west the open-cast mining in the Mesabi Range has yielded millions of tons of iron ore. Beyond lie the great wheat lands of the U.S.A. and Canada. As a result a great flow of freighter traffic passes through the "Soo" Canal, between Lakes Superior and Michigan, carrying wheat from Thunder Bay, and iron ore from Duluth to the lakeside steel towns and Pittsburgh. There is a great movement of freighters within the whole lakes system. The St Lawrence Seaway now links the industrial zone of the Great Lakes with those of the St Lawrence valley, with the raw materials of the Canadian north-east, and with the Atlantic sea-routes. The Great Lakes have an economic importance unrivalled by any other inland waterway. They lie at the heart of an extensive industrial region: their chief problems are winter freezing and industrial pollution.

The Oceans.—As waterways they present, within the limitations of the vessel, a free choice of routes. The old sailing vessels closely followed the wind-belts and ocean currents, but modern shipping, despite occasional interference by weather, is relatively free from such controls. Even the most formidable of barriers, ice, can be partly overcome by ice-breakers, and, although the famous North-West Passage is never likely to be kept open, the Russians have managed to

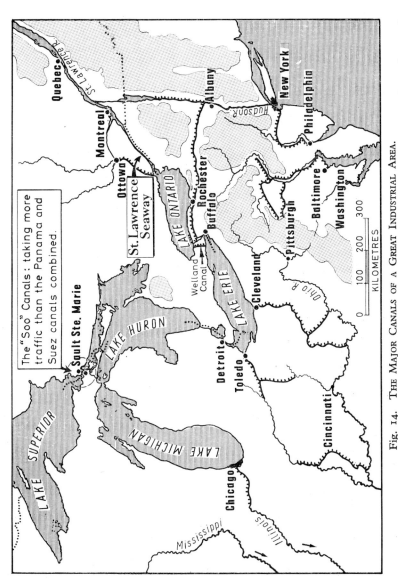

The "Soo" Canals: taking more traffic than the Panama and Suez canals combined.

St. Lawrence Seaway

Fig. 14. THE MAJOR CANALS OF A GREAT INDUSTRIAL AREA.
The canals carry internal trade and industrial raw materials; some, like the St. Lawrence Seaway, are outlets to the Atlantic for the produce of the lakeside industries, the Middle West, and the more distant Prairies; others form links with the lower Mississippi Basin.

achieve regular sailings along the north Asiatic coast by the north-east route, while nuclear-powered submarines travel beneath the surface ice barriers of the Arctic.

The most permanent indications of man's ocean travels are the ports, the termini of the major routeways, with their warehouses, and other installations, and the land communications converging upon them.

The routeways themselves, and the extent to which they are used, are governed by three sets of facts:—

(a) *Those relating to the "homeland."* The direction and nature of overseas trade depends on: (i) the standard of living; (ii) the extent of industrialisation; (iii) the resources available "at home"; (iv) policies in relation to tariffs and trade agreements.

(b) *Those relating to the land overseas.* The actual countries with which the homeland trades depends on: (i) which countries can supply raw materials and finished products required by home markets; (ii) which require raw materials or finished products from the homeland.

(c) *The actual location of ports at home and abroad* (c.f. Chapter VII, page 147).

Commodities are carried chiefly by liners, vessels which run along regular routes, or "lines". Some carry passengers as well as cargo. Some large bulk carriers are chartered on a long-term basis, by steel or oil companies, for example to obtain more favourable terms from the owners. Some trading and manufacturing companies own shipping. There are also tramp ships, that is merchant vessels with miscellaneous cargoes, which ply from one port to another as the opportunity for trade occurs. Smaller ships, or coasters, serve in home waters.

Some small vessels make surprisingly long journeys to carry local produce to collecting centres. In the Indian Ocean, dhows still trade and even large canoes travel six or seven hundred miles without compass, to take dried fish and copra to Colombo or Mombasa.

The Air.—The first air-line company was a Danish one, started in 1918. The early air-lines of Europe and North America were generally confined within continental limits; but in the 1930s routes were established from West Africa to Brazil, then across the Pacific, using islands for refuelling, and across the North Atlantic between Ireland and Newfoundland.

As the flying range of aircraft increases, so it becomes easier to avoid restrictions which hamper land and sea transport, giving the airman almost unlimited freedom of travel. Airstrips can now be constructed and maintained in the most unlikely areas; and although the length of runway required, in relation to the prevailing wind, is usually a limiting factor, vertical take-off is already with us.   However, there are other considerations which tend to restrict long-distance travel to certain routes:—

(*a*) Although man overcomes physical difficulties with prodigious efforts, all too frequently he raises political barriers.   Nations can cause

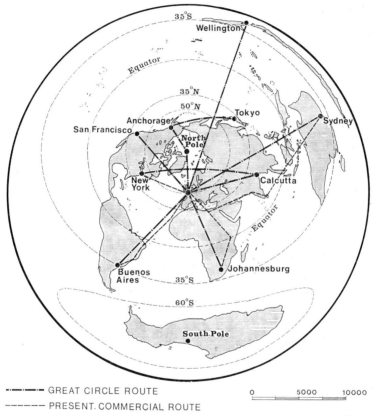

------- GREAT CIRCLE ROUTE

------- PRESENT. COMMERCIAL ROUTE

Fig. 15.   COMMERCIAL AIR ROUTES FROM LONDON COMPARED WITH GREAT CIRCLE ROUTES.

The straight lines from London are Great Circle Routes (distances shown by the scale).   Notice the use of such a route to San Francisco and the Polar Crossing to Alaska.

The need for serving large centres of population, political barriers, and the limited range of some commercial aircraft largely account for the differences between actual and Great Circle routes.

(The Great Circle route from New York to Calcutta is not to scale, but indicates the shortest distance between the two cities.)

the major air-routes to deviate by hundreds of kilometres from their direct course, simply by refusing to allow flying over their territory.

(b) Lines of air communication are likely to follow well-defined routes which converge on the world's great trading cities. There, also, the many technical facilities essential to a large airport are most readily available. Although, theoretically, the whole air is available, the necessity of carrying a pay load on both outward and return journeys may make it profitable to forgo the advantage of the shortest route and call at intermediate commercial airports.

(c) Although the routes of long-distance aircraft may pass over high mountain ranges, some short-distance lines find it uneconomical to attain the necessary height, and in consequence, wherever possible, choose routes to skirt mountains.

(d) Uncertain meteorological conditions still add to the difficulties of navigation, particularly near the poles. But the use of high altitude flying and navigational beams enables fast passenger air-lines to use the shorter Polar crossing (pages 258-60).

There is considerable internal freight transport in the larger countries like the U.S.A. and Australia; particularly valuable where other forms of transport are backward, as in much of Brazil. Not all goods can bear the high cost of air transport, but in most countries the volume of freight and the numbers of passengers carried by air is increasing. Millions of people are flown across the Atlantic each year.

The importance of airways in opening up or removing isolation from regions otherwise very difficult of access cannot be too highly stressed. In Guyana, for instance, regular flights take place between Georgetown and settlements in the interior to which there are as yet no road or rail connections. Food, hospital equipment, and mail regularly reach the inland mission stations; courts of law make their circuit by air; equipment goes to the mining districts (the parts of a 500 ton gold dredger have been flown in, to be assembled in the interior); tourists visit the great Kaieteur Falls. Return flights carry gold and diamonds, balata from the forests, and beef from the southern savannahs.

The use of aircraft for military purposes involves the construction and maintenance of special bases, whose strategic siting relative to possible targets *on the globe*, is vital to the defence of modern states and allied groups of states (Chapter XII).

Pipelines.—These are now used to transport fluids on a massive scale. Networks of pipelines arranged continentally and inter-continentally carry petroleum, gas, and refinery products, and of course, water. Some on a smaller regional scale, as in Switzerland, carry milk. This form of transport is already extended to powdered solids, *e.g.* crushed coal.

Types of Transport—A Comparison

Air Transport.

(*a*) The ability to fly above terrestrial obstacles gives a wide choice of routes.

(*b*) The vehicle is relatively small (though "jumbo" jets operate), but its speed enables it to make frequent runs.

(*c*) The need of airports roughly corresponds to the ship's need of harbours and port installations. The position and siting of the airports relative to population clusters, and as refuelling bases, is important.

(*d*) Despite the use of radar and high flying, weather conditions still impose limitations.

(*e*) It is most suitable for passengers and mail, or for small articles of high value.

(*f*) The vehicle is expensive to develop, build, and maintain; forward-planning for new forms of air transport is a long-term necessity, but suffers from the difficulties of making accurate forecasts.

Ocean Transport.

(*a*) Within ocean limits there is also a wide choice of routes.

(*b*) It requires port installations, but little or no attention to the "highway", in contrast to road, rail, and canal.

(*c*) It is a relatively slow form of transport, but can carry a great deal of freight per trip.

(*d*) It is the cheapest way of carrying bulky goods, but it needs a near capacity load.

(*e*) Large vessels are cheaper to build and maintain, and consume less fuel on a capacity-cost basis; fewer men are needed to handle them than for their equivalent in small freight carriers.

(*f*) Terminal port charges are high and quick turn-round essential; here containerisation of the load helps, and specially designed bulk carriers can be handled quickly.

(*g*) Limits to the size of vessel are set by the depth of water in port approaches and by available berthing facilities.

Somewhere between air transport and water transport is transport by *hovercraft*. These vehicles successfully carry passengers over fairly short journeys more rapidly than other sea vessels. They have also proved of great value in the exploration of difficult lowland territory, as in the basins of the Amazon and Orinoco rivers.

Inland Waterways.

(*a*) River transport, in particular, may involve devious journeys. The routes are inflexible.

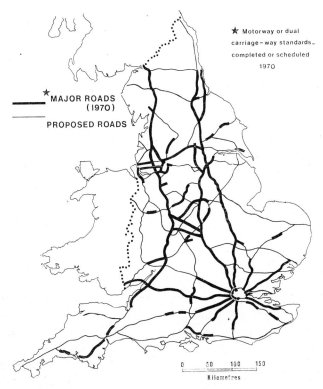

Fig. 16.   ENGLAND'S ROAD HIGHWAY NETWORK.
Motorways and routes designated in 1970 for improvement and construction.

(*b*) Transport is slow, but cheap under favourable conditions.

(*c*) Heavy, imperishable goods, such as coal, iron ore, and cement, can be transported cheaply.

(*d*) The construction of canals requires much capital. They also need constant maintenance and perhaps dredging.

PLATE V

Above: Celtic Fields—early settlement on the downlands of Dorset. (*Photo by J. K. St Joseph. British Crown Copyright Reserved.*)

Below: An abandoned medieval village, Ingarsby, Leicestershire. An air photograph shows up the form of a village of the "grassy shires" which was abandoned when enclosures deprived many agricultural labourers of their means of livelihood. (*Photo by J. K. St Joseph. British Crown Copyright Reserved.*)

PLATE VI

Above: Cultivation and forestation in West Bengal. Arable farming follows the line of the water-courses. Cultivators of small holdings live in villages amid tree clumps. In parts of West Bengal irrigation from the Damodar (page 213) supplements the erratic rainfall. (*Aerofilms.*)

Below: Caste in Indian agricultural industries. The red and white striped markings show the caste of the owners of this mill at Madura—the priests of Shiva. Zebu oxen move the heavy stones which grind and compress sesamum grain to obtain oil for cooking. (*Aerofilms.*)

(*e*) Differences in level means the use of locks or, to avoid these, the construction of canal tunnels or the use of a roundabout route.

(*f*) Navigation may be impeded by frost.

Road Transport.

(*a*) Modern motorways are direct, but road transport must often leave them to follow a route which, in long-settled countries, is determined by ancient tracks, field boundaries, or obsolete trade requirements.

(*b*) Roads need constant maintenance. Costs are high, bearing in mind the amount of surfacing, drainage, and bridging involved, though largely distributed throughout the community by taxation; so that overheads for the individual road haulier are low compared with those of a railway company.

(*c*) Operating costs for a road haulier vary in almost direct proportion to the number of vehicles in use.

(*d*) Because of the intricate network of roads there is considerable flexibility of movement. Most roads are suitable for light loads carried over a short distance, though in many countries heavy long-distance haulage has become increasingly important as new, or improved, trunk roads are constructed, and roll-on/roll-off ocean transport carry laden lorries from one country's motorway system to another's.

(*e*) Roads are widely used by private vehicles, which may hamper the free movement of transport vehicles, especially at rush-hour periods near large urban centres.

Railway Transport.

(*a*) The railways can move passengers and freight in large numbers and volume at high speed, over long distances or within a close network of routes, picking up and delivering at scheduled places at scheduled times.

(*b*) Railroad construction and operation are very costly. Installations, equipment, vehicles, and track, are expensive to maintain. Fixed costs of operation are, therefore, high.

(*c*) Fixed costs do not vary whether the system is used a lot or a little.

(*d*) Traffic flow is variable—especially commuter flow near a large urban area.

(*e*) Lines and networks established in the early days of railway transport may become obsolescent and a financial burden.

(*f*) Rail transport is comparatively inflexible.

(*g*) The greatest economies are obtained when freight is moved long distances at capacity load; for this purpose special freight-liners are developed.

(*h*) In linking up existing networks, differences in gauge may necessitate passengers and goods changing trains at certain points. The Australian railway system suffers from this drawback.

(*i*) The railway can be a direct and speedy means of land transport. In Great Britain it is the most used form of public passenger transport from town to town, but most journeys are made by road.

(*j*) The ability of the goods train to carry large quantities of freight has had enormous influence in opening up the "new lands", and in the siting of industries in the "old".

Pipelines.

(*a*) Generally a cheap form of transport, but the cost of installation is high.

(*b*) A continuous flow can be carried at a constant rate.

(*c*) The cost varies with the terrain, pipeline diameter, and viscosity of fluid.

(*d*) The rigidity of the system can be a disadvantage in changing economic conditions.

(*e*) Pipelines may be disrupted by malicious action. Even when buried they may suffer from frost-heaving or earth movements, and are difficult to inspect for deterioration.

Transport Systems

An efficient transport system operates through closely-integrated movements of different forms of transport over a variety of routeways, and aims to move passengers, small or bulky consignments, perishable goods, valuable articles, etc., as cheaply and quickly as possible.

Though individual forms of transport, on road or rail, may compete, people are best served where the integration of each form within the system is most successful. Many people and goods make journeys involving successive movements by road to rail, rail to road, road to airport, and then a plane journey followed by a succession of land movements. The siting of airports in relation to urban terminals and railway stations is thus an important consideration for millions travelling through such a system.

Conclusion

Communications are the arteries on which the very existence of the vast majority of mankind depends, and in any region are visible signs of man's occupation of the earth. The forms of transport considered above have been reviewed in terms of their significance to the "modern world". There are, however, many primitive forms of transport, just as important locally to millions of people. Human porterage is still used on a large scale in China, and in those parts of West Africa where the tsetse fly makes it impossible to use draught animals, as in some of the cocoa collecting districts. Throughout south-east Asia and Indonesia the bullock cart is the most used and most characteristic form of transport for the peasant and his produce. It is very easy to consider human activities only in terms of "Western Civilisation", forgetting that well over half of the world's population has neither the outlook nor the material possessions considered "normal" in the "West".

CHAPTER V

FEATURES OF SETTLEMENT— AGRICULTURE

Examine an aerial view of an occupied region. The most evident changes wrought by man upon the natural landscape will be the pattern of his agriculture. In open country will appear signs of tillage, crops, vegetation modified by grazing, or, perhaps, clearings stand out in the forested areas. (Compare Plates III, VI, and XVI).

The actual agricultural land-use in these areas will, of course, vary with the region observed. Man's fundamental need is to obtain food, and its production engages about three-quarters of the world's population. Side by side with this goes the production of industrial crops, notably those which give fibres and vegetable oils, and also the rearing of animals for milk and meat, wool and fur, hides and skins.

The agriculture in any particular area, and the extent to which it is developed, depends on a combination of facts and conditions:—

(1) Climate.

(2) Soil.

(3) Methods of cultivation (whether by primitive peoples or those able to use machinery, selected stock, fertilisers, etc.).

(4) Organisation of labour (on peasant holdings, farms, or plantations).

(5) Local economic facts (land rent, transport costs, market prices, etc.).

(6) World conditions (such as a glut or shortage of a commodity, government controls, tariffs, quotas, or support).

(7) Other facts (including social and religious customs).

It is these facts taken together which are responsible for this or that form of agriculture practised in a given area.

CLIMATIC AND OTHER LIMITS TO CULTIVATION

It is not as easy to explain why certain crops are predominant in various regions as it is to account for the distribution of natural vegetation; for, although the climate strongly influences the distribution of cultivated plants, there are other, and sometimes more compelling, reasons for cultivating one crop rather than another, some of which are considered below.

(*a*) The distribution of any agricultural crop is subject to two different limits:—

The absolute climatic limit, beyond which, under conditions of frost, drought, or other elements, it is impossible for the plant to survive.

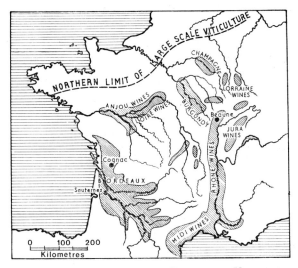

Fig. 17.   THE NORTHERN LIMIT OF LARGE-SCALE VITICULTURE.

All the principal centres of wine production lie to the south of this limit, although grapes may be gathered from outdoor vines in more northerly regions.   Excellent table grapes are produced in the hot-houses of Reykjavik, Iceland, and in numerous places of Northern Europe where an "artificial climate" is made under glass; but the economic limit of modern viticulture is as shown.

The economic limit, beyond which it is not profitable for man to cultivate the plant.   This is usually where the yield per plant becomes too low to justify it occupying the acreage devoted to it; a limit which may vary with changing economic conditions.

(*b*) The widespread use of irrigation, and of intensive farming methods with fertilisers and glass-houses, which create "artificial soil" and "artificial climates".

(*c*) The influence of pests which may bring about the shifting or abandonment of a particular crop. Since the advent of the boll-weevil in the U.S.A., the principal areas of cotton cultivation are no longer in the south-eastern States but in areas west of the Mississippi which are less affected by the insect. Coffee plantations in Sri Lanka were also devastated, in this case by a fungus, and planters have long since turned to tea cultivation; much the same has taken place in Java, though rather more slowly.

(*d*) There are often many soil types in quite a small area, so that one form of cultivation may give way to another more suited to the particular mineral contents.

(*e*) Various social and economic reasons, some of which are local and are described below; but particularly significant are the ways in which demands for industrial raw materials can vary, and in which demands from other countries whose home production is subject to periodic failure may fluctuate. Thus when China's harvests fail, she places large-scale wheat orders with Canada and Australia.

All these can bring about modifications of the general distribution otherwise controlled by the climate. There are always local variations in climate within any broad climatic region, so that the form of agriculture may change with, say, variations in the quantity and seasonal distribution of rainfall, and with regional differences in temperature.

THE SOIL

Man probably feels closer to the soil than to any other part of his natural surroundings for, at least, he may tend it, and, to some degree, alter its composition to suit his own requirements. It is a natural asset which may be conserved and improved by careful management, but which, if plundered regardlessly, will rapidly deteriorate, no matter how rich its virgin state.

Constitution of the Soil.—The soil is fundamentally composed of mineral particles of varying size such as sand and clay derived from a parent rock or variety of rocks. A mixed soil, such as alluvium, or the lighter glacial soils, provides a variety of essential minerals. Between the mineral particles are air and water with various salts in solution. Mixed with this is humus, the product of vegetable and animal decay, brought about by innumerable bacteria. Through the agency of nitrifying bacteria, for instance, the decaying matter provides the plants with nitrogen as soluble nitrates. There are also other living creatures, such as earthworms, which assist in aerating and mixing the soil. From this complex mixture the plants absorb soluble mineral salts.

The plants flourish and may be eaten by animals, which discharge their waste upon the soil, and finally die and decay. The plants drop their leaves to rot upon the surface and then themselves suffer final decomposition. Each process returns to the soil compounds of nitrogen and other elements needed for fresh plant growth.

Man may break this natural cycle. The vegetation is removed to feed people remote from the soil itself. In modern civilisations, neither man's waste products—returned to the rivers via sewage works—nor his own remains are returned to the soil. By contrast, the peasant farmers in China and south-east Asia do make use of human waste upon the fields, though in these closely populated lands there is the risk that this may spread disease. The great danger arising from man's interference with natural soil stability is that without replenishment of substances essential to plant growth the soil will become useless for agricultural purposes, and, stripped of its natural plant cover, will be at the mercy of the weather, with the likelihood of subsequent soil erosion.

METHODS OF CULTIVATION

Early Development.—Cultivation with the aid of irrigation is known to have been practised in the flood plains of North Africa and south-west Asia over seven thousand years ago. With the retreat of the great European Ice Sheets these lands had become progressively more arid, and it is probable that groups of hunters and gleaners began to settle near the rivers. Varieties of millet, barley, and wheat, were collected from the wild state and cultivated along the Euphrates and the Nile. In south-east Asia men had begun to cultivate roots and bananas, and to use rice as a food plant, though exactly when it is impossible to say.

In the forest areas a shifting agriculture developed. A patch of land would be cleared, exploited, its soils depleted, and finally deserted, to return to scrub, or perhaps inferior forest. In Europe, too, cleared patches were similarly used, though early agriculture was less widespread, mainly due to the more rigorous climate, the difficulties of clearing, and the lack of native food plants.

Along the Nile strings of villages were established with more or less permanent holdings, and here the early ploughs lightly broke the hard-baked crust of the flood-plain. The use of the plough spread to the alluvial plains of northern India and northern China, and was used on the lighter soils of Europe.

Until the advent of iron tools the forests of northern Europe were not easy to clear, and the heavier land was difficult to plough. However, clearances were made and pastures developed; the pig and the sheep were the domestic animals first associated with these early settlements. Later, new stock was introduced from Asia, where, on the edge of the steppes and in the broader flood-plains, such as Mesopotamia, pastoral activities had developed along with cultivation.

We must leave a more detailed description of the cultivated plants, their origins, and their present uses, to be studied separately. Also, to trace the details of development from primitive to modern agriculture, requires a series of separate studies for each region where this has taken place; but a glimpse of the progress made in England will help to show the continually changing relations between men and the land they occupy.

The Development of Agriculture in England.—The first farming peoples must have arrived, four or five thousand years ago, to find aboriginal hunting and fishing communities living in a land which was closely forested, especially over the lowland areas. The first agricultural settlements were on the uplands of southern England, where grazing must have halted the natural regeneration of the light forest growth upon the chalk and limestone.

During the advent of a succession of invading groups from the Continent the clearing of the forests continued in these areas, and pastoralism became centred chiefly on the chalk areas on and around Salisbury Plain. The cultivation of grain increased during the last millenium B.C., and some of the lighter soils were ploughed into rough rectangular fields, near which small farmsteads with fenced yards were built (Plate V).

In the fifth century B.C. iron tools began to be used. With improved technique, enough grain was harvested to allow storage in pits, to be drawn upon in winter by the population, which by this time had increased rapidly by immigration. Small clusters of farmsteads were appearing.

Shortly before the main Roman occupation, tribes from the Low Countries introduced improved iron tools, and with them spread cultivation to the heavier valley soils. Fresh and extensive inroads were made into the forests and the agricultural possibilities of these heavy loams and clays were exploited for the first time, with the aid of large iron wheeled ploughs yoked to teams of oxen. The environmental influence of chalk and limestone upon settlement was weakening, though only slightly as yet.

Under the Romans privately-owned villas replaced many of the old farmsteads. These were sometimes converted from the older buildings, or were new self-contained farms, with barns and labourers' quarters. The long open plots, which owed much in origin to the heavy Belgic plough, continued to be used as the basis of a farming system, which provided bread, animal produce, and wine. Use was made of "fallow", a short rest period for the soil.

The Roman villas represented a much more stable form of settlement than their artificially-created towns, which, like the planned road system, were designed both for military purposes and to serve as symbols of authority. But, because of their isolation, the villas were easy prey for subsequent invaders.

In most of the old areas of settlement peasants still lived a primitive existence, using the old types of plough, but gradually extending the numbers of small fields.

Anglo-Saxon invaders came to Britain with a previous experience of life in forested country and made great progress in clearing the lowlands. They penetrated along the rivers and occupied the valley sides—in some parts of England terraced them. During this period there was a downward movement of the native population from the old hill settlements. In both Saxon and Danish agriculture long open strips were ploughed, and the open-field system which evolved became the basic pattern of medieval agriculture.

The manorial system, partly begun, allowed the family to farm a strip in each of the large fields which lay around the manor house and the nearby dwellings, and also common use of the water meadow (Fig. 18). Three fields were generally under plough and a rotation of crops,* in which the family could share, was thus made possible. The nature of the soils was reflected to some extent by the use of a three-field system on the better soil and the two-field system, giving a longer fallow period, on the poorer.

The lands of the manor and village contained a population which had little intercourse with neighbours, for cow downs and sheep pastures lay beyond the tillage area, as part of the waste ground separating one community from the next. Meat came chiefly from swine, cows being kept for milk, and sheep for wool. Lack of winter fodder led to the slaughtering of many cattle in the autumn, the meat being stored in brine. Most of the produce went to make the manor self-supporting.

Thus there were established rural settlements supported by a specific adjacent rural area, which was extended as population increased. As the outer limits became too distant for economic cultivation from the small settlement, groups might migrate to clear and settle elsewhere.

---

* Rotation of crops is often practised in quite primitive communities and although frequently looked on as relatively modern in conception, had its roots in the trial and error plantings of early agriculturalists. Primitive tribes on the Nigerian Plateau evolved a rotation system, and also used animal manure.

[In many countries open-field cultivation is in common use today; and in some it is customary to divide the unfenced land between heirs, creating the problem of diminishing size of holdings. Such a problem is very real in the Middle East, in parts of France, and elsewhere. The plots are not only small, but a man's holdings may be far apart, scattered around the village (page 68). Good ground is wasted on paths and boundary ridges, and much time is lost in getting from one plot to another.]

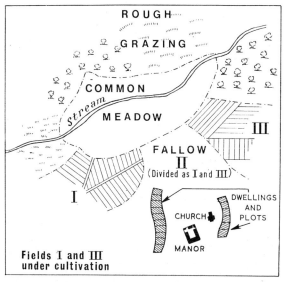

Fig. 18. THE MEDIEVAL MANOR.

Around the fortified manor house, with its enclosed courtyard and church, lay the less substantial peasant hovels, most of them with small garden plots. Beyond the cluster of dwellings were the three fields, the common meadow, and, further afield, the rough pasture.

In England the fourteenth century saw the beginning of a great turnover from arable farming to the more profitable sheep rearing. High returns were obtained from the pasture lands, which naturally required enclosures. These enclosures became more common as the number of landholders increased, following the Peasants' Revolt and the decline of feudalism, and, because wool retained its high place in the country's exports, the numbers of sheep continued to increase. Unfortunately many landless labourers became redundant as there was less demand for work upon arable land, and much migration took place from the "grassy shires" of the Midlands, where the sites of abandoned villages can still be traced (Plate V).

The pattern of the fields changed as larger, more compact, holdings were formed about large individual farmhouses. From Tudor times there was a continuous, though variable, increase in the number of enclosures. In the mid-eighteenth century the Enclosure Acts brought about the fencing of millions of acres, although even in the early nineteenth century there was agitation for completion of the enclosures, particularly in the Midlands.

During the sixteenth and seventeenth centuries many vegetables and root crops were introduced from the Continent. The legumes, such as clover, with their nitrifying bacteria, were a very important innovation. Enclosure had made possible the control of their use and, in the early eighteenth century, the four-course rotation, or "Norfolk" system, was introduced. Wheat was followed by turnips to feed sheep, which manured the land for barley in the third year, while in the fourth year legumes returned nitrogen to the soil.

About the same period, enclosures also made possible a new approach to stock breeding, and Midland tenant farmers were able to produce the now famous breeds of English sheep and cattle.

The nineteenth century saw the shipping of fertiliser from abroad, and the twentieth century has brought great developments in agricultural machinery and in soil science.

***Geographical Facts Behind Agricultural Developments.*—** Although many different political and economic factors have affected the development of English agriculture through the centuries, the basic facts of soil, climate, and relief, have been the foundations of rural life and their effects are always apparent in the rural scene.

The order of clearance of the forests and the positions of the early settlements were strongly influenced by the underlying rock and soil type. Other demands upon the woodland, of course, accelerated the clearance; buildings meant a steady drain of timber; early industry called for charcoal, and later for pit-props, particularly near the iron ore centres of the Forest of Dean and the Weald; and the expansion of the mercantile navy had an effect on the rate of clearance.

The influences of climate and relief were reflected in the initial distribution of scattered farmsteads in the more pastoral west, and the compact villages of the manorial lands of the south and east, on soils which are more suited to arable farming. Here the holdings tended to be arranged according to soil conditions: meadows on the colder, heavier soil, and crops on the lighter soils, depending, of course, on the availability of such land and on earlier settlement.

The actual boundaries of the enclosed fields closely followed the changes of relief or parent rock. The hedge, or else a stone wall, was a characteristic feature of the English countryside. The hawthorn, beech, hornbeam, holly, or oak, have all been planted according to the local conditions of sub-soil and climate. The type of stone in the walls, the method of hedging, and the different standards in the hedges vary from region to region.

Economic Facts Behind Agricultural Land-Use.—When the carriage of goods depended on head loads and animal transport, journeys to market, and to and from the fields, took a considerable time.

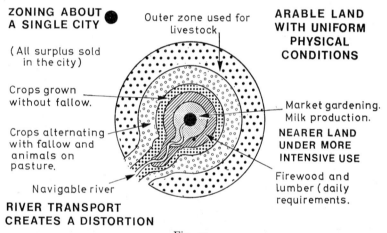

ZONING ABOUT A SINGLE CITY

(All surplus sold in the city)

Crops grown without fallow.

Crops alternating with fallow and animals on pasture.

Navigable river

RIVER TRANSPORT CREATES A DISTORTION

Outer zone used for livestock

ARABLE LAND WITH UNIFORM PHYSICAL CONDITIONS

Market gardening. Milk production.

NEARER LAND UNDER MORE INTENSIVE USE

Firewood and lumber (daily requirements.

Fig. 19.

Where a particular crop, or a dairy cow, required much attention, it was likely to be located as near as possible to the homestead, hamlet, or village. A recognisable zoning of land-use tended to develop about each rural settlement, with those activities requiring only occasional attention located further from the centre. Such patterns may be seen today about villages in the Mediterranean lands, the plains of India, and wherever agriculture is carried out from small nucleated settlements.

In 1826 J. H. von Thünen, who managed an estate near Rostock, in north-eastern Europe, published a book which analysed the relationships between various forms of agricultural activities and their distribution about a single place. He postulated an "isolated state"— one city surrounded by arable land with uniform physical conditions. Each farmer sold his produce in the city and each bore the costs of transport by horse-drawn vehicle. Also, each farmer wished to obtain the highest possible net return from each particular piece of land, and so would put it to the most profitable land-use.

Net returns from market gardening, milk production, lumbering (wood cutting), livestock farming, and various forms of arable farming were considered. The result, summarised in the model (Fig. 19), reflects a substitution of forms of land-use: as distance from market

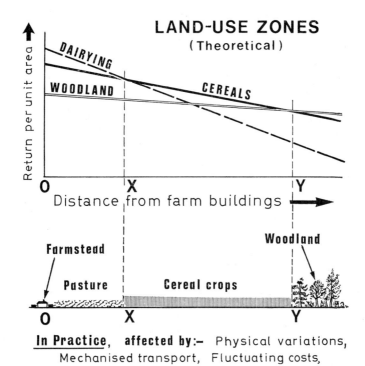

Fig. 20. *Return-Distance Relationships in Farming. The more distant land is put to a less intensive form of land-use.*

increases, the return per unit area from one form of land-use falls to a point where it is profitable to substitute another.

In von Thünen's time wood was much used for fuel, and could return higher profits per acre than, say, rye, if transport costs were low. Types of arable farming of decreasing intensity lay further out. Lower production costs offset the higher costs of transport. Beyond these was livestock farming, the least intensive of the uses.

It is generally still true, especially in peasant lands and about nucleated agricultural villages, that the nearer fields are preferred for more intensive forms of cultivation.

Land-Use about a Farm

Theory. If we again assume uniform physical conditions, and a farmer is looking for an optimum return, seeking to maximise his return for the effort he puts in, we might expect to see evidence of zoning about his farm-house (Fig. 20).

In the case of dairy farming, the cost per unit area increases rapidly with distance from the farm buildings; for the animals are brought in for milking, supplied with fodder, or the grazing controlled, and time is part of the farmer's input. The "friction of distance" is great, and the return to the farmer is higher per unit of land nearer the centre. The more distant land is put to a less intensive form of land-use. Arable crops require less regular attention, so that the return per unit area falls less rapidly with distance. Woodland requires only occasional attention, and so it may be profitable to leave the outer parts to provide an income from timber.

Practice. Such considerations undoubtedly influence land-use distribution. But as market prices fluctuate, returns from various forms of land-use will also fluctuate. Mechanisation allows the farmer to travel rapidly to attend to different parts of his land, and extra fuel is likely to be only a minor consideration.

Some parts of his holding may be physically more suitable for one form of land use rather than another. Changing costs of seed, stock, fertiliser, and altered quotas or subsidies, will influence the farmer's decisions concerning the most profitable arrangement.

The return-distance factors we have noted may act to produce a zoning of forms of land-use, but the pattern is likely to be much modified by so many other considerations that in intensive, temperate mixed farming, it is usually difficult to detect the results of individual influences.

Nevertheless, clear zoning is often apparent about agricultural villages in the less capitalised farming lands. In Cyprus, for instance, the zone close about the village houses, and often including the rooftops and house gardens, is usually devoted to vegetables, household vines, citrus trees, mulberries, almonds and other plants needing careful and frequent treatment. Beyond are olives and carobs, with land ploughed beneath for grain-growing; vineyards tended periodically, beyond this; and further off, perhaps under old olives, are grassy pastures, where flocks or herds of goats are tended. Finally, between villages is rough, stony country, grazed more extensively.

DIVISION OF LABOUR—THE MAIN TYPES OF FARMING ORGANISATION

The progress from the peasant's small holding and communal village land to the larger isolated farms with a system of hired labour that came to exist in England is not typical of the world as a whole. Over much of the world, especially in eastern Europe and Asia, the majority of the cultivators are peasants. The way in which land is held and the method of using available labour varies from region to region. The following is an outline of the main types of farming organisation, related to the various regions in which they are practised.

Shifting agriculture, although still practised in the equatorial and monsoon forests, and to some extent on the savannahs, does no more than give means of subsistence. In some cases, however, as in parts of West Africa, foodstuffs are obtained from shifting cultivation of the land around a settlement, while a cash product is gathered from trees, chiefly from the cacao and oil palm.

Peasant Cultivation.—Whether they are tenants or not, their land usually consists of small holdings on which the family labours, first to subsist and then, if possible, to produce a marketable surplus.

(i) In much of monsoon Asia production is merely at subsistence level, although where possible surplus crops are sold off the land. The relative prosperity of the peasant depends on the proportion of his land which he is able to devote to a cash crop, and this varies, of course, with his geographical location. There is a world of difference between the bare subsistence obtained by the peasant in the drier inland regions of Mysore, and the high standard of living in some of the coastal districts of Madras, where three crops of rice may be obtained during the year. In general, however, the population pressure is so great in the rice areas as to make the holdings very small.

In the more fertile irrigated areas peasant production of sugar or cotton makes for a higher income. Unfortunately, owing to harsh conditions of tenure and personal debts, this does not necessarily lead to a higher standard of living.

(ii) In Central and South America the peasant holdings are usually very poor. There has been as yet little incentive in the way of a good market for cash crops from peasant sources, for peasant produce must invariably come into competition with that of the great plantations of the southern U.S.A., West Indies, and Brazil.

(iii) In West Africa, by contrast, the produce of some peasant farmers finds a ready market in Europe, especially for the cocoa and palm oil produced in Ghana and Nigeria. It would perhaps be better to call many of the peasants "collectors" rather than farmers, and one of the causes of inefficient production is that the careful treatment and attention which the farmer must give to all crops is too often denied to the local trees. As with most types of peasant farming the chief disadvantages are the use of primitive tools and backward methods of production. In the case of palm oil the peasant has come more and more into competition with plantations. He crushes his fruit in a large stone mortar, or a simple form of handpress, and obtains a yield of oil which is well below that he could obtain by using up-to-date methods of extraction.

A great drawback in the peasant system is the difficulty of introducing innovations which would undoubtedly benefit the crop as a whole. In Ghana an attempt to legislate for the removal of cacao trees suffering from swollen root disease, in order to isolate infected areas, met with such resistance that voluntary efforts were substituted. Even treatment by insecticide (hannane) at first proved difficult to carry out in the face of local apathy.

Modern methods are difficult to apply to small holdings, scattered haphazardly. The technical knowledge and skill has come mainly from western Europe. It appears, therefore, that only overall government control, sponsoring the provision of tools and materials, carrying out research, and creating better transport facilities and market organisation, can make for all-round improvement. Among the priorities must be better local education.

(iv) Eastern European state-imposed "collective" policy has aimed to effect a radical change in the peasant's status, with greatest initial success on the former large estates and richer lowland areas, but less in the more remote districts.

(v) In the lands surrounding the Mediterranean, the climate does not favour the growth of grass and fodder crops throughout the year and limits pastoral activities, although in some regions transhumance is practised. The peasant holdings are again small, and there is generally a lack of capital for the production of commercial crops, though the olive, vine, and citrus fruit, may be cultivated in combination with the usual subsistence crops. Competition from other "Mediterranean" regions, where ready capital is available (California, for example) is lessened to some extent by the accessibility of nearby European markets, by local currency advantages, and by the different time of the growing season in comparable regions in Australia and South Africa.

(vi) In north-west Europe and in North America subsistence farming is not a general practice. However, in certain areas there are small holdings where the peasant comes near to a meagre self-sufficiency;

PLATE VII

Left: A regular group of "beehive" huts of Chavante Indians in the Amazon Basin; thatch covers bent saplings. Like all who adopt a settled way of life, these primitive folk create a landscape pattern by their clearings, tracks, and habitations. (*Pan American World Airways System*.)

Right: A Swiss mountain village, Saas-Fee, of both stone and timber, with roofs of slate and of shingles. Note the stone "mushrooms" in the foreground to guard against rats. In such country, villages may have to be carefully sited against avalanches and land-slides. (*Swiss National Tourist Office*.)

PLATE VIII

Two compact settlements. (*Above*) Blanchland, Northumberland, of eighteenth century planning—in country where the clustered form of village often stems from the need for protective, stockaded settlement. (*Below*) Ashmore, high on the Dorset downs; where surface water is scarce the rounded village lies about a pond. Notice the different region character of these settlements in their Pennine and chalk downland settings. (*Aerofilms.*)

but more generally the farmers, however poor, are engaged in different forms of what may be termed "Temperate Mixed Farming" (page 66).

Plantation Agriculture.—The first great expansion of sea trade in the sixteenth and seventeenth centuries brought to Europe many products from the tropics. The great Trading Companies brought back raw materials which were largely the produce of peasant cultivation. The increasing demand for spices, coffee, tea, cocoa, and sugar, was further encouraged by the rise of European industries. Fibre, vegetable oils, and rubber, became essentials.

Long ago the Portuguese established plantations in Brazil and on islands off the West African coast, and in the Americas cotton plantations were worked by slave-labour. But in south-east Asia, the organisation of native agriculture and native labour under direct European supervision was not firmly established until the late nineteenth century, except in Java, where from 1831 the peasants cultivated one-fifth of their land in accordance with Dutch stipulation, the produce of which was delivered as taxes. However, by establishing a firm control over the trade in local produce, Europeans obtained a political control over many of the productive agricultural regions of south-east Asia. The transfer of cultivable plants from one tropical region to another, such as the establishment of Brazilian rubber (*Hevea*) in Malaya, helped to bring the plantation system into being.

Plantation and Peasant Cultivation—A Comparison.—
(i) Plantations are large economic units. Capital is needed for land, for initial clearing and planting, for roads, accommodation, machinery, pesticides, and a host of other modern aids to cultivation, harvesting, and processing such crops as rubber, coffee, and sugar, before shipment.

(ii) Labour for the plantations is often imported from afar. This may be due to lack of indigenous labour, through scarcity or disinclination, or because of the skill of certain peoples in a particular form of agriculture. Thus Indian labour has been used on coffee and tea plantations in Trinidad and Natal, South Africa, and in the tea and rubber plantations of Malaya.

(iii) Unlike the products of peasant agriculture, the cash crop is all-important on the plantation, and much of the food for the workers is brought from outside.

(iv) Many crops are grown both by peasant cultivation and plantation methods, and sometimes, as in the case of Fijian sugar, the peasant sells direct to the mills.

I. TO H. G.   5

Cacao is mainly a plantation crop in Brazil and Indonesia but a peasant crop in Ghana, where the marketing has been successfully organised by the large cocoa firms. The labour organisation in the case of cotton and cane-sugar production also varies from one land to another.

(v) The social structure of the plantation system is apt to be a potential source of political friction. An "aristocracy", often European, a foreign labour community, a different foreign trading element, and the local population, all live side by side at different economic levels. Thus in Malaysia there may be British supervisors, Tamil rubber tappers, Chinese traders, and a local Malay population.

With the peasant system, the population remains more or less homogeneous, shares any increases in living standards, and, by taking a part in trade, may develop its own leaders.

(vi) The desire of plantation owners to exploit to the full the continuous growing season of the near-equatorial regions has, in some cases, led to over-cropping and a deterioration in soil conditions.

In well laid out plantations the organic replacement by natural leaf fall is often lacking. The soil may also be exposed to extremes of heat and torrential rain, with consequent leaching and erosion. Many rubber plantations allow secondary forest to develop between the trees, or as an alternative legumes are sometimes sown. Among the natural vegetation pests act on each other in a balanced biological control, which may be upset by clearing. By removing a species of plant completely, insects associated with it may also be removed; but they may have attacked, and thus controlled, other harmful insects. A single cash crop in unprotected rows may be liable to violent pestilential attack, as from the fungus which destroyed the coffee of Sri Lanka.

The "disorderliness" of native gardens may give a small but constant yield, yet in the long run prove more efficient than the clean-weeded plantation. In Malaysia there has been a great increase in the number of small holdings producing rubber, for not only have small rubber estates been established by Asiatics, but rubber trees are also grown by small-holders side by side with rice or cassava. At present nearly half the rubber produced comes from small holdings. Erosion due to over-cropping is by no means confined to equatorial regions: many of the original coffee and cotton lands in São Paulo State, Brazil, have sadly deteriorated through misuse.

Temperate Mixed Farming.—(i) Mixed farming as represented by English agriculture has already been considered. The chief characteristic is a wide variety of crops, which are sold off the farm, often to large processers or packagers, sometimes in a nearby market town.

(ii) The huge demand for fresh foods by urban populations means that near the towns there is intensive market gardening, poultry farming, and, in many cases, dairying. Further afield lie the areas of mixed arable farming and bigger cattle farms.

(iii) Much capital is needed for modern intensive farming, where fertilisers play their part in assuring a high yield and agricultural machinery is used, if the size of the holding and the relief permit. Although after a time fertilisers and machinery more than pay for themselves, the initial cost is heavy.

(iv) Holdings vary in size, from great estates to the small strips of many French farmers.

In France, where about a quarter of the working population is employed in agriculture, compared with less than a twentieth in Britain, the size and nature of the farm vary from region to region. Farming practices are adapted to the natural environment, which often changes abruptly, and consequently there are marked regional differences. In the north large arable farms, run by tenant farmers, produce wheat and sugar beet. In Normandy, the dairying, moist pastures, and orchards of cider apples, are reminiscent of south-west England. Brittany provides early flowers and vegetables from small fields near the sea, but much of the upland soil is thin and acid, derived from crystalline rocks of which the low farm buildings are built. Poitou, though fertile, has suffered from the pernicious system of division of the inheritance. "It is nothing uncommon for a peasant cultivating twenty acres to have it in fifty separate pieces scattered all over the commune, some of them three or four miles from his homestead . . . In France wheat costs nearly twice as much to produce on a field of two-fifths of an acre as on a field of three acres."*

A policy of *remembrement* has helped to overcome this severe fragmentation. In this the small scattered holdings are combined with adjacent land, and after consolidation the larger units are reallocated. But the practice described by Yates underlines the inefficiency inherent in such systems which are common in other parts of the world.

Other parts of France have developed distinct regional characteristics in agriculture: the cooperative systems of the great dairying region of Charentes; the vineyards of Bordeaux and the flower growing of Provence; share cropping in the Midi. In marked contrast are the bleak limestone mountains of the Causses and the Massif where,

* P. LAMARTINE YATES, "Farming in France", *Geogr. Mag.*, vol. **19**, p. 375.

through the ages, peasants raised sheep and cattle; and again there is the transhumance of the dairy herds in the Savoy Alps. Thus France provides ample illustrations of the contrasts and variations to be found with this type of agriculture.

(v) The actual amount of land cultivated, and the proportion of arable to pasture, depend not only on the climate and the soil but on all

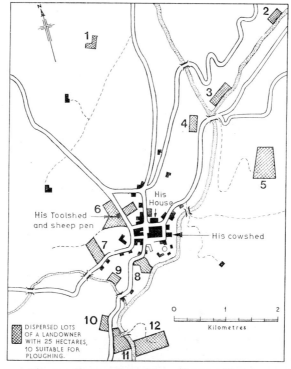

Fig. 21.   Beaufort—in South-Eastern France.

A small village where the division of land under the Laws of Inheritance produced scattered holdings. A shortage of agricultural labour adds to the difficulties of the small farmer. Here the landowner divided his time and labour between twelve widely scattered lots. In many parts of France, redistribution and consolidation of farm holdings has made headway.

kinds of economic and political considerations, which may make it necessary to concentrate on one form of agriculture rather than another.

Extensive Farming—The More Recently Settled Lands.—
These are the lands which received the majority of the European emigrants during the last century, and include Australasia and much of

North and South America. To these may be added much of the U.S.S.R. and southern and eastern Africa. A large part of the farming in the lands of eastern Africa, with marked social differentiation between the settler and native labourers, has resembled the plantation type already considered.

Grain Production

Initially, large tracts of grassland and open scrub were put down to grain, usually wheat. In the maize belts of the U.S.A. and South Africa, there was extensive use of black labour, and the agricultural organisation of the latter is essentially different.

The rich chernozem soils of the temperate grasslands at first allowed the growth of successions of grain crops without rotation or improvement. But such continuous demands upon the soil ultimately brings loss of fertility, and most of these regions have already turned to large-scale application of fertilisers or the use of rotation systems.

The part the great wheat lands play in feeding foreign populations, particularly in Europe, tends to obscure the dangers of soil exhaustion. A survey by the United States Soil Conservation Service has indicated that in the entire country, including the great prairie lands, the land which can be safely cultivated without the risk of serious depletion is only about one-and-a-quarter times the area of Great Britain. All the remaining agricultural land requires protective measures to prevent erosion, water-logging, or harmful accumulation of salts.

There has been a marked trend towards diversification on the grasslands of Canada, Argentina, and the U.S.S.R. In Argentina, wheat growing is usually associated with alfalfa, barley, and green fodder cultivation, and therefore with pastoral farming. The dangers of monoculture, entailing large risks from the vagaries of climate, pests, and the fluctuations of world markets, are well appreciated by farmers, who, through bitter experience, are now less willing to put all their eggs in one basket.

A variety of crops means a more efficient use of land and labour throughout the year; with monoculture the demand for labour is largely seasonal, being greatest at harvest time. The low yield per acre obtained from these extensive lands indicates that farming on such a scale cannot in the long run be efficient, though broadcasting fertiliser and pest-controlling chemicals and the use of selected grains helps to raise the output.

Quota Systems

Governments may fix quotas for grain production from certain regions and this may be broken down to allow each farmer to meet his own particular quota, usually with a guaranteed minimum price—although prices, like quotas, vary or may be fixed annually. If a farmer delivers his quotas to a local storage elevator and has surplus, he may or may not be allowed to deliver that surplus at less advantageous price.   Yields are difficult to forecast and at government level demands for grain from other countries fluctuate; there is thus an element of risk, and where this becomes too great a farmer may, if he can, adopt an alternative form of land-use—increasing his proportion of stock or, possibly, diversifying his arable production.

Extensive Pastoral Farming

Pastoral farming is a major occupation on the great natural grasslands. On the drier grasslands this is of an extensive nature, and large expanses of ranching country are needed to provide sufficient grazing for the herds.   In Australia and North America many cattle are sent to fattening areas before slaughtering, though the creation of irrigated pastures within the drier grazing lands is counteracting this.

In many parts of these countries, however, where the moisture is sufficient, pastoral farming takes place on contained and fenced grassland, with sown pasture and the help of fodder crops.   On the Humid Pampa of Argentina, for instance, the naturally fertile soils, the ubiquitous wind-pumps, the growth of leguminous plants (alfalfa) and European grasses, and an excellent railway network make possible a very large cattle industry.   The introduction of quebracho posts and wire fencing allowed selective breeding of cattle, and consequent improvements in the quality of the stock.   The need for plentiful and regular watering points is obvious; the wind pumps of Argentina and Uruguay and the artesian bores of Australia are essential for the development of pastoral industries.

Over large marginal areas of the Australian outback sheep farming is the dominant occupation; elswhere extensive wheat and sheep farming go together.   In some countries sheep and cattle have a zone of contact for large-scale grazing, and competition for pastures has led to considerable friction.   Sheep crop closely, and may produce plant associations unsuitable for cattle; they are also more likely to create conditions leading to erosion.   On the eastern slopes of the Rockies in the "mid-eighties", the friction between cattle and sheep ranchers led to serious skirmishing, and much the same took place in the early days in southern Australia.

The pastoral industries have been much affected by outside influences.   In the 1870's disease in the British herds, the rapid expansion of the American home market, and the Homestead Act, which enabled ranchers to settle at low cost and range their cattle over adjacent land, combined to cause a great increase in the number of cattle on the prairies. The type of stock changed as the road and rail pushed westwards. The Texas Long Horn, which could thrive on sparse foliage and stand the long drive to the fattening areas, was replaced by stockier pure-British breeds which could now be carried by rail. In any case, the actual size of the horns of the Texas stock made them unsuited to close packing in railway wagons.

One of the greatest influences on land-use on the grasslands was the advent of the refrigeration ship in 1882. Distance from the big European markets became as nothing. Where once live cattle were imported into Europe for slaughtering, or meat was received salted, refrigeration chambers in railway wagons and ships delivered barrelled, canned, or frozen meat. This was particularly revolutionary in the cases of New Zealand and the Argentine, where flocks and herds greatly increased, and changed in type and quality as it became profitable to keep good meat-producing stock. Unfortunately, in New Zealand, where the grasslands had been cleared from forest, this resulted in over-grazing and soil erosion.

Communications

The occupation of these vast primary producing areas forged ahead as the railroads pushed further inland. Rail systems focused on the outlet ports. In Argentina an extensive railway network developed with the maritime centres of refrigeration and grain storage as its foci. In each of the countries a grid pattern of roads subsequently developed.

Other Farming Occupations

Large-scale grain production and ranching are not the only agricultural occupations in the newer lands. Near the cities are areas of intensive agriculture which give way to mixed rotational farming, with the accent on grain production. This latter system has been brought into use throughout the Ukraine, as well as in the Americas.

Also, of course, in other parts of these lands there are climatic regions with conditions favourable to other crops. To cite a few: in Canada there is the fertile Ontario Peninsula with its small holdings, and the long strips of farms, with mixed farming, along the St Lawrence Valley; in Australia there are the fruit farming districts of Tasmania, and the sugar-growing coastlands in eastern, tropical Queensland; each has distinctive forms of agriculture. Many of the newer agricultural regions had the advantage of a planned economy from the start. The citrus industries of Florida and California, tobacco growing in Rhodesia; cotton in the irrigated areas of the Uzbek Republic,

U.S.S.R., are all examples of development in territory where there have been few problems resulting from former occupation.

WORLD CONDITIONS

In most parts of the world the area under cultivation, and the amount of land devoted to any particular crop, are responses to world-wide social and economic conditions. In Chapter IX the question of world population and food production is examined in some detail. Among the general facts which may decide the amount and distribution of crops in any region, other than suitable physical conditions, are:—

Attempts to Control Production.—The densely-populated industrialised nations in temperate latitudes import foodstuffs from primary producing nations—grain from Canada, wool from Australia, sugar from the West Indies, coffee from Brazil, cocoa from West Africa, among them. Sometimes the economy of these exporting countries is closely tied to one or two crops which leaves them open to the consequences of depressions and overproduction. The large producers are very vulnerable to any contraction of demand. On the other hand, the small-holder, selling such a commodity merely as surplus, is in a stronger position in the event of an economic crisis. In a general depression those countries which produce "luxury" commodities are hard hit.

Technical Developments.—These may create a particular demand for a certain raw material, such as that of the car industry for rubber. Conversely, they may bring about the decline in the use of certain commodities, in the way that synthetic aniline dyes ousted natural indigo dye, when the work of a group of German chemists changed the form of agriculture practised by thousands of Bengali peasants, who formerly cultivated the indigo plant. Between 1895 and 1913 India's annual export of indigo fell from 18 700 tons to 1 110 tons. Again, with the production of synthetic threads the "silk" industry no longer depends entirely upon the mulberry tree.

Political Insecurity.—Insecurity may cause a nation to strive for agricultural independence and self-sufficiency, and wartime conditions accentuate this. In Great Britain in World War II the need to cut down imported grain and animal foodstuffs caused the farmers to bring marginal land into production, at a high cost in fertilisers and extra mechanisation. Much permanent pasture was converted to arable, which was largely devoted to fodder crops to help to maintain milk production.

LAND USE—GREAT BRITAIN, 1939-45

HECTARES ('000)

	ARABLE	PERMANENT GRASS
1939	5225	7643
1945	7766	4389

The area under beet-sugar, already subsidised, was also greatly increased. In the interests of survival, many crops were subsidised, for cost had to be a secondary consideration in the effort to achieve self-sufficiency.

Area Available Relative to Other Countries.—Increasing foreign competition may bring about a change in a nation's economy. Denmark is a small country whose climate and soil can give an exceptionally high yield of wheat (over 4000 kg per hectare). Yet, in the face of a volume of cheap grain from the newer lands, where average yields were of the order of 1500 kg per hectare, the government voted for a change to a dairy farming economy, for which produce the dense populations of industrial north-west Europe provide ready markets; this now forms the basis of the country's economy.

Cooperative Schemes.—Many farmers have formed cooperative organisations to help them obtain, improve, and market, their produce, and compete successfully at home and in the world's markets. These may be relatively small concerns as in the Irish creameries, or on a much bigger scale, as in the production of wheat in France, the U.S.A., and elsewhere. (Other systems of cooperation are considered in Chapter IX.)

Tariffs.—Laws, Tariffs, or Quotas, imposed by governments to restrict imports and to increase home production of various crops, obviously have a direct effect upon land use. The repeal of the Corn Laws, for instance, caused a major reorganisation of British agriculture.

OTHER INFLUENCES UPON AGRICULTURE

The small farmer and peasant may be heir to customs, or to inescapable conditions of land tenure, which have very restricting effects upon his methods of agriculture. The life of Asian peasants, for example, is interwoven with a host of such factors, some of which are indicated below.

Religious Influences and Tribal Customs.—One of the most outstanding examples of direct religious influence is the reluctance of the orthodox Hindu to introduce restrictive breeding among the millions of cattle. This results in serious overstocking and in the perpetuation of poor stock. Also, the great numbers of Indian cattle which are left to die a natural death not only spread disease but consume already scarce grazing.

In China the veneration of ancestors and ancestral property tied the bulk of the population very firmly to the land of their fathers. Burial took place within the small family holdings, so that burial mounds occupied part of the precious land, upon which the population presses ever more severely. Cemeteries are, of course, part of the unproductive use of many lands. Asiatic peasants are notoriously conservative in outlook and resist land reforms, but young Communists have reacted to ideological persuasion, and so broken close family ties, redistributed land, and run new communes; in many provinces large flat fields have replaced the old irregular plots and mounds.

In Indonesia rice is a symbol of fertility, and in Bali, in particular, many still insist that paddy fields may not be defiled by fertilisers. Fortunately most of the lowland soils are extremely rich.

Many tribal peoples have customs or long-standing practices which must needs be discarded before agricultural productivity can be increased. One form of uneconomical practice is the custom of regarding cattle as a form of wealth in themselves, which is still prevalent throughout the African grasslands. As they are used as a basis of exchange, quantity rather than quality of the cattle counts most. This leads to overstocking and overgrazing, and is responsible for much deterioration of the grasslands.

Debt and the Effect of Social Functions.—The three major occasions in the life of the peasant, birth, marriage, and death, are often commemorated in a manner far beyond the means of the family. The result, especially in India, is that the farmer becomes heavily in debt to the money-lender, who exacts an exorbitant rate of interest. This reflects upon the land, as less and less capital is available for improvement, for new tools, seed, or stock. Government-controlled loans at low interest rates, and the actions of cooperative societies, are helping to meet this situation, but only, as yet, in a minor way. The problem of debt is shared by farmers the world over. Farming needs capital for improvement, and in many countries there are cooperative societies which make loans or hire out equipment for this purpose.

Land Tenure.—Where peasants are cash tenants, they are often deterred from making even those capital developments they could afford. This can be overcome through a payment, or allowance, for land-improvement, but as yet this is not usual in the East. Peasant owners are often tempted to acquire land at the expense of land-improvement, which generally means that even more land is held by impoverished owners.

Share cropping, or *métayage*, under which the tenant repays a proportion of the produce, and may receive equipment or stock from the landowner, often benefits the peasant. But it is obviously open to abuse, and may lead to a sense of insecurity in the tenant.

Ignorance.—Modern methods of farming can only be introduced, and the soil accorded proper treatment, if education is spread correspondingly. Conversely, as far as the peasant and small farmer are concerned, educational development must be backed by something concrete in the form of capital advances or the loan of tools or machinery. It is difficult, for instance, to convince him of the necessity of returning dung to the soil while it remains virtually his only source of fuel, and while he remains too poor to buy and maintain a small stove.

Man and the World's Forests

Depletion.—We have already seen the extent to which the forests have been cleared in England. All over the world the progressive depletion of forest resources continues. Human occupation, with its needs for arable land, building materials, fuel, and vehicles, has long made serious inroads into the forest cover; and in these respects alone demands for timber have increased by virtue of the rapid growth of world population. There are, in addition, requirements for the production of paper, pit-props, and a host of synthetic products obtainable from cellulose. The present timber resources of the world are being used more quickly than nature can replace. In fact, nature alone cannot replace them, for the cleared areas tend to become covered with secondary bush and low growth, rather than with high forest; in this way the sal forests of India have largely been replaced by grass jungle, or open woodlands. Trees grow slowly, and replacements need man's care and protection. Over half a century is needed for most softwoods to become of economic value, and at least twice as long for the temperate hardwoods. The softwood *pinus radiata*, reaching a height of 30 m in thirty years is an exception and is a valuable rotation tree for timber and pulp.

In the lands of early settlement, the Mediterranean and the Near East, little remains of the former forest covering. In north-west Europe almost all has been destroyed. In Europe as a whole, only Sweden and Finland preserve half their forested area, though, of course, there are large areas of valuable forest deliberately planted in otherwise unproductive areas, like those of the Landes in south-west France.

The extent of exploitation depends upon the type of timber and its accessibility. The *coniferous forests* are relatively quick growing, easily cut and transported; but because of the many uses to which the wood can be put they are being rapidly depleted—despite the large stands available in North America, Scandinavia, and the U.S.S.R.   Shortly after World War II the U.S.A. was reported to be using up her timber resources at a rate of 50 per cent. above the

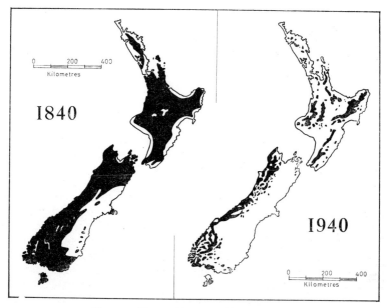

Fig. 22.   VIRGIN FOREST IN NEW ZEALAND.
The extent of the forest clearance in a single century is clearly shown by these two diagrams.

total annual growth of new timber; replanting was being carried out, but not in all areas of felling.   In recent years, however, forest conservation has become much more effective.

Short stretches of road and railway, water flumes, and cable ways are all part of the pattern of "destructive exploitation".   On the other hand, rows of young saplings, watch towers and telephone lines as fire precautions, are evidence of some comprehension on man's part of the necessity for conservation and replacement.   Fire, incidently, takes a tremendous toll of the world's forests.

The deciduous hardwoods of the temperate forests include the oak, elm, beech, and most of their timber is consumed by the industrial lands "on the spot".

The tropical hardwoods, such as teak and mahogany, are more difficult to procure because of uneven distribution of the species within the forest. Having been felled, they must each be brought to some central track or waterway, for transportation to the saw mills. Their exploitation is at its greatest in the neighbourhood of coasts and rivers.

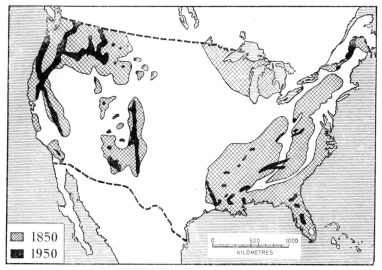

Fig. 23. VIRGIN FOREST IN THE U.S.A.—IN 1850 AND IN 1950.

The areas shaded in black show the only stretches of virgin forest remaining in the U.S.A. A vast amount of clearing has taken place for settlement and agriculture, and to obtain timber for industrial purposes.

They are slow-growing and long-term plans must be made for their replenishment.

Man collects a variety of substances from forest trees without necessarily causing damage. Latex from the hevea, sugar from the maple, quinine from the cinchona, and cork from the cork oak, are a few examples. Few of the tropical species occur in pure stands and so, for ease of collection, they are sometimes cultivated as plantation crops, rubber and the oil palm, for instance.

Conservation.—To conserve world resources of timber, trees must be treated as a crop, with a definite period of growth. Selective logging must be practised, taking only the mature trees or stands, except where thinning is essential.

In the softwood industry about 10 per cent. of the log is lost as sawdust; yet a variety of chemicals and textiles can be produced from pulped waste material. Many pulp factories do use sawdust, but much of that lost could be used in place of freshly pulped timber, and thus help to conserve the forests.

CHAPTER VI

FEATURES OF SETTLEMENT—VILLAGES: THEIR FORM AND DEVELOPMENT

The Growth of Rural and Urban Settlements

"Cities are emblems of that settled life which began with permanent agriculture, a life conducted with the aid of permanent shelters, permanent utilities like orchards, vineyards, and irrigation works, and permanent buildings for protection and storage." (Lewis Mumford, *The Culture of Cities.*)

Those geographical facts which we have seen to be associated with permanent agriculture also have close connections with the nature and distribution of rural settlements. Such settlements, for instance, are most likely to be concentrated in areas of good soil and easily cultivable terrain. The growth of a village or town is closely related to the number of functions it is required to perform. As the centre of a rich region it may become a stronghold to safeguard local wealth (or in modern times house large banks); local industries will almost certainly develop, and it may accommodate those bodies which administer the region as a whole. To fulfil these, and other, functions satisfactorily, nodality and good communications must rank high amongst the geographical advantages which it has over neighbouring settlements.

However well endowed the settlement may be geographically, whether it will actually flourish or not will depend also on a host of social, political, and economic considerations, which naturally vary from time to time and place to place. Thus, a market town, however firmly established in relation to its surrounding region, may suffer decline if the staple local commodity is superseded in world markets by substitutes, or by a glut from other regions.

The majority of villages and towns have evolved from earlier and simpler forms of settlement, although this does not necessarily mean that there is always a regular transition from hamlet to city.

Distribution of Rural Settlements

If we return for a moment to the Anglo-Saxon village and look on its fields, common land, and adjacent woodland, as parts of a tributary area supporting the settlement, we may also envisage similar places with their own tributary areas taking up more and more of the available lowland as colonisation proceeds.

Supposing all the land were occupied, in theory a pattern like that in Fig. 24 (1) will have evolved; except that tributary areas of hexagonal shape allow the greatest density of settlement with the shortest distance from each central place to the perimeter of its territory: Fig. 24 (2) represents a more likely theoretical pattern of occupation.

(1)   **(2)**

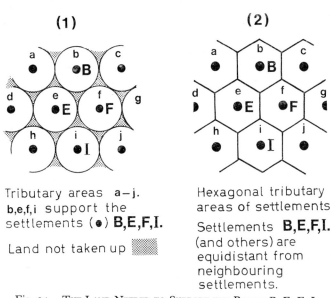

Tributary areas a—j.
b,e,f,i support the
settlements (•) **B,E,F,I.**

Land not taken up ▨

Hexagonal tributary
areas of settlements

Settlements **B,E,F,I.**
(and others) are
equidistant from
neighbouring
settlements.

Fig. 24.   THE LAND NEEDED TO SUPPORT THE PLACES B, E, F, I
AND NEIGHBOURING SETTLEMENTS.

With time, the newly-established settlements acquire tributary areas which, if circular, would leave "wasteland" uncolonised.   In practice they vary in shape with physical conditions and human acquisitiveness—but, in theory, the hexagonal would allow an ideal equable distribution.

Market Functions and the Growth of Central Places

As the well-placed settlement begins to develop as a small trading centre, collecting and distributing produce and offering the services of local craftsmen to neighbouring places, it will compete for local custom with places of a similar size and intent.

Such a central place will offer those goods or services for which people in surrounding settlements will travel the few kilometres to its market, stores, or workshops.   This distance is the "range" of its services or goods.   If there is sufficient demand, it might obtain goods from larger centres and offer them for sale in its market.

In turn, the larger centres will stock goods which are less frequently in demand, but available for people who are prepared occasionally to travel considerable distances.   These goods have a greater range.

PLATE IX

Above: Aigues Mortes. A bastide town in the Rhône Delta, its fortifications and planned layout remarkably preserved, with little extension of settlement beyond the walls. (*Ministère des Travaux Publics et des Transports.*)

Below: Polperro, Cornwall. A fishing village with a naturally sheltered ria harbour further protected by sea walls. The long village follows a deep coombe. Beyond, the small enclosed fields and scattered hamlets are typical of the more gentle uplands of south-western England. (*Aerofilms.*)

In order for a central place to offer a particular good or service, there must be sufficient demand for it within the area served by that place. The number of customers needed before the commodity or service is offered is the "market threshold" of that particular good or service.

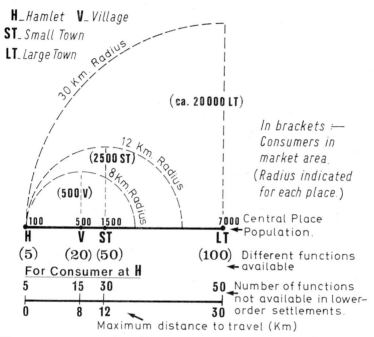

Fig. 25. POPULATION, FUNCTIONS, AND MARKET AREA OF VARIOUS ORDERS OF SETTLEMENTS.

We can see, in terms of modern settlement, that the market threshold for goods in daily demand, such as bread and expendable household commodities, is likely to be small—so that small settlements will usually have a store offering these "convenience goods". For more expensive or "durable goods", required less frequently, people will travel some distance to an urban centre on, "shopping expeditions".

In terms of services, much the same applies. Small settlements may have an inn, but are unlikely to have a hotel or restaurant, or service garage (though they may have petrol pumps). People will travel some distance to make use of a town's hospital, branch bank, solicitor's office, and other services which have a range greater than the distance separating the smaller hamlets and villages.

As a central place acquires more functions, so its population tends to increase. Each function may employ several people, and some quite a number, who will probably reside locally with their families. So there is usually a marked step-up in population between hamlet (with few functions), village (with several), town (with many), and

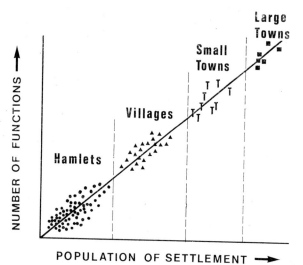

Fig. 26.   Hypothetical Statistical Distribution of Central Places.

Ideally, each rank in the hierarchy is clearly distinguished in terms of numbers of different functions and size of population. (The lowest order provides only a limited number of goods and services; the highest will supply normal local services and also additional special services for the whole area—perhaps those of a hospital, department store, insurance office, etc.)

larger town/city (with a great many). Fig. 26 shows in a theoretical way how such relationships between function, threshold, and size and number of settlements lead to a hierarchy of central places.

Spacing of Settlements—Christaller's Models

A German geographer, W. Christaller, put forward, in 1933, a theoretical arrangement of market central places, based on the observations of retail/service and market areas in southern Germany. He postulated a uniform distribution of population, purchasing power and resources, uniform physical conditions, and equal transport facilities in all directions.

Fig. 27 shows central places equidistant (at the vertices of equilateral triangles) each with a hexagonal hinterland. It can be seen that the custom of each hamlet may be regarded as shared between three villages from which it is equidistant; each village thus has six one-third shares of custom from the six surrounding hamlets—which, with its own, gives it a custom of $\frac{6}{3} + 1 = 3$ units. Such an arrangement is termed a $k = 3$ pattern, and, in fact, hamlets are three times as numerous as villages, which are three times as numerous as towns of the next higher order. Such a town has three times the hinterland of the village, three times the population, and three times the purchasing power. If the villages are d km apart, then the towns are $\sqrt{3} \times d$ km apart.

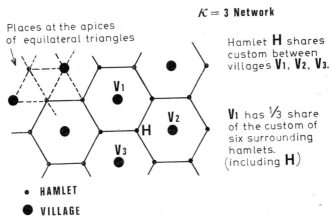

$K = 3$ Network

Places at the apices of equilateral triangles

Hamlet **H** shares custom between villages **V₁, V₂, V₃**.

V₁ has ⅓ share of the custom of six surrounding hamlets. (including **H**)

• HAMLET

● VILLAGE

Fig. 27.   *Each village has one-third share of the custom of the surrounding hamlets and that of its own population.*

This is, of course, a theoretical model, but in southern Germany a general relationship of this type was observed—with villages 7 km from one another and small townships $\sqrt{3} \times 7 = 12$ km apart, and similar relationships in population. The hexagonal spatial pattern continues up to the largest city, which provides very special goods, services, and overall administration.

The $k = 3$ arrangement is based on a regular marketing principle, with higher settlements distributing goods of a greater range to their appropriate hinterland. On p. 116 we see another possible arrangement, more likely perhaps in these days of rapid transport; for Christaller's towns and villages in southern Germany (like so many in western Europe and in densely-settled agricultural lands elsewhere) were established as settlements in the days of head loads and animal transport, and a market range for convenience goods was a physical one, in terms of distance that could be travelled in one day.

The Value of Such Models

We may observe that in most cases the conditions postulated by Christaller do not prevail (although those typical of settled lowlands in Medieval Europe and on the Indo-Gangetic plains of recent times are not much different). We may say that local central places are not the only providers of goods, in these days of mail-order and plentiful individual mechanised transport; and that, anyway, the "sphere of

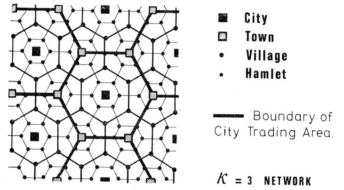

City
Town
• Village
• Hamlet

▬▬ Boundary of City Trading Area.

$K = 3$ NETWORK

Fig. 28.   *The hierarchy $k = 3$, based on Christaller's marketing principle. Boundaries of the trading areas of city, town, and village are indicated.*

influence" of neighbouring central places overlap. We can point to the effect of large cities, which so dominate the whole local pattern that settlements of intermediate size do not have some services which would simply duplicate those of the city.

These may be valid observations and, if true, mean that the $k = 3$ network is unlikely accurately to represent the actual settlement pattern. But the model still has value: it can make us aware of such observed discrepancies and stimulate us to ask why these occur. The use of models in general has greatly influenced geographical thinking, and has often created, by simplification, an awareness of order which would otherwise be difficult to appreciate.

These theoretical considerations should not prevent us from looking at each settlement in the light of its particular geographical setting and historical growth. So many facts affect human settlements that each should really be the subject of a local study.

As we shall see, generalisations and overall classification can be very misleading: for instance, it is not always advisable to classify and consider groups of settlements in terms of their similar functions, important as a knowledge of their functions may be. What were "market" towns at the end of the eighteenth century may still be principally market towns: but they and their neighbouring centres may have changed their character almost beyond recognition, with the acquisition of dominant industrial functions during the nineteenth and twentieth centuries. In the British Isles, many former rural and market towns have, almost unawares, acquired a preponderance of industrial workers. So that a strict classification by principal functions can have no lasting value.

Before any comparison between settlements can be made, a great deal must be known of their history and the conditions of their development. First, therefore, let us look at the village as something which has grown in a particular geographical environment, and which may continue to grow or may decline; and then compare villages with different physical settings, housing peoples of different cultural backgrounds and different stages of economic development—far from the uniform conditions depicted in the models (though some, like the Chinese lowland settlements are part of a recognisable "Christaller $k = 3$ hierarchy").

In the following pages the development of the earlier forms of rural settlement in north-west Europe are considered, largely because here much virgin forest remained until well into historical times, whereas the forest cover had been cleared from much of the "older" lands of south Asia and the eastern Mediterranean before historical times, which consequently do not show the pre-urban forms of settlement quite so clearly.

Background to Rural Settlement in North-West Europe

The form of the pre-Roman settlements underwent changes which roughly corresponded to the variations in the early types of agriculture. The relative ability of the occupants, the metals they could work, and the weapons and tools they could fashion, had a powerful influence on the location and nature of the early farmsteads and villages. The form and location of the settlements changed as the land was occupied by the early Beaker Folk, the Celts, and later by tribes of the Germanic or Gallic peoples. The introduction of iron implements into Britain by the later Celtic folk meant more effective means of cultivation, and also a greater solidity in the farmstead. With increased grain-yield, storage places became larger, and around them clustered the first of the true upland villages. A consequent shift in the position and siting of settlements occurred as the Belgic tribes with their heavier ploughs brought the valley sides and lowlands under cultivation, although a great number of upland villages remained, even after the period of Roman occupation.

Under Roman rule fundamental changes in the occupation pattern took place, behind a screen of fortified posts. The careful siting of encampments and towns, usually in relation to a planned network of roads, created for the first time large settlements which had not "grown from the soil". The *villae* were also introduced into the countryside as artificial creations, and from the third and fourth centuries, as Roman power weakened, many of these self-sufficient households, set amid their cleared agricultural land, became the centre of small independent provinces.

Long before the final breakdown of the Roman frontier zone in eastern Europe, tribes had been attempting to move into the richer lands of the Empire, especially from the north-east. Eventually a great westward movement brought peoples from this quarter, from east central Europe, and from the steppelands north of the Black Sea into territories which had formerly been under Roman control. Such migrations by different routes, and over a considerable period of time, involved tribal units of contrasting race, tongue, culture, and economy (Fig. 70, p. 178). Thus while the Germanic tribes consisted largely of agricultural and pastoral folk seeking new lands in which to settle, others, such as the Huns of the steppelands were pure nomads.

The reason for the migrations from the forest, marsh, and heath of the north-east was probably over-population. A wet climatic period may have made these poorer lands even more unattractive to a people who, besides raising stock, were developing arable farming. Because of the weakening Roman control they were prompted to move into areas which had already been settled, rather than clear new lands.

The movement of horsemen from the steppes, in the fifth century, was almost certainly caused by successive droughts which reduced the supplies of grass. In central Europe the movement, by folk who probably came from the area of the Pripet River, was slower and more diffused.

In north-west Europe sporadic settlements grew up in contrast to the planned occupation of the Romans, although existing routeways, fields, and pastures were undoubtedly made use of. Mountains and hilly regions, such as the Ardennes, were usually avoided, as were marshy areas and many of the former settlements on the short-grass uplands, a type of country with which the settlers were unfamiliar. Naturally, soils were chosen which were easy to work, but gradually the areas of occupation extended into the forest lands, where compact nucleated villages were formed in clearings.

In England the Anglo-Saxons penetrated through the river valleys, re-established towns at road-river crossings, and spread outward away from the banks. The forested clay lands of the Midlands were cleared and colonised. In France and Germany, although the forests were also extensive, they did not remain unexploited, for hunting and trapping, charcoal burning, fuel collecting, and the provision of acorns and beechmast for swine, all formed part of the rural economy. Here, too, land was claimed from the forest to add to existing villages, while new settlements were formed within the forest, many of them by monastic bodies.

Throughout the lands north of the Mediterranean, there were few large towns; but, gradually, peoples such as the Norsemen and the Danes, used to life in maritime towns, stimulated urban growth in occupied regions, including the north-east and north-midlands of England. On the whole the countryside was characterised by rural settlement, and in England the actual sites and distribution of the hamlets and villages were basically those of the present day. This is a generalisation, but, nevertheless, substantiated by a study of the Domesday record of 1086. England, however, is unique in this respect, for though the plague and changes in land-use following enclosures had their effects on the fortunes of small rural settlements, the country did not suffer such wars as have devastated many closely-settled regions in the continental countries.

Rural Settlements and their Distribution

These may be broadly classified as large independent *homesteads*; *hamlets* with few functions beyond housing the local pastoralists or tillers of the soil; single, large nucleated *villages*, probably with a church, periodic market, inn, craftsmen, and other functions. In any agricultural area the proportion of such settlements depends upon the combination of natural geographical features, economic circumstances, and other human influences within that particular region, some instances of which are given below:—

(*a*) Economic relationships with other rural central places, as outlined above.

(*b*) Long periods of freedom from military invasion, and a consequent sense of security, which has favoured the spread of homesteads outwards from an earlier nuclear settlement. Conversely, troubled times and insecurity, which may have led to a concentration of dwellings for common defence.

(*c*) The difficulties of farming in rugged country and rough pasture which may have caused farmsteads to be dispersed over the upland areas, with more concentrated settlement along the lines of valleys or lowland strips, as, for instance, along the fiords of Norway (Fig. 29). Conversely, in lowland areas of fertile soils, there are likely to be nucleated villages which have many advantages: peasants, or hired labourers, remain in easy reach of the fields and yet can enjoy the social amenities of village life; whereas in those upland pastoral districts, where hamlets or homesteads are scattered to take advantage of small areas of better soils, social gatherings are less frequent.

(*d*) Lack of available surface water has often brought about a concentration of settlement along a river line or around a well, while in other areas ample surface water has favoured dispersal (Figs. 6 and 7).

(*e*) Historical influences have often decided the location of a hamlet or village; in some instances, a Saxon village, coextensive with the manor, occupied the site of an ancient villa. Many manors developed from the home of an overlord elected by invading groups. The churches built by lords of the manor received tithes from local tenants and the church itself acquired a parish whose boundaries were often those of the manorial possessions. Monastic bodies also cleared land and developed farmsteads around which villages eventually grew up.

As settlement spread, some of the early parishes were subdivided, and long after the churches had become "village churches" their parish boundaries were, and still are, altered for administrative convenience, or because of the changing fortunes of the settlement itself.

These are but a few of the reasons why rural settlements are distributed as we observe them today. Usually the pattern is far from allowing a simple explanation, and the conditions outlined above have frequently interacted, causing apparent anomalies. While it is true that, in general, large nucleated villages predominated in the lowlands of the south and south-east of England, and that small dispersed villages were more common in the south-west, by modern times many scattered hamlets had developed into small villages, especially in the south-west, with the result that the rural countryside of today presents a very different appearance even from that of, say, the eighteenth century. Since that time further enclosures have taken place, and throughout the countryside the large individual farmhouse is the typical unit controlling the agricultural land-use, co-existent with the pattern of villages and market towns established long ago.

The Siting of Rural Settlements

In early times the life of most men was closely connected with the soil, and consequently the rural settlement was normally sited to give ease of access to the cultivated or pastoral areas. The actual siting depended upon local features. Marshy land was usually avoided, although settlements developed on islands within the English fens, and in Flanders early drainage schemes saw the rise of scattered hamlets along the dykes. Where there was relatively flat land, and where clearing had been extensive, the presence of shelter and water became

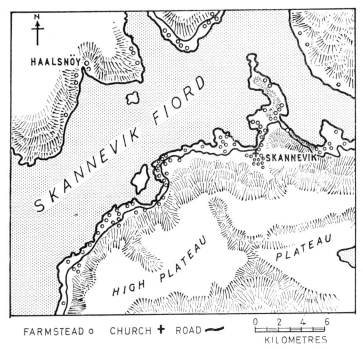

Fig. 29.   Settlement along the Skannevik Fiord in Western Norway.
The farmsteads are dispersed along the first gentle slopes, except where the fiord sides rise sheer from the water (east of Skannevik and on Haalsnöy). Skannevik, the largest community and the religious centre, is regularly visited by people from the more distant homes, by road or by boat. (Note the scale of this map.)

prime considerations, so that men made use of a slight hill or of a wood which would break the force of the wind upon houses huddled in the lee.

Where the alluvium of river valleys proved easy to till, men often made their homes where gravel terraces provided well-drained foundations. Springs were an obvious inducement to settlement, particularly if adjacent to cultivable land; accordingly, villages became strung out along a spring line, as at the foot of the chalk and limestone scarps of southern England. Elsewhere, where deep valleys have east-west trend villages are more commonly found on the sunny south-facing slopes.

The necessity for defence often occasioned the use of prominent features of the landscape.   Extreme examples of this are found in the *puys* country of the Central Massif of France, where small villages lie under the protection of a castle perched high upon an old volcanic core, and in some of the ancient Indian settlements in New Mexico, where the villages appear almost to grow out of the rocky buttes (Plates XII and XVI).

But, as regular trade routes developed, settlements with predominant market functions grew up.   Some had particular advantages; perhaps because of a cross-roads site, and later many of these expanded into market towns, with hinterlands, or service areas, related to the competitive economic circumstances outlined above.

The form of the village has usually been adapted to the natural features of the site, generally being as compact as the topography would allow.   Over most of north-west Europe, the church has been the centre of social life, and usually dominates the houses which are clustered close by, sometimes flanking a roadway, sometimes around a green or square.   Variations are seen in those settlements which have followed the planned layout of earlier defensive villages, either on the sites of old Roman camps, or, usually on a larger scale, as the remains of the medieval fortified towns of south-west France, the geometrically planned *bastides* (Plate IX).   The following are some of the more usual village forms but there are innumerable variations and their present shape may have genetic significance, or not:—

The Squared or Round Village.   There are many varieties, but in general most of the houses surround a green, pond, market place, or church compound.   Often they clustered close to a manor or, in later days, near a great house, as at Kimbolton, Huntingdon.

In some cases the shape is a relic of protective stockades.   The round village, of a ring-fence type, is very common in eastern Europe, while in the north of England there are good examples of villages conforming to the old square stockade of the Border country.

Long Villages.   These generally grew up along lines of communication, either because it was naturally convenient; or that line of houses with holdings turning back from the road was a spatially sound arrangement; or simply because the relief did not allow lateral development.   In this last category come the villages along riverside terraces beneath high banks, such as are found along the middle Rhine and the Elbe.   In narrow valleys, villages usually follow a line above flood level.

Cross-Road Villages.   These show infinite variety according to the angle formed by the roads, but basically the houses form "wings" along two or more adjacent roads, with secondary streets subsequently running between them.

There is obviously an endless variety of village forms, many of which are combinations of the types indicated above; some "double" villages are formed around opposite bridgeheads, or on either sides of fords; fishing villages respond to the feature which gives shelter to the

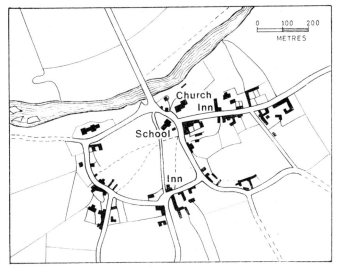

Fig. 30.   BRIDGEHEAD VILLAGE—FELMERSHAM, BEDS.

An old village with its limestone buildings grouped around the bridgehead. The bridge itself is at a nodal point in the road system.

harbour, houses clustering beneath a headland, or running inland along steep and narrow streets (Plate IX).

The functions of a village are usually slow to change, so that the general form and size have often remained basically the same for centuries; this is especially so where a great house has helped to maintain a semi-feudal structure until quite recent times.   In some cases, however, villages have been victims of changing rural economy, and have either suffered shrinkage or have been abandoned (page 58). Others have acquired additional functions and expanded to become larger rural centres—or occupy a higher order in the hierarchy of central places.

More Recent Changes in Rural Settlement

Since the Middle Ages there has been a steady movement away from self-sufficiency, and farms, hamlets, and villages, have become increasingly dependent on local market centres. Most of these small trading towns have developed from the occasional village, whose favoured position enabled it to collect and market the produce of the peasants, or of the craftsmen who lived locally, or sometimes in the surrounding hamlets.

In Britain many of the great landowners of the eighteenth and nineteenth centuries planned and built villages. Materials were usually obtained from local sources, and as their purpose was for agricultural dwellings, they usually conformed to the character of neighbouring settlements.

Nowadays many of the inhabitants work in local industries or travel daily to the towns. In addition many townsfolk use the villages for residential or "dormitory" purposes, travelling daily to their business in the towns or cities so that the simple relationship between the village and its rural surroundings has, in many cases, ceased to exist.

SOME VILLAGES IN THEIR REGIONAL SETTING

Just as the individual house reflects the character of the region in its form and materials, so the rural village possesses features which are characteristic of its own particular environment. Fields, villages, and country paths have become as much a part of the landscape as the hills, valleys, and streams. Thus it is possible to recognise agricultural scenery as typical of a certain region. Cotswold villages with their sturdy yet mellowed houses, built from local limestone, by good craftsmen, and in roughly the same style, are set among fields bounded by stone walls; the grey stone is evident in quarries, cuttings, and broken and scattered over the surface of the soil, so that the whole forms what may be called a "typical Cotswold landscape". (Compare the villages in Plate VIII).

In truly agricultural regions the world over, the net result of man's long-standing occupation has been to create a landscape which can be recognised as characteristic of his own particular part of the world. This is illustrated in the following pages, where a few villages are considered in their regional setting. That they can be recognised as typically "Chinese", or "Iranian", or "Swiss", is due both to their environment and to the cultural activities of their occupants.

It is possible to comment on only a few of the multitude of village types in existence throughout the world. The following have been

carefully chosen so that there may be a variety in the cultural backgrounds of each (*e.g.* in West Africa, China, Switzerland); that there
may be some comparison where different physical conditions prevail
within one broad region (*e.g.* in different regions within China, Iran,
and West Africa); and that several may have an environmental feature
in common (*e.g.* a river valley).

China.—*Settlement in the Yangtse Delta.* Innumerable waterways
run throughout the flood plain, forming in the Delta itself an intricate
network, whose total navigable length has been estimated at 40 000
kilometres.

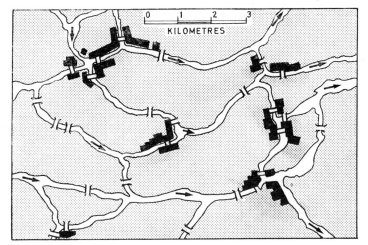

Fig. 31. PATTERN OF SETTLEMENT IN THE YANGTSE DELTA.

*Small settlements of wattle, rush, and bamboo construction lie at the junction of
waterways. Rice and mulberry trees are cultivated on the alluvial flats.
A small market town usually serves twenty or thirty small places.*

The flat alluvial land is held by family groups whose holdings are
often fragmented and scattered, and whose dead lie within grave
mounds upon the fields themselves. Irrigation ditches run through
the fields, to which water may be brought by scoops on the chain of a
treadle-wheel. Rice is the main crop, and the many mulberry trees
are the basis of a widespread silk industry; both benefit from a growing
season of about 300 days. Fishing is the whole-time occupation of
some families.

Most of the very dense population live in hamlets or small villages
distributed more or less evenly throughout the countryside. Travel

by boat is convenient, and consequently houses generally lie alongside the streams, and villages have grown up around the junction of water-ways.   Local wattle and rushes are used in construction, but through-out the Yangtse Valley bamboo is the chief building material.   Light timberwork bridges cross the canals and lead to the surrounding farmlands.

Produce goes to a collecting centre, usually a small town which serves twenty or thirty such hamlets and distributes in return manu-factured goods from the cities, sometimes via 'standard' markets in the larger villages.   Skinner* has shown that a similar arrangement in Szechwan, south-east of Cheng-tu, of intermediate market town, standard market villages, and small hamlets yields the $k = 3$ network of Christaller, which is what one might expect under these particular rural circumstances.

Villages in the Loess Lands of North China.   The villages in the valleys of the upper Hwang-Ho and its tributaries have a very different appearance from those of the Yangtse Delta.   The physical surround-ings are obviously dissimilar.   In the north-west the Hwang-Ho cuts its way through thick layers of loess which, though of great natural fertility, can be cultivated only in river basins, or where terraces keep erosion in check.   Here, large nucleated settlements are separated by intervening ridges.

In Kansu Province, dwellings are burrowed deep into cliffs of loess, or dug out of the sides of sunken roads; thus they find shelter from the bitterly cold winter winds, and remain cool in the heat of summer. Villages of sun-baked mud are strung out along the narrow valleys but where the basin is large are grouped around a small market town. The nucleated settlements are almost always walled, as protection against both flood water and the large-scale banditry which for so long harassed the villages of the northern border lands.   In the carefully terraced fields the characteristic crops are wheat, beans, and kaoliang millet.

Cultural Influences

Despite such contrasts in climate and topography, and the differences in agriculture and occupation, there is in each of these regions an essential Chinese quality, undoubtedly due to customs and traditions common to the villager throughout China.   The broad acceptance of a common language and literature, the spirit of Confucianism, and the slow evolution of a civilisation against the background of frugal agri-cultural existence, have a great deal to do with this.

* G. W. SKINNER.   "Marketing and Social Structure in Rural China". *Journ. of Asian Studies* 34. (Nov. 1964).

In the villages and towns certain architectural traditions help to create likenesses which may be recognised in villages as far apart as those of Shensi and Yunnan. Among traditional features are the decorated roofs and balustrades, the widespread use of tiling, distinctive walls for house compounds and for towns, and the *p'ailou* or commemorative archway. Yet most small towns, villages, and hamlets, though incorporating such features, seem to be a natural growth from the soil, a happy blend of human and natural environmental influences.

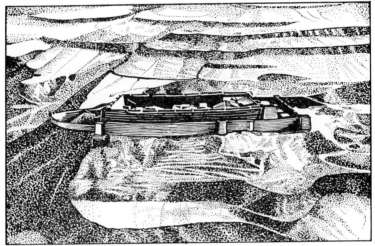

Fig. 32.   VILLAGE IN THE LOESS LAND OF NORTH CHINA (near Lanchow).

The peasants constructed the mud walls along the crest of a residual loess hill as a precaution against banditry, and as a protection against sudden floods.

The terracing has checked erosion to some extent, but there is not enough vegetation to prevent gulleying.

Switzerland.—*The Rhône Valley.* Along the upper Rhône and its tributary valleys are a variety of village types, whose appearance, position, and functions, depend closely upon the geography of their individual surroundings. Changes in altitude or in the direction of a valley have caused significant changes in the form and function of the village.

In the main valley the original settlements avoided the alluvial plain, which was frequently flooded, and sought rather the coarser alluvial fans of the affluents, or else the outcrops of hard rock, which in places project from the valley sides. Although the danger from flood has been minimised, by means of controlling dykes in the upper valley, the slight elevation has the added advantage of raising habitations a little above the extremely cold air and river mists which gather in the valley bottom in still, cold weather (Plate XIII).

In general, stone is the chief building material, although in the upper valley there is a greater prevalence of wooden houses on basements of masonry. Below Martigny, the valley is open to the prevailing north-westerly winds, and the villages are surrounded by wooded country, of beech and chestnut. Here the occupations are

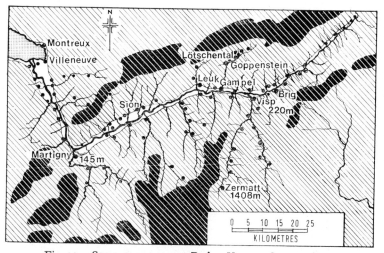

Fig. 33.   Settlements in the Rhône Valley, Switzerland.

Note carefully the situation of the small villages. [The valley drops steeply to Brig, and the more gentle fall between Brig and Martigny is indicated by the heights shown. Except along the tributary valleys, the surrounding mountains rise steeply to over 3 000 m, while many of the heights in the main ranges (dark shading) are above 4 000 m.]

mainly agricultural, or connected with the summer tourist trade. Above Martigny, the sheltered valley has a south-west-north-east trend and becomes very hot in summer. Rainfall is slight but maize, tobacco, vines and strawberries are cultivated with the help of irrigation. The great majority of the settlements are situated on the south-facing slopes among crops which here obtain full benefits from the sun. Many villagers possess dairy cattle which, after spending the winter in the village, move upwards in the spring to the high pastures—usually up and along the valleys on the left bank of the Rhône. The cattle are in the charge of a few herdsmen who occupy small chalets near the grazing grounds. The *Föhn* winds, so common along these southern valleys, clear the snow relatively early in the year.

PLATE XI

Above: Maiden Castle, Dorset. This huge triple-ramparted camp (900 × 450 m) used the natural strength of a flat-topped hill. Some of the ramparts are 20 m high, with entrances guarded by a maze of earthworks. Its origin is pre-Roman (Celtic—*Mai Dun*), though the Romans strengthened the fortifications. (*Photo by J. K. St Joseph. British Crown Copyright Reserved.*)

Below: Woodcuts, Dorset. An Early British settlement on the Chalk. (*Photo by J. K. St Joseph. British Crown Copyright Reserved.*)

PLATE XII

Left: Le Puy, Haute Loire, France. One of the three volcanic plugs about which the town is built. This one carries the church, another the castle. *(Paul Popper.)*

Right: Wengen with Lauterbrunnental, Switzerland. The houses are situated above the valley floor, dispersed to make use of relatively gentle slopes,

PLATE XIII

Above: The Middle Rhône Valley, Switzerland. Blick, and Gampel across the valley, both lie on the first slopes and, although the valley is cultivated, settlements tend to avoid the flood plain. (*Photo by G. Schneiter, Thun. Swiss National Tourist Office.*)

Below: A pagan village near Bauchi, Nigeria, built mainly of earth and thatch for, despite appearances, timber is scarce on this stony plateau. Most villages are clustered, many with a cactus stockade, for "Bauchi" means "country of the slaves" and memories of raiding are still fresh. (*E.N.A.*)

PLATE XIV

Above: Village in the Foothills, Iran. Water is deep and wells few. The village, built of local materials, with its domed roofs for protection against the sun (see Plate XVI), blends with the hills and even the parched fields scarcely disturb the countryside.

Below: Village in the Plains, Iran. Here ground water from the hills issues from *qanats*. The fields are greener and produce a variety of crops. The houses are more substantial, and some have formal gardens. (*P. H. T. Beckett.*)

The Higher Villages. In the tributary valleys, such as the Lötschental, the villages are usually found on the first slopes. A powerful factor affecting siting is the frequent occurrence of avalanches, which cause the brown larch wood chalets to cluster together in the few safe areas. In this valley it can be seen that the change in direction near Goppenstein allows the higher settlements the choice of a south-facing slope; there, around the houses, hay, brought from the lower water meadows, is allowed to dry in the sun (see Plate XII).

In the case of the high villages the reduced atmospheric density allows direct sunlight strongly to warm ground and body, although the air remains cold. Although cloudier than the lower valleys in summer, and snow covered in winter, the upland areas escape much of the mist which persists at lower altitudes. It is here, therefore, that the villages have developed into winter resorts; but, as in the case of Zermatt, they have lost much of their original character with the spread of tourist amenities.

Among the settlements which have increased in size and importance are those which command routeways, such as Martigny, which lies at the lower end of the route up to the Grand St Bernard Pass, and Brig, which commands the entrance to the long Simplon tunnel.

Villages Along the Gambia River.—Here again the villages are situated so as to avoid the lower flood plain, and in this case the variety of soil types has an important effect upon settlement.

Gambia consists of a narrow strip of country measuring about ten kilometres from each bank of the river. Groundnuts form about nine-tenths of the exports, and are produced by local Africans with the aid of a considerable seasonal labour force from beyond the borders.

Settlements are of two main types: the rural village, and the small collecting and trading centre lying alongside the river. The site of the agricultural village is strongly influenced by the topography and the geology. Alluvial flats, with mangrove, grasses, and reeds, lie along the river's edge, and although much used as paddy fields, they are generally unsuitable for habitation. Inland lies a low plateau of sandstone, covered with bush, but giving a poor soil, on which millets, sorghums, guinea corn, and maize, are grown. The main area of cultivation is a belt of light sandy soil lying between the flats and the plateau. Here groundnuts are grown as well as the upland type of food crop, and here lie the majority of the villages.

In the village several huts form a compound. They are constructed from saplings, closely arranged in circular form, and generally have a thatch of grasses or fronds. Each compound has a small garden which provides vegetables, as addition to food grains which are grown beyond the village; and around the whole village there is usually a fence of split bamboo.   The nucleated settlements afford protection, and allow men to share social occasions and cooperate for work on the farms.

The trading settlement usually occupies a suitable ridge near the river, and shows European influence in its less compact form, in the number of brick buildings, and in the use of corrugated iron for roofing.

Fig. 34 shows the settlement and land-use in the vicinity of Kuntaur, a village which lies close to the navigable limit for ocean-going ships.

Some Iranian Villages.—Away from the river valleys water sources are scarce, and men must devise means of bringing water to enable them to establish fields and maintain village life in potentially fertile areas.

In the arid parts of Iran, therefore, settlements exist only where man has obtained sufficient water, and to do this he has learnt carefully to observe the drainage pattern above and below ground, for the surface flow is usually intermittent.   (Compare the villages in Plate XIV.)

In some of the high basins in the mountains a well has been sunk, around which huddles a small stone village.   A few folk cultivate poor soils, but it is chiefly a place where the shepherds may bring their sheep or goats, to be folded at night behind walls which deter the panther.

The gravelly bare foothills absorb the rain draining from the mountains, and streams flow only in late winter.   In the valleys, however, the water is nearer the surface, and shelter can be obtained from the winter cold.   Here larger villages are situated.   They are surrounded by small fields growing corn, vegetables, and opium, and the inhabitants make carpets from the wool of the mountain flocks. The houses are rectangular and of stone, surmounted by a mud dome, timber for rafters being practically unobtainable.

Along the fringe of the plain, at the edge of the outwash from the mountain, a deep stone-free soil is formed, and here, therefore, is a belt of large villages, often with small bazaars.   Beneath the plain, the water-bearing gravels usually lie deep, so that a system of irrigation has been evolved to make use of water from wells sunk nearer the mountains.   The water-table below the deeper gullies in the hills is reached by a wide well, and from this level a horizontal tunnel is bored and lined, eventually reaching the lower plain lands.   The point at which the water emerges has usually become the focus of the village; and from this point branch channels carry the water between the houses and to the fields.

Contrasts in West Africa

Villages on the Nigerian Plateau.   Among the rugged hills of the Nigerian Plateau the sites chosen for settlement are traditionally those which can easily be defended. Clusters of round mud-walled huts with steep thatched roofs are constructed on hill tops, scarp faces, or rocky shelves. The houses and granaries are clustered together, for further protection the whole is tightly contained within walls of mud or stone, or enclosed by thick cactus hedges (Plate XIII).

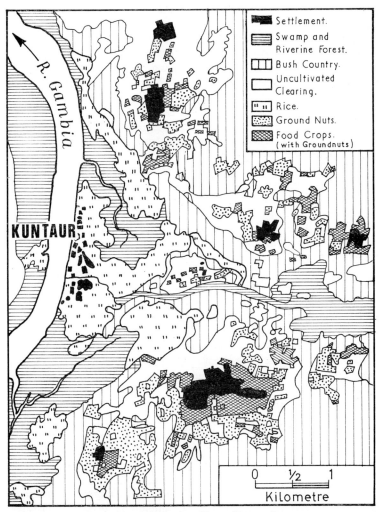

Fig. 34.   SETTLEMENT AND LAND-USE IN GAMBIA.

The villages lie on a belt of light sandy soil above the riverside swamps.   Only the collecting and trading settlement, Kuntaur, lies near the river, close to the navigable limit for ocean-going vessels.

The villages are separated by neutral ground, although as local warfare and slave-raiding became less frequent small farms and hamlets spread outwards from some of the centres. Despite their isolation, the villagers cultivate a variety of crops, using terraces, manure, and employing simple rotations. They have developed well-balanced systems of subsistence farming, for self-sufficiency was a pre-requisite of life in these more remote parts of the country.

Rural District in Ashanti. There is great contrast between the relative isolation of these independent groups on the Nigerian Plateau and the close settlement and intermingling of the peoples of southern Ashanti. The natural vegetation of southern Ashanti is rain forest, though much of this has been replaced by secondary bush, cocoa, and food farms. The region produces a large proportion of the world's cocoa, which is grown on peasant smallholdings. A variety of food crops is grown, including plantains, cassava, yams, and maize, much of it by shifting cultivation.

The population is well-distributed, with concentration around the market towns, especially in the vicinity of Kumasi. The village is the basic unit of settlement, and although many men find employment elsewhere, they remain members of their village and are usually named after it. A wide range of occupations is pursued within the village, and cocoa farming may be a secondary source of income. Little skill is required to tend the trees once they are established, and, when necessary, extra labour can be hired, and housed within a special section of the village. Food plots, on which women do much of the work, are established in clearings around the settlements.

Because few men are rigidly tied to a plot of land, the attraction of a new road can cause a considerable shift in population and the establishment of new villages. Fig. 35 shows how, over twenty years, new road construction can bring about a change in the pattern of settlement. Scores of new villages grew up along the roads, and habitations became more dispersed. At the same time, many villages away from the roads stagnated, partly because the tsetse fly remains such a scourge that the only alternative to mechanical transport is human porterage.

There are signs that the location of the smaller settlements is becoming more rigid, as shifting cultivation slowly gives way to more permanent forms of land tenure.

The Smaller Settlements in Lands of European Colonisation.—The early settlers almost always attempted to recreate features of their native towns and villages upon the soil of their new land. Villages, place names, and the style of architecture in the marginal regions of early occupation such as the St Lawrence Valley, New

England, the south-west of the Cape Province, and the coastlands of New South Wales, bear witness to the nationality of those who succeeded in establishing themselves in hitherto unknown lands.

Adaptation to a New Environment. But often their new geographical environment would cause them to modify the type of settlement with which they were familiar; and the form of their rough and

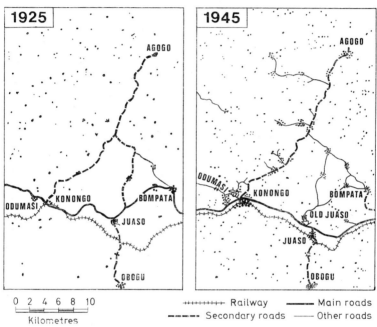

0 2 4 6 8 10
Kilometres

+++++++ Railway   ━━━ Main roads
▬▬▬ Secondary roads   ━━━ Other roads

Fig. 35. THE EFFECT OF IMPROVED COMMUNICATIONS UPON SETTLEMENT DISTRIBUTION IN AN ASHANTI DISTRICT.

The new roads led to a dispersal of settlement, and new cocoa farms became economically possible over wider areas. In those twenty years many roadside villages became towns, whereas older, now isolated villages, declined in population. (R. W. STEEL, "The Population of Ashanti", *Geogr. Journ.* **112**, p. 64.)

ready homesteads and their methods of agriculture would conform to local influences. In French Canada, the early settlers in the St Lawrence Valley had to adapt their farmsteads to the narrow belt of clearing between the river, the main channel of communication, and the forested lands bordering the edge of the Canadian Shield. The family holdings formed narrow rectangles running back from the river to the virgin forest; arable land near the river gave way to pasture further back, and finally to uncleared land which supplied timber as a building material and as a cash crop.   Each holding thus gave on to the river thoroughfare.   The farmsteads lay along the riverside, or inland and parallel to it, so that the road which ultimately linked them followed the line of the river, producing in effect a village strung out along the roadside (Plate XIX).

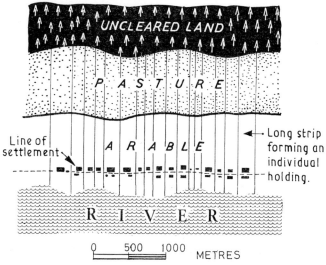

Fig. 36.   SETTLEMENT IN THE ST LAWRENCE VALLEY.

The seigneuries established by the French in Quebec Province contained farms which extended in long cleared strips from the water's edge to virgin forest.   The farmsteads usually lay back from the waterfront, and were connected to neigh-bouring farms by a road parallel to the river, so that they formed what was, virtually, a long straggling village.   This pattern has survived.

The Influences of Communications.   The rate of development of the great grasslands—the American Prairies, the Pampas of Argentina, and those of the Murray-Darling Basin increased rapidly with the coming of the railroads.   In the absence of strongly marked relief features, lines radiated from earlier marginal settlements like Buenos Aires.   As lines like the Canadian Pacific and the Union Pacific of the U.S.A. extended across the continent, they became axes of settle-ment, with villages spaced along the main or branch lines.   Today, the overall pattern of communications and field boundaries is related to the original rectangular layout of the roads, which were generally orientated to the cardinal points of the compass.   Individual farm-steads are more or less regularly distributed along these and minor roads.   The centres of the rural communities have the nature of small "service" townships, rather than agricultural villages.   These small

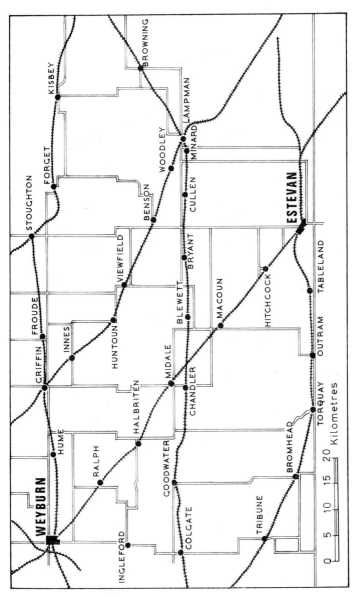

Fig. 37. Detail of Settlement on the Canadian Prairies (Saskatchewan).

A characteristic pattern of occupation on the Prairie Lands, with small settlements more or less evenly spaced along the railways. The diagram shows the distribution at the end of the nineteenth century, when the railway was the principal form of industrial transport. Despite an increase in the number and size of farms, and the coming of modern road transport, the rectangular pattern of the roads remains.

towns, usually situated at a junction of major roads, have a rectangular
system of streets lying to either side of a long "Main Street"; in this
central thoroughfare the local farmer and his family can obtain the
majority of his requirements in the way of goods, services, and local
entertainment.

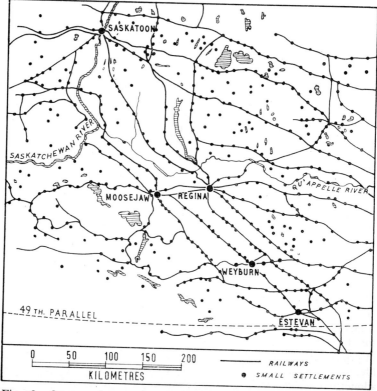

Fig. 38.   Settlement on the Canadian Prairies—Saskatchewan in 1900.
*The majority of the small settlements were along the line of the railways,
acting as halts and grain-storage depots. The basic settlement pattern was
established before the introduction of modern road transport. (Fig. 37 shows the
framework of the rectangular road system, and gives further details of the clusters
of population between Weyburn and Estevan.)*

The Development of a Hierarchy of Settlement.   Here once more
we see a hierarchy of central places.   The smallest units are the
individual farms.   Serving these are small centres of a few hundred
folk.   Here farmers may drive in to obtain "convenience goods";
though most of the shopping is done at the larger "shopping goods"

centres of, say, two thousand people; these are spaced further apart. Next in the hierarchy, perhaps thirty kilometres or so from each other, are the towns (5-10 000 population) which will stock speciality goods not available in the smaller settlements, but for which at this level a threshold of demand is reached. Still further spaced, are the regional centres, and finally, the larger cities, which distribute commodities wholesale to other settlements; these provide a large number of professional services and amenities unavailable in the small towns, or only available in restricted form—branch offices, branch libraries, etc.

The small settlements, therefore, have restricted roles as centres of community life, and with the advent of deep-freeze, mail-order deliveries, and several cars to the family, they are often by-passed as providers of goods and services.

Compared with the older villages of Europe, the Far East, and south-east Asia, there is at first a degree of artificiality about the type of rural community thus developed; but in the Americas men have made their own individual impress upon the region they have come to occupy. In Nebraska, for instance, where a high proportion of the folk are of German extraction, with many others from Scandinavia, and where some counties are "almost solidly" Czech, each former national group has managed to achieve, within the familiar standardised layout, a distinctive landscape which incorporates features from their original cultural background: a type of barn, a means of fencing, or maybe the form of their place of worship.

The hierarchy from small town to regional city, with regular "orders" of settlement, does not necessarily develop in all countries of recent colonisation. In the Australian outback, there are many small townships, from a few hundred to a few thousand people, which are central places for shopping, local schooling, repair facilities, and temporary storage of primary produce (wheat bins); in these there is strong community life, and here families from widely-scattered homesteads, and local administrative committees, meet. But though such centres are spaced some thirty or forty kilometres apart through the "sheep and wheat belts", there are relatively few towns of a size intermediate between these and the cities (Fig. 39).

The headquarters of the farmers' organisations, banks, insurance offices, etc., are in the cities. There, too, are the larger schools and universities, the great shopping centres, larger sports grounds, and so on. Periodic journeys are, therefore, made to these large centres, or goods ordered from them for local delivery or occasional collection. This makes for a few very large places, and a great many small ones of roughly similar size. In such lands, the "Rank-Size Rule", discussed on pp. 168-70, scarcely holds good.

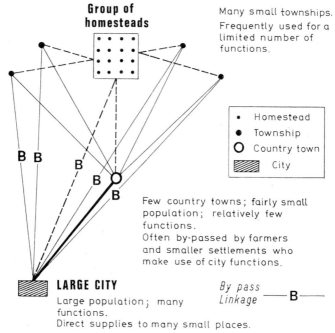

Group of homesteads

Many small townships. Frequently used for a limited number of functions.

- • Homestead
- ● Township
- ○ Country town
- ▨ City

Few country towns; fairly small population; relatively few functions.
Often by-passed by farmers and smaller settlements who make use of city functions.

LARGE CITY
Large population; many functions.
Direct supplies to many small places.

By pass ——— **B** ———
Linkage

Fig. 39. Diagrammatic Representation of the Functional Linkages Between Australian Settlements.

Goods and services do not necessarily move in a series of steps through each central place—city to district town, town to township, township to homestead, nor in reverse order—as was the case in Christaller's southern Germany.

The Character of Small Settlements.   It is easy to lose sight of man except as an economic influence, when considering spatial patterns and settlement "orders".

The villages described above are representative of those in their own particular geographical region.   Each village has its own blend of environmental features, which have combined to give it its distinct character; but by comparing them with one another, and with other villages which we may come to study, we can form some idea of the general effects of various features of the environment, as well as of those of economic competition.   Though the small townships in the agricultural outback of Western Australia may superficially resemble those of comparable size on the Canadian prairies, and perform similar functions, they are very different in character.   The Australian township does not experience the winter conditions nor the necessary variations in community life between mid-summer and mid-winter.

The Canadian township does not wake to the screaming of galahs in the eucalypts, nor its workshops fit "roo-bars" to dented vehicles, liable to be wrecked by a kangaroo on a day's journey.

Human geography must not lose sight of man in his regional setting, nor forget that his way of life there may also be influenced by wider economic or political considerations: a withdrawal of subsidies can affect the rural settlement as drastically as a drought.

CHAPTER VII

FEATURES OF SETTLEMENT—
URBAN DEVELOPMENT

The initial growth of towns in the valleys of the Tigris and Euphrates, the Indus, and the Nile, represented a cultural advancement beyond the stage of the early agricultural settlements. Each phase of culture has produced typical urban forms, depending both on geographical environment and on the particular social heritage. To investigate the influence of natural features on the origin and growth of cities such as Ur, or those of the Greek states, is very much a part of Human Geography, but beyond the scope of this Introduction.

The geographer not only studies the town as part of a region, considering the effects of regional environment on its site and its growth, but also the way in which the town serves the region and the extent of its influence throughout the surrounding countryside.

The town, like the village, arises from the need of mankind to congregate for purposes of security, social welfare, or trade. It may become a common centre for administration, marketing, and for religious, educational, or other social activities, and is often a centre for specialised craftsmen, and for banking. In short, it combines many and varied functions which are usually intimately connected with the surrounding region, for the town generally serves surrounding villages, the number of which varies according to the density of rural population and the state of local communications.

Ancient Cities. The ancient cities were limited in their growth by the fertility of the surrounding region, for on this largely depended the density of the farming population. Their growth was also limited by the means of transport. The city would have to draw its basic supplies from a radius of some thirty kilometres if land transport alone were used—that is porterage or animal transport. The population of most cities was of the order of tens of thousands, rather than hundreds of thousands—although where water transport, by river or sea, enlarged the economic transport radius, supplies could be brought from afar to support larger numbers.

It has been pointed out that, in general, the modern city, with its large population, and divorced from its immediate environment, did not really exist before the nineteenth century; for few local areas were sufficiently productive of the diverse requirements to support as many as 100 000 people. There had been larger cities than this, of course; ancient Rome probably contained more than a quarter of a million people at the height of its power; but only a particular combination of overall power and integrated and controlled transport systems allowed such numbers to live together in an urban environment.

The Growth of Towns in North-West Europe

Roman Towns.—The Roman conquests brought a common culture to the scattered hamlets and villages of north-west Europe, and the effects of road building, developments in agriculture and mining, and the creation of towns on favourable sites, have left their mark on the human geography of Europe.

In Italy, towns had been created by both the Etruscans and the Greeks, and later, as part of their first northward movement, the Romans established many of their fortified towns on the site of captured Etruscan strongpoints. With the power of Rome in the ascendant, sites were also chosen with a view to commanding future trade routes. The urban expansion and prosperity which followed a wise choice of site is instanced by the rapid growth of Aquileia, the predecessor of Venice, which was founded to the north-east of the Po Delta, and became a focus of land routes and a flourishing port. As the Roman conquest prospered, so Aquileia was linked with rich and fairly tranquil regions. Commercial goods arrived from the new towns in the north, and into the port flowed merchandise from the Roman provinces around the Mediterranean.

As the Empire was extended, towns were set up at strategic points behind a series of fortresses established along the border zone. Previous tribal centres were frequently chosen, with the hope of retaining tribal loyalties. Roman stations were also created where an intersection of routes was deemed to be of strategic importance, at Strasbourg and St Albans, for example. Naturally, not all the "obvious" route towns were once Roman settlements; some of the present "gap-towns" in the chalk surrounding the London Basin were established in Anglo-Saxon times, Dunstable and Dorking, for instance.

The relative value of a site is apt to change with the years, and depends upon man's ability to make use of it. Thus the site of Lyons was not occupied until Roman times, and long lay at the boundary between unfriendly tribes, so that its possibilities as a strongpoint and focus of routeways remained latent. Many of the great modern trading cities had a humble origin, thanks to the Roman peace which first allowed a steady flow of commerce through their region. The extensive development of London, during Roman times, as a communication centre and a port was directly due to the Roman road system, and to the increase of continental trade. The main features which influenced the exact location of a settlement at this point were the two gravel hills between the Lea and the Fleet which were well-drained sites above flood level, at the head of a navigable estuary, and near the lowest crossing point of the Thames.

The plan of the towns was usually along formalised lines corresponding to Roman camp layout (Fig. 40), and towns such as Arles or

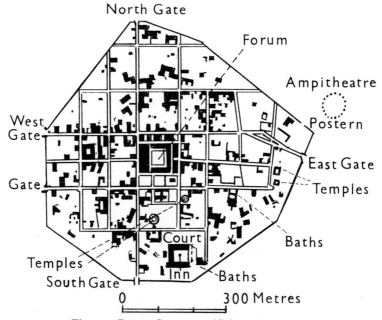

Fig. 40.   ROMAN SILCHESTER (Calleva Atrebatum).

A Roman town, in Hampshire, which has not survived in a modern form. Today its walls enclose fifty hectares of ploughland, though an air photograph shows up its rigid town plan with the central forum and the grid system of roads as they were laid out when it was a flourishing district capital. (Town and Country Planning Textbook, *ed. APRR, pub. Architectural Press.*)

Nîmes clearly show this type of foundation. The actual pattern on the ground depended mainly upon the topography, religious auspices, and local defence requirements. Merchants collected in and around the garrison towns, so that from Britain to beyond the Danube there already existed the nuclei of future trading towns. Despite their deliberate creation, the original appreciation of geographical facts was made so carefully that many modern towns occupy the actual sites of former Roman settlements.

Medieval Towns.—Of the many villages of medieval Europe some, by virtue of their nodal position, were particularly suited to become the trading and cultural centre of an agricultural region, and here, as the years went by, new markets were set up, churches built, and walls erected to protect the valuable workshops and commodities.

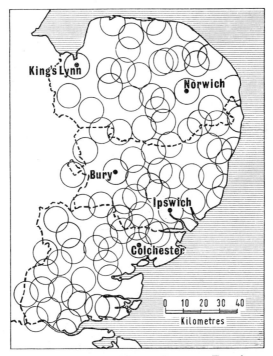

Fig. 41.   THE MEDIEVAL MARKET TOWNS OF EAST ANGLIA.

The circles show a radius of some six kilometres around each small town, indicating the approximate area served by these small markets.   Twelve kilometres portage in one day was far enough when the journey was made on foot over the very rough roads and tracks of those days.

(*From R. E. Dickinson, City, Region, and Regionalism, Routledge and Kegan Paul Ltd.*)

Here we return again to the concept of the ordered arrangement of commercial central places, and of competition between places of similar order.   Where the system of transportation was well-developed, the sharing of custom between markets resulted in a more or less regular pattern of central places.   We see such a pattern in East Anglia, and notice the small hinterland—a radius of some six to eight kilometres—served by the lowest order commercial centres, usually a small market on a green or in a square near the church (Fig. 41).

Not until the late eighteenth century, or early nineteenth century, did development in road transport, and improved road surfaces, see the closing of many of these small markets and a concentration of the central market function in towns like Bury St Edmunds and Stowmarket (Fig. 42).

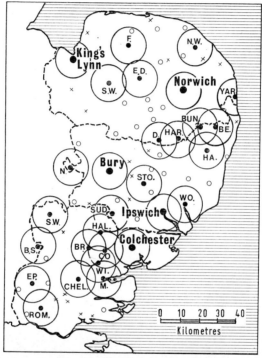

Fig. 42.   THE MARKET TOWNS OF EAST ANGLIA ABOUT 1834.

The developments in road transport and the improved road surface of the late eighteenth and early nineteenth centuries resulted in the concentration of marketing in fewer towns.   Those nodal settlements in rich agricultural areas, with good communications, were the most fitted to survive; other markets fell into disuse (see also Fig. 117).

Not all medieval towns developed from the village by a spontaneous process.   Many villages became associated with a great family, religious order, or dignitary, and consequently increased in stature and population.   Some towns had been occupied since Roman times and probably continued to serve urban, as opposed to purely rural, functions; Canterbury, for instance, maintained a civic life throughout the "Dark Ages".

PLATE XV

Landscapes reflect customs and traditions as well as methods of land-use. (*Above*) The Chinese landscape in Yunnan shows the pattern evolved by generations of farmers—though modern political and social outlook assents to ploughing up the burial mounds seen in the fields. (*Below*) In the Murray-Darling Basin, settlers laid out a rectangular pattern of agricultural holdings and communications in virgin territory. Fields cut into forest cover, and fruit orchards replace the eucalypts. (*Aerofilms.*)

PLATE XVI

Above: A village house in Iran, where sun-dried bricks are built into arches, which together form a cupola, for timber is unobtainable. (*P. H. T. Beckett.*)

Below: Walpi—Arizona. Centuries ago the Hopi built this village on a defensible site 200 m above the plain. The old houses of local stone and adobe, cool in the heat of the day, appear almost part of the rock. (*E.N.A.*)

In Britain, most of the major Roman towns were revived, and all but three of the original tribal capitals are important towns today. This has much to do with the excellence of the alignment and the permanence of the Roman roads, and with the attraction which many of the sites at river crossings had for the Anglo-Saxons.

The Site and Plan of the Medieval Town. The Roman pattern did not persist in the plan of the medieval town, and the streets were often irregular, narrow, and winding. The houses were usually wooden, or half-timbered, although local stone was used for the more important buildings.

In medieval England the streets were aligned according to relief features, or perhaps to through routes, and almost certainly related to the position of the central market. The grouping of central market, church, inns, meeting hall, and adjacent streets devoted to the shops, stores, and houses of local craftsmen, is typical of most towns of rural origin. As many towns lay close to a river, often at a bridgehead, the site made use of natural features above flood level or marsh land. In many cases a castle or church occupied a prominent feature, so that the town nestled below, or perhaps spread up towards it. In Norman England many such castle mounds were deliberately raised, and still grace the centre of many towns. On the continent, with the northward spread of Christianity, cathedrals were centrally situated within the town and were often fronted with a square; Amiens and Chartres both have this feature, and each expanded rapidly during the medieval period.

Some settlements prospered on account of the fairs which were held there at certain times during the year. In eastern and central Europe there are many such towns, usually situated at the place where earlier trade routes crossed. Augsburg, on the Lech, commanded the great Danube route from Basle to Vienna; and roads led thence to the mines at Salzburg, and into the Inn Valley. By late medieval times it had become a powerful trading town, with merchant connections in the east, and subsequently with the New World.

Some towns were planned, however, and at the time of Edward I many military townships were constructed in England and France. Few have survived in Britain, though Hull and Flint still show some of the regularity of their military origin; but in France some fine examples of the *bastides*, as they were known, survive today, especially in the vicinity of Bordeaux, although the majority are now simply small rural centres. Towns such as these, created to fulfil a specific function, survive only if their sites permit the changes which must follow man's technical advances, or if they occupy a site which is in the position to serve a prosperous region. Kingston-upon-Hull, military settlement and port, long provided a good haven for the relatively small vessels of earlier days, and when sturdier ships of greater draught were built, they found a deep water channel available right inshore.   Later, the growth of the industrial centres of Yorkshire and Lancashire gave Hull considerable importance as a point of transhipment for goods passing to and from the north of England.   As it was connected to a hinterland (which included the Midlands) by natural waterways, and later by canals, its continuance as a flourishing port was assured. By contrast, another east coast port, Boston, whose commerce in the fourteenth century exceeded that of Hull, not only lacked a deep water channel but suffered from considerable silting, and is today of little economic importance compared with Hull.

Later Developments.—From the sixteenth century onwards the influence of royalty and nobility helped to create many notable cultural centres.   The presence of royal courts brought rapid growth to the capital cities, while, under the patronage of prominent nobility, provincial centres grew well beyond the size of the average medieval town.   Theoretical town plans were approved by patrons, and their adoption led to formalised layouts around the original nucleus of the town.   These, however, were for the dwellings and amenities of the wealthy and the aristocracy, rather than for the mass of the poor, who continued to overcrowd the older quarters.   Nancy was just such a court residence, with planned extensions beyond the medieval settlement; while some, such as Mannheim and Karlsruhe, were new cities laid out to a rigid plan, to serve as the permanent home of a prince and his court.

The firmer the consolidation of political power in the "royal cities" the more rapid the increase in population.   At the end of the sixteenth century London had more than a quarter of a million inhabitants, and Paris about 200 000; whereas purely trading cities, such as Bristol and Norwich, remained small in size and population.

From medieval times onwards, stone and half-timber had gradually replaced the flimsier structures of wattle and daub, or of wood, so that even though the plan changed but little, the general appearance of the towns had altered considerably.

Military progress, particularly in the power of artillery, brought about changes in the defensive arrangements, more especially on the Continent.   Walls were often doubled, extended, or set at angles to lessen the chance of direct hit, and to give all-round defence. Obstacles were set up beyond the walls in the form of field defences or wide moats (Plate XXII).   Here again the increase in the degree of centralised political control gave an overall security to large areas, so that the protection of a market town lay in the strength of the new frontier towns, rather than in its own walls, which, in many cases, fell into decay. Frontier towns, such as Lille and Strasbourg, were replanned and designed to hold a large garrison; and in many other towns the inclusion of barrack and parade ground, for state troops, was followed by the widening of streets for parades and for the increasing amount of wheeled traffic.

The increasing use of watering places, or spas, by the wealthy, turned many an older settlement into a fashionable centre. As the fashion of "taking the waters" increased, Karlsbad, Bath, and Tunbridge Wells flourished accordingly, and among the many new buildings fashioned for the patrons, were the crescent, square, and arcade.

During the first half of the eighteenth century there was little to foreshadow the coming of the great red rash of mean houses which were to surround the industrial centres; though here and there were towns which had already acquired something of an industrial character. At Norwich over 70 000 people were employed, largely in the production of worsted, and towns in the West Riding were also engaged in worsted production. Birmingham had long manufactured small metal ware for agricultural purposes, and specialised in forging; with the introduction of coke smelting many of its craftsmen were becoming skilled in iron and metal working.

Improved Communications, Transport Costs, and the Pattern of Settlements.—As road surfaces improved and forms of transport became speedier, especially with the aid of mechanisation, the development of direct well-used lines of communication between the more important centres suggested that the overall pattern of settlement would better be represented by a $k = 4$, rather than $k = 3$, network. Fig. 43 shows that in such a $k = 4$ network, based on the transport principle, once a hexagonal distribution of centres is derived, the next lower order of centres is at the mid-points of the transport routes running directly between these centres. In this arrangement, as many important places as possible lie on one traffic route between the larger towns, and the route is established as cheaply as possible.

Each centre shares its custom with two larger ones, which thus each receive $\frac{6}{2} = 3$ shares, plus their own, making four in all ($k = 4$). The market areas of the ordered settlements would be expected to increase by a rule of fours: 1, 4, 16, 64, . . .

It can be argued that the value of using such models is that one sees how settlements might arrange in response to economic laws, and then observe variations from the expected pattern, in response to such factors as relief, soil variations, and so on. When we come to consider urban growth which has taken place since the Industrial Revolution, this argument is less effective as far as the networks we have considered are concerned. The latter are based on an evolution of commercial central places under certain uniform conditions; the location and growth of complex industrial areas seem to require a different approach.

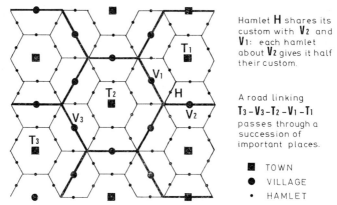

Hamlet **H** shares its custom with **V**2 and **V**1: each hamlet about **V**2 gives it half their custom.

A road linking **T**3 – **V**3 – **T**2 – **V**1 – **T**1 passes through a succession of important places.

■   TOWN
●   VILLAGE
·   HAMLET

Fig. 43.   *The hierarchy k = 4 (traffic principle), where one traffic route may link many important places as cheaply as possible.*

Modern Urban Growth

The Industrial Revolution.—By the latter half of the eighteenth century an "industrial revolution" was gaining momentum within the British Isles.   Besides introducing the use of coke for smelting, technicians were placing such devices as mechanised looms, and steam engines and pumps, into the hands of the new industrialists.   A significant redistribution of population was taking place, as people began to concentrate in areas adjacent to the factories.

The Advantages of Earlier Specialisation.   Towns which already possessed small specialised industries, and had established trade connections, received impetus from mechanisation.   Birmingham had the advantage of brass manufactures developed in the early seventeenth century and rapidly gained a supremacy in the brass and copper industries.   But it was on the coalfields that the most rapid growth took place.   Small industrial settlements, which formerly had used water-power, switched to steam, and, with the benefit of their previous specialisation, prospered accordingly.   Thus Sheffield grew up in a region where small iron implements had been made as long ago as the fourteenth century.   Local iron ore and charcoal were smelted together, and five small streams had been used to provide power to turn grind-stones, which were fashioned from the nearby "millstone" grit.   With the coming of steam-power, and the introduction of blast furnaces, this inherited skill of the local metal workers proved a very great asset.

By contrast, many towns away from the coalfields lost former industrial functions and declined in importance. This was the fate of many former woollen towns in East Anglia and the west of England, and in the Cotswolds the industry has survived only in a few places, notably at Witney and Stroud.

The Industrial Slums. In the industrial centres the factories were soon surrounded by row upon row of mean and closely-packed houses. Slag heaps and dumps became the daily prospect, and too often fumes destroyed what vegetation remained; at Swansea, for instance, the sulphurous fumes from copper smelting destroyed the vegetation for miles around. Factories, needing water for manufacturing, lined canals and rivers, which became heavily polluted with industrial waste— much of which could have been converted into valuable by-products. Laws have now been introduced to prohibit the liberation of poisonous fumes, but drabness remains in many modern industrial cities, and numerous forms of industrial pollution are still with us.

Many continental countries did not develop really large industrial areas until later, but, though this meant that technical developments which had proved their worth could be incorporated from the start, the urban sprawls which resulted were much the same, in their over-crowding and lack of planning, as those in the British Isles. The newer countries of European settlement had, to some extent, a double advantage, because they were able to profit from their knowledge of the horrors of haphazard growth, and because they could combine the inventions of the electrical age with schemes of town-planning (although this does not apply to much of the industrial north-east of the U.S.A.).

Where the poverty of the masses of the east has been exploited for industrial purposes, the most abject squalor has resulted. The over-crowded tenements of Bombay and Calcutta, more than equal in wretchedness the slum conditions which once prevailed in, say, Glasgow or Pittsburgh.

The Growth and Structure of Modern Towns.—Apart from the industrial urban growth which took place particularly on the coalfields and along the estuaries of north-western Europe in the nineteenth century, many rural towns which had increased little in population and size over the centuries, acquired new functions and grew accordingly.

Small engineering works, printing establishments, factories using a local resource, now mechanised and employing more workmen, retail establishments, increasing in number and size, reflecting a national growth of population and wealth, and the increasing ease of transporting raw materials and finished products—all these, and other developments of an administrative and civil nature, were causing towns to grow. At the same time they were making for movements from the rural settlements into the towns.

Much of the new industry in urban areas was near a railway, and this and the main station was usually off-centre, for the line skirted the edge of the old town. Close to the factories, row after row of small red-brick terraced houses were built for workers in the expanding industries. Other rows of similar houses tended to be established as close as possible to the old town centre, but usually clear of those parts of the town regarded as "well-to-do"; the latter generally possessed amenities in terms of aspect, elevation, distance from the industrial development, and up-wind of factory pollution. Solid, three-storied houses of the middle and upper-middle classes were also being built outward from the town centre.

Near the centre itself, the High Street and streets immediately adjacent, formed the chief shopping centre, and here, and about the old town square, were the professional offices, Town Hall, and business houses.

As time went on, the land values and land rents of this central area, generally termed the Central Business District (C.B.D.), which usually included areas devoted to wholesaling and warehousing, have increased. Access to this central area is desirable for businesses and certain professions, and so values are usually highest near the centre, and diminish away from it.

Today, about the centre of the old towns there is usually the ring of earlier residential development, much of which, both the poorer terraced housing and the more solid Victorian-Edwardian buildings, is deteriorating. Private residents cannot afford the high rents of the centre, and, in any case, under conditions of modern transport, such housing and the alignment of the old roads, tends to create traffic problems and bar ready access to the shopping, business, and entertainment facilities of the central district.

Hence there has been much clearance about urban centres, followed by replacement by high-rise buildings, whose extra floor space gives a better rent return, or by the development of new shopping centres, bus depots, and multi-storied car parks. Some of the old, inner middle-class housing has been converted into offices, surgeries, clubs, or used for other functions which can afford the rent.

In the nineteen-twenties and thirties much speculative building created housing beyond the older Victorian developments; usually the new higher-class housing continued outward beyond the previous well-to-do districts. With the coming of private motor transport, some commuted to the urban centre from houses built on the urban fringe or in nearby villages.

As light industries have been freed from the ties of power-source locations and sites near the railway, factories and industrial estates tend to be established in the outer zone, away from inner urban congestion, and in many cases on a ring-road about the town.

In more recent times, many of the outlying villages have increased in size, as urban "two-car" families use them as "dormitory settle-

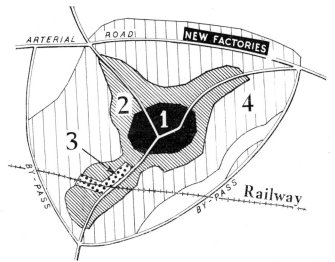

Fig. 44. STAGES IN THE CONCENTRIC DEVELOPMENT OF A MODERN TOWN.

(1) *The Old Town, now largely non-residential and a business centre.*
(2) *19th Century Suburbs Extended along the Old Roads; many of the terraces and houses have become offices or flats.*
(3) *20th Century Residential Growth; with new industries, especially along the by-pass roads.*
(3) *19th Century Industrial Growth; near the railway, with working-class housing nearby.*

ments" or commuter bases, and so enjoy a rural environment but use the employment opportunities and amenities of the town. In fact, small estates are now appearing in the villages themselves.

Models of Urban Development.—We have seen that progressive urban changes have created certain patterns of business, industrial, and residential areas. Various models of urban structure have been put forward, and it is instructive to consider the concepts of three of these. Rent values tend to decrease with distance from the city centre, about which are grouped those functions which can afford high rents, and multi-storied buildings enclosing much floor-space.

In 1923 an American, E. W. Burgess, put forward a theoretical model of a *concentric theory* of urban structure, using descriptive terms.   About the inner zone, or Central Business District (C.B.D.) was a "Zone of Transition"; beyond the older zone of working men's houses was a "Zone of Better Residences"; while outside the main urban area lay a "Commuter's Zone".   This pattern, in the broadest

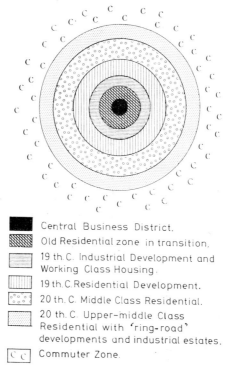

■ Central Business District.

▨ Old Residential zone in transition.

□ 19 th.C. Industrial Development and Working Class Housing.

▥ 19 th.C.Residential Development.

▦ 20 th. C. Middle Class Residential.

□ 20 th. C. Upper-middle Class Residential with 'ring-road' developments and industrial estates.

C C Commuter Zone.

Fig. 45.   *A Model of Concentric Urban Development applied to English central places of ancient foundation.*

sense, is seen in many towns and cities.   His zone of transition included the many deteriorating properties being renovated for new functions or demolished to make way for new buildings.

H. S. Hoyt suggested, in 1939, that city growth might take place, partly at any rate, in terms of "*expanding sectors*".   Thus, as one part of the town acquired certain characteristics, these would tend to be maintained as the sector which contained them developed outward with urban expansion.   Thus high-class residential areas would develop outwards along established routeways, beyond the older high-class houses, which might in time be used for other purposes. Certainly, in many towns, the sector which included nineteenth century industrial development, close to the railway and goods yards,

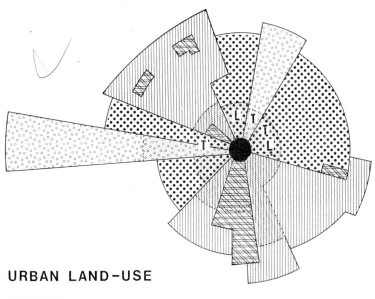

URBAN LAND-USE

OLD 20th.C.

Central Business District.
Lower-class Residential.
Middle-class Residential.
Upper-middle Class Residential.
Industrial.
T   Transition to Offices and Flats.
L   Transition to Lower-class Residential.

Fig. 46. *Expanding sectors of five types of development about a town centre, showing a simplified view of* 19*th century and* 20*th century stages of development.*

has tended to spread outwards along the line of the railway and roads parallel to it.

There is, however, a tendency for functions displaced from the inner zone to reappear in the outer areas. This "leap-frogging" by industries and working-class residences (sometimes combined in industrial estates) may bar certain outward growth along established sectors. Also, within the urban areas are various clustered functions located about nuclei which particularly suit them: dockside activities near a water-front; component manufacturers near larger factories; sports complexes near parks and games fields; and financial offices deriving mutual benefits from clustering.

C. D. Harris and E. L. Ullman published their views on urban structure in 1945 in terms of agglomerations of many different functional clusters, each developed about favourable nuclei within the

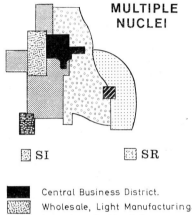

MULTIPLE NUCLEI

▦ SI   ▦ SR

Central Business District.
Wholesale, Light Manufacturing.
Low-class Residential.
Middle-class Residential.
High-class Residential.
Heavy Manufacturing.
Outlying Business District.
SR   Suburbs – Residential.
SI   Suburbs – Industrial.

Fig. 47.   *A Multiple Nuclei arrangement as drawn up by Harris and Ullman* ("Annals of the American Academy of Political and Social Science", **242** (1945), 13.)   *The cellular structure may be shown thus, illustrating development about various growth points within the urban area, and, of course, is realistically applicable to quite complex urban areas.*

city.   Descriptions in terms of *multiple nuclei* were able to include activities which had "leap-frogged" and were part of the general land-use patterns developed around discrete centres in the urban area as a whole.   Such nuclei, therefore, formed the basis of distinct districts: the C.B.D. itself; light industrial districts, districts with many medical/dental establishments, a university campus, dormitory suburbs, and, on the outer edge of the urban area, the airport, are cases in point.

Models such as these are not necessarily mutually exclusive, and the zones and patterns they each emphasise may be seen, at least in part, within most large urban areas of historic growth. They are useful generalisations about urban structure which make it easier for us to observe, describe, and analyse features of land-use and urban expansion.

Rural-Urban Fringe. On the outskirts of most urban areas there is usually a zone, or perhaps sectors, in which land has not been fully developed, or has been taken out of agricultural use and apparently neglected.

Anticipating urban expansion, farmers may be reluctant to invest in capital improvements; while those speculating on a future demand for land for building purposes, buy but do not develop, waiting for the most profitable time to sell. The so-called "rurban fringe" is, therefore, apt to appear an untidy, somewhat neglected zone, neither urban nor rural in character.

Suburban Centres. The C.B.D. contains a variety of retail establishments offering a wide choice of convenience goods and durable goods; besides large stores, there are banks, insurance offices, local government departments, etc. But with modern traffic congestion, suburban householders are likely to make a shopping/business trip to the centre only once or twice a week (unless, of course, they are employed there). Local shops in the suburbs provide their convenience goods; once it was the "corner stores", or local post office-cum-store. But with suburban expansion, more and more suburban shopping centres have been established, with groups of shops, branch banks, branches of large stores, sub-post offices, etc.; and in new, large estates, planned shopping centres are commonly established as the housing is built. Such centres are mainly concerned with a regular turnover of convenience goods, in daily demand, though there may be some stores dealing in a limited range of more expensive goods and including many durables.

In recent years, large, self-contained suburban supermarkets have been built, complete with parking facilities, covered pedestrian ways, and large shops which offer a wide range of goods. There is usually easy access to these from a broad suburban area, via ring roads or along arterial roads leading to the town centre.

Recent Trends—A Summary.—In many of the larger towns and cities there has been a movement of residents outward from the centre. Since 1900, the tendency to move outwards to the suburbs has led to ribbon development along the main roads, and to the growth of housing estates in the wedges formed by the roads. The buildings around the old market square, or central parade, have become offices, and administrative in function. As central areas have been cleared for new business property, so in the move to the "suburbs" the wealthier have migrated to new residential areas, or outer "commuter sites" in the country, and the less well-off to suburban estates. In fact, there is a daily movement of peoples of all classes into and out of the business centres of the really large cities, and considerable commuting to and from most towns. Tens of thousands commute daily into the metropolis of New York from settlements as far off as the eastern part of Long Island, just as thousands travel daily into London from the towns of Hertfordshire and Kent.

In the most general terms we find that the large urban areas have, as a result of the tendencies described above, at least three marked zones:—

(i) The original site of the historic town which has become the non-residential heart of the city, and is usually deserted by night. In many continental cities, such as Paris, Brussels, or Vienna, the line of the old surrounding walls has been cleared to form wide boulevards. In most cities the outer part of the old town, close to the urban centre, has become the fashionable shopping area and entertainment district.

(ii) The first of the suburbs, which were once fashionable, have now become flats, and rows of old terraces harbour offices, or have been replaced by high-rise buildings.

(iii) An outer zone which contains new industries, many of them attracted by the growing urban market, discontinuous residential areas with local shopping centres, playing fields, cemeteries, etc.

⌐Gradually the urban sprawl extends into the surrounding agricultural land, especially as many modern industries are situated on the outskirts of the big towns. The widespread electrical grid system has enabled fairly heavy industries to be established in towns other than those of the coalfields.⌐ The construction of arterial roads, passing along the periphery of the towns, has also favoured this dispersal of industry, and obviates the necessity for a concentration of industrial vehicles in the heart of the town; although where docks reach into the city centre, heavy traffic must pass through miles of streets to serve them.

Beyond these are likely to be dormitory settlements, or, about the large cities, satellite industrial/residential towns, and much land taken up by the runways and complex buildings of a modern airport.

Urban Fields.—Towns offer goods, services, and amenities which are acquired or used by people who live within the "field of influence" of the town. In outlying areas, some will, of course, go to one town for one service and to another town for some other function. But, in general, most people regard a particular urban centre as their "local town" and shop there with some regularity.

Much depends on the accessibility of the centre, and this is perhaps best viewed in terms of time rather than distance. A family living 50 km away may, by using a nearby motorway, reach the town centre more quickly than those in an outer suburb, who must thread their way through congested streets. An isochronous map, show equal average times for the journey to the town centre, is usually a significant one.

Each central function will have a different range of diminishing influence away from the centre. For each it is possible to conduct a survey to ascertain the area served by that function, whether it is the local newspaper, sports club, or store's delivery service. It is unlikely that their fields would coincide. In any case, the limits of an urban field fluctuate, and instead of "hinterland boundaries" there are usually zones, in which neighbouring centres competing for the supply of goods and services have dominance in some commodities and functions, but not in others.

Break-points between Settlements.—One theoretical method used to establish a likely point at which the influence of competing centres will be equal embodies a generalisation based on Reilly's law of retail gravitation. If the two centres are of equal size, the break-point is likely to be midway between them. If not, then the larger centre will have the greater attraction for retail trade, and the break-point will be further from it. For towns A and B this may be expressed as:—

$$\text{Distance of break-point from } A = \frac{\text{Distance between } A \text{ and } B}{1 = \sqrt{\dfrac{P_B}{P_A}}}$$

(P_A and P_B are the populations of the settlements.) (See Fig. 48.)

Applied to roads leading outwards from a town centre, this can denote a break-point on each road to a neighbouring town of reasonably comparable size; and thus a general theoretical area of influence may be established about the town.

Within this theoretical "hinterland" surveys may then be made to try to establish shopping habits, etc., with more accuracy, by sample surveys in the outer areas or in the town's C.B.D.

The Towns Coalesce.—In many great industrial regions the outskirts of adjacent cities coalesce, resulting in a continuous built-up

SPHERE OF INFLUENCE

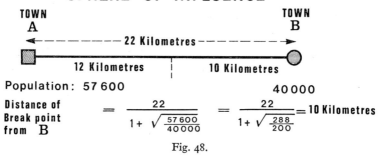

Fig. 48.

area, termed a "conurbation". In Great Britain there are several such extensive groupings: central Clydeside, Merseyside, south-east Lancashire, Tyneside, the West Riding of Yorkshire, and the west Midland group of towns which surround Birmingham and Wolverhamp-

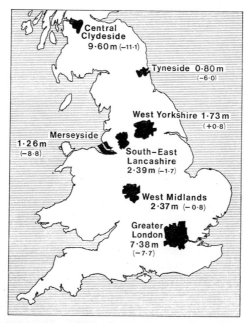

Fig. 49.   CONURBATIONS OF GREAT BRITAIN—AS DEFINED IN THE 1971 CENSUS

Population figures and the percentage intercensal increase/decrease are shown. There has been a notable movement out from the heart of the conurbations to new towns and to existing towns beyond the outer limits of the large city-clusters. A zone of rapid growth from East Anglia through the south-east Midlands, for instance, is due to outward movement from the metropolitan suburbs as well as to the "south-east drift" from the old industrial regions.

ton. Though multifunctional, each conurbation tends to have a typical group of occupations. Greater London is in a class by itself.

The overlapping of industrial centres occurs elsewhere: in the U.S.A. there is a continuous industrial belt along the south shore of Lake Michigan, from Gary to Chicago; in Germany more than six million people live between Duisburg and Dortmund, in the manufacturing area of the Ruhr: the two Japanese conurbations of Tokyo-Yokohama and Kobe-Osaka together contain more than twenty million people.

As these conurbations grow outwards, men try to limit or channel their growth so as to preserve as much open land as possible, and as close to the city centre as possible. The London County Council Plan of 1935 aimed to establish a "green belt" around the capital city.

Green Reserves and Urban Corridors.—A number of other cities have tried to maintain open spaces for the public and recreational areas in belts about the urban core. Unfortunately, there is a tendency for housing and industry to leapfrog this belt and to spread at a greater radius from the centre; and also for roads cutting through the belt to be followed by urban development. Once the green belt begins to "crumble" then an untidy sprawl results.

Others have suggested that the main radial routeways should indeed be axes along which development is encouraged and planned. There would be a check on any tendency towards lateral spread, and green, preserved countryside would occupy the wedges between. New towns might then be planned to grow, with good communications, at places within this "urban corridor", though perhaps in scheduled development areas, rather than in continuous strips.

New Towns. In all these considerations transport and communications loom large. Rather than creating satellite dormitory towns, with people travelling long distances into the city for work, planners have aimed to create *new towns* in which to live and work, with more space and less travelling. Stevenage, created just after World War II, and still growing, is such a town, with "neighbourhood" residential areas and employment for tens of thousands. Crawley, south of London, Harlow and Hemel Hempstead to the north, were developed as new towns soon afterwards, and, later, Basildon to the east, and Bracknell to the west of London.

Many other new towns have been built in various parts of Britain— Cwmbran in south Wales, and the architecturally bold town of Cumbernauld in Scotland among them. Others are planned, such as Milton Keynes, which will have the expanding town of Bletchley on its outer industrial fringe, and is a good example of expansion between the radial routeways of the M1, A5, and London-Midlands railway.

Other towns are chosen in *Growth Areas*, and for these there is to

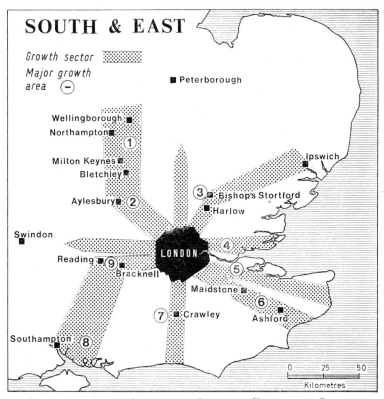

SOUTH & EAST

Growth sector
Major growth
area

Fig. 50. STRATEGIC CORRIDORS OF INDUSTRIAL/RESIDENTIAL GROWTH

These have been put forward as pattern of a plan to encourage development along main radial routeways, thus limiting lateral spread into the intervening "green wedge". Among the centres designated for planned development are these nine areas where considerable growth is likely. These are not all the areas where potential growth is recognised and is likely to be encouraged, but they include the major growth areas of the south and east.

be planned expansion. Such *expanded towns*, as Aylesbury, will have acquired new status, many new industries and planned housing estates without the enormous expense needed to create a completely new town with planned centre and services developed from scratch.

PLATE XVII

Above: Norwich in 1570. This map reveals considerable information of the life around sixteenth-century Norwich. The countryside, already rich agriculturally, shows that much enclosure had been made, although open fields are under plough. The shepherd and his flock are significant in view of the city's prominence as a wool market. Windmills are already a feature of the countryside.

The Norman Cathedral and the Castle are easily recognisable, and in front of the latter is the market, with the roof of the Guildhall standing out. (The city is viewed from the north.)

Below: Compare features on the map of sixteenth-century Norwich with those of Norwich in the mid-twentieth century (as seen in the vertical air-photograph).

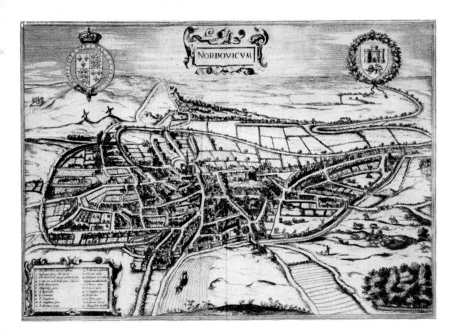

(1) The Castle on its Mound; (2) the Market; (3) is the modern City Hall, but between (2) and (3) lies the old Guildhall; (4) the Goods Yards occupy the land shown in the middle distance beyond the river. Between (4) and (5), and over a new bridge, runs the road which is shown to the right of the Cathedral (itself just off the photograph—bottom left).

These features remain, though the last twenty years have seen much clearance and further commercial redevelopment of central Norwich. [*Hunting Aero-surveys Ltd. (through Aerofilms).*]

PLATE XVIII

Above: Kano—the old City. The form of the houses and their enclosed compounds have changed little over the centuries. (*B.O.A.C.*)

Left: Mount Vernon (20 000), in the mid-twentieth century, a typical small town in the U.S. Middle West, a commercial central place in an agricultural area. Main Street runs from the lower right to the upper left; the other roads run parallel, or at right-angles to this. (*USIS.*)

Dependence on Non-Urban Areas

The great town or city, although exerting its influence over a very wide area, seems to stand apart from the rural countryside. But with its huge population, which must be fed, clothed, and housed, and which receives benefits in the form of power, water-supply, and sanitation, it is astonishingly dependent on non-urban areas and on the supply of commodities from far afield. For all necessities, and amenities, the population must turn fundamentally to the primary food-producing areas: to the great wheat lands, to the nearby market garden or truck farm; and to the primary extractive industries, for gravel, cement, coal, or metal ores.

The majority of the people take the city and its functions for granted, unaware of the fact that continued prosperity may depend on a supply of commodities which may become difficult to obtain, or on markets which fluctuate with world affairs; heedless also of the fact that a city never stands still—it is either developing or in decay.

TOWNS AND THEIR DIFFERENT FUNCTIONS

Classification by Function—Some Considerations

Towns are apt to be placed into categories according to their size, status, or main functions. A town's functions and size are often inter-related, but it is often extremely difficult to point to a town's dominant function, even if there is one, and in any case these are apt to change with time. Most towns are multi-functional. It is possible to point to specialisation by calculating a *location quotient* (L.Q.) for a particular function. This shows whether or not a place has a greater than average share of a particular function. It compares the proportion of its occupants employed in that function with proportion of the country's population so employed. But there may be also specialisation in a number of other functions in the town.

One must always be sure of the purpose of classification; is it to rank places in order of economic importance, or of their administrative status, or to compare them in some way with other towns with similar functions—ports, resorts, or ecclesiastical centres?

While principal functions provide some basis for comparisons between towns, further studies may reveal that some towns have acquired important functions almost fortuitously, rather than because of the influence of specific geographical factors.

Birmingham may have had a metallurgical history favourable to the growth of modern vehicle production, but this was certainly not the case with Oxford, where population figures show the effect that vehicle production has had upon the city. In 1921 this old university city had a resident population of 67 000, but by 1940 it was 100 000, and it is still increasing. New clusters have grown up to the east and north of the old heart with a combined population greater than that of the entire city in 1900 (49 000). The geographer cannot ignore

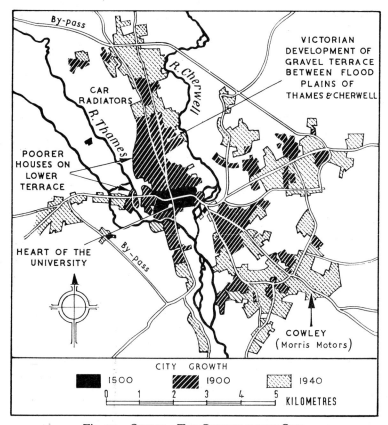

Fig. 51. Oxford—The Growth of the City.

The car industry and its subsidiaries have greatly expanded during the last thirty years, and urban estates have filled in most of the rural fringe east of the city. A link to the southern by-pass has helped to create an outer residential arc extending from the south-west to the north-east of Oxford.

that the growth of the last few decades is intimately connected with the fact that the future Lord Nuffield was born in Oxford and not elsewhere, and in his youth became interested in things mechanical, leading later to the creation of the Morris works in the suburb of Cowley. He would also find that a considerable proportion of the population is

Welsh born, due to the fact that the car industry was still expanding in the 1930s, when unemployment in south Wales sent thousands of Welshmen to the newer industries of the Midlands and south of England.

However urban functions are acquired, their presence in a town causes men to group themselves in a particular way to carry out those activities connected with it.   The overall character of a town depends on the nature and proportion of its various functions; and so we will examine a number of types of towns which have certain important functions in common, but which are located in different regions. First, let us look at a number of functions which are only occasionally dominant, but which are found in some form in most large towns.

Functions which Today are not Generally Dominant

Religious Functions.   Many towns are spiritual centres in the sense that they contain religious bodies, religious buildings, or religious symbols, the influence of which extends over a wide area.   Some, such as Rome, Banaras, or Amritsar, have renowned religious functions and are the centre of pilgrimages, but at the same time house a large permanent population, with considerable numbers of people engaged in administrative, commercial, and industrial business.   In others the religious function is still most significant.   There are many such centres in the Middle East and southern Asia, of which Mecca is the outstanding example; while the great monasteries of Tibet, which had populations of up to ten thousand, were townships in themselves.

Scholastic Functions.   The origin of the older university towns of Europe was probably connected with fairs, at which learned mendicants would gather, or sometimes with religious bodies, who set up places of instruction.   Later they included in their body foundations proclaimed by papal or royal charter, or established through the offices of a patron. Oxford, Cambridge, and Heidelberg, are representative of this type.

Today the older universities are being hemmed in by industrial growth, while many modern universities (especially those with a scientific bias) have been established in large industrial towns.   But in most sizeable towns there is a variety of scholastic centres, technical colleges, schools, and various cultural societies and other organised educational bodies.

Military Functions.   The possession of an occupied fortress or a large garrison have earned some towns the title of "military" or "defence town".   Few today have a purely military function, but most large regional capitals contain barracks and the headquarters of the local regiment.   Some, such as Portsmouth and Aldershot, are widely known as centres of the armed forces, while the smaller "specialist" settlements on the edge of training areas, such as Tidworth on Salisbury Plain, and Woomera on the Australian rocket range, are even more truly towns with a dominant military function.

Communication Centres. While some towns retain their pre-eminence as communication centres, technical advances in road building and modern airport construction are such that almost any flourishing town can be classed as a route centre. Nodality, or control of gaps, is still a great asset to a settlement, however, and Chicago, Crewe, and Dijon each fulfil the role of a major transport centre which is theirs by virtue of their favourable situation in relation to major routeways. But, again, we must remember that the presence of a prosperous community is likely to stimulate inter-communications with other centres.

Some Towns in Their Regional Setting

The following towns show between them a number of dominant urban functions such as marketing, commerce, industry, mining, administration, and the functions of port, capital city, and resort. Most combine several of these functions, and have large social and residential areas. Though each is representative of a certain type of town, it can properly be studied only in relation to its own region.

The Market Town.—*Norwich.* Norwich is the regional capital of East Anglia, fairly centrally situated at the junction of the Wensum and the navigable River Yare; sea-borne coal can, in fact, be delivered direct to its power station. For centuries it has been first among East Anglian market towns, in a predominantly agricultural area, and evidence of its success as a regional capital is found in the intense local patriotism throughout city and countryside.

Although a mint was established there in Saxon times and though it later became a Danish settlement, it was in the Norman era that Norwich began to stand out in importance, ranking next to London and York. The Normans built the great cathedral and raised the castle on an artificial mound (Plate XVII).

Being in easy touch with northern Europe, it became a major centre for wool exports, and the growth of a great wool-weaving industry owed much to the personal interest of Edward III. Later it sheltered refugees from Europe, and the skill of Flemings, Walloons, and Hugenots, helped to build up the woollen industry.

By the thirteenth century the market place, which is still the focus of many of the city's activities, was regularly receiving wool and a variety of produce from settlements throughout East Anglia. Its continued association with a rich agricultural region is reflected today in the number of food industries which are based upon local produce, including mustard manufacture and brewing, and also in the production of agricultural implements and wire-netting.

The industrial revolution brought unemployment and a decline in the staple trade, as the distance from the coalfields of the Midlands and the North, and the effects of the competition of the power looms of Yorkshire, proved too great for the local wool-weaving industry. Fortunately, the craftsmen soon adapted themselves to the manufacture

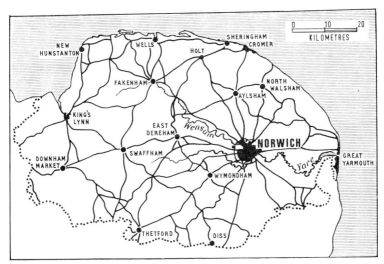

Fig. 52. NORWICH—A COUNTY TOWN.

The pre-eminence of this city as a market and regional centre is amply illustrated by the pattern of the roads, and by its size in comparison with that of the country towns.

of footwear—the "uppers" frequently require textile covering—and the boot and shoe industry still employs thousands. The production of high-grade silk and crepes remains as a specialised form of weaving. Printing is an important industry and some of the larger works occupy former woollen mills.

A regional centre of any character is usually also a cultural centre, and Norwich is, in fact, the only city in Britain whose name is associated with a School of Painting (which flourished under local patronage in the nineteenth century). Now the University of East Anglia makes a cultural and economic impact on the city.

The city has a large banking and insurance business, befitting its role as the largest central place in East Anglia serving, through the ages, the hierarchy of rural settlements, from hamlets to large market towns, fairly regularly spaced over one of Britain's most fertile lowland regions.

Kumasi. With over 300 000 people, Kumasi is one of the largest market towns in the cocoa-belt of southern Ashanti in south-central Ghana. This area, which has been described on page 100, has an ample rainfall and close vegetation, compared with the drier northern districts. The small rural settlements are widely distributed, as many of the cocoa farmers produce their various food crops by a shifting agriculture, and need pay only periodical visits to the cocoa trees. From the many scattered holdings the cocoa is brought to collecting points and thence to rail-head at Kumasi.

The town was the seat of the ruler of Ashanti during colonial times and became prominent in commerce and administration. It soon became a centre of attraction for the young Ashanti seeking to advance beyond the confines of village life, and for the absentee farmer, employing seasonal labour for the cocoa, and finding other work for himself in the town. Its growth has been spectacular. In 1911 its population was 18 000; in 1921, 23 000; in 1931, 35 000; in 1951, 80 000; in 1961, 180 000; and in 1971, 350 000.

There are distinct districts related to its different functions; some urban districts are associated with commerce, some with administration, some with the activities of the ruling group, others with residential needs and local retailing.

The roads throughout Ashanti converge upon the town, while, to the south, railways link it with Accra, Takoradi, and Tema.

Within its region, like Norwich, it is a primate settlement, very much larger than the other central places. But, whereas Norwich serves many sizeable towns whose descending orders are arranged in close accord with the $k = 3$ market pattern, Kumasi dominates an area of many small market centres and very many scattered family groups: it serves a region where an overall network of communications has yet to develop, and where local markets remain small collecting points selling relatively little to cultivators, whose women-folk bring in the surplus of a semi-subsistence form of cultivation.

Towns on the Plains of the Middle West of the U.S.A. Rural towns of from one to five thousand inhabitants follow a distinctive pattern throughout the Middle West of America, with only slight local differences. They are almost all cross-road towns. Many have their origin in the corner store at the centre of older, and cruder, trackways. The pattern of the cross-road remains, though one street is usually established as Main Street, exhibiting today a line of modern store fronts with neon signs, disguising brickwork and stucco of earlier buildings, with here and there a taller modern building.

There are few hills, and no skyline is seen from the centre of the town. Usually the brick houses of the centre give way to neat clapboard dwellings bordering tree-lined avenues, finally merging into the countryside, which seems so close to the heart of the small town. A town of this size serves rural communities over a radius of perhaps 15-20 km, which would mean that its shops and services would cater for some 3-4 000 people, besides its own population. This means that, whereas the smaller townships might have a grocery store, filling station, restaurant, bar, post office, church, and perhaps grain elevator, this large number of consumers would warrant the provision of other functions, such as banking and insurance facilities, large drug-store, funeral parlour, hardware and furniture stores, doctor's surgery, and so on.

The next order of towns tends to have a population of 5-10 000, with a radius of perhaps 30-40 km, and a trade area with a population of the order of 20 000. If it is a county town, then there will be government offices, and local newspaper, and retail stores specialising in goods with a larger threshold, including high-priced durable goods, and luxuries like jewellery among their stock. The C.B.D. is likely to include large buildings.

Up to the level of the smaller regional capitals, these central places tend to retain many small-town characteristics, and are closely linked with agricultural activities; they generally include small light engineering industries.

The big cities of the central plains have been likened to national capitals, their "country" being the surrounding areas of plain-land, and also to "ports—serving a great ocean of prairie—all linked by bonds of steel rail and concrete highways". Such are Omaha, St Louis, Kansas City, and the more marginal cities, *e.g.* Chicago.

Such cities produce machinery and other manufactured goods for the rural population, for use and distribution in the small towns, and for the inhabitants of the city itself. At the same time they serve as gigantic markets for primary agricultural produce, and for grain and fattened livestock, converting them into consumer goods in mills and meat-packing factories. Being of rapid growth, their centres are often of haphazard development, but show the zoning referred to on page 120. As in most big cities, different social and racial groups have come to live in their own particular districts, according to the level of the citizen's economic or social status. The less well-to-do usually live in a zone about the old centre or close to the railroad tracks, while the wealthier lie a little farther off.

Summary. A market town must be in a position to serve the rural community, by providing a centre and facilities for the exchange of commodities, the sale of agricultural surplus, or the purchase of consumer goods. Industries may be set up to cater for the needs of the farming community, and to process local raw materials. Its stores provide convenience goods, durables, and luxury commodities, and the town offers various amenities according to the number of consumers in its market area and their purchasing power.

One of the larger regional markets may become the administrative centre; or, conversely, a town, being an administrative centre, may become prominent as a market or commercial settlement.

As the prosperity of the market town is closely connected with the surrounding region there is generally a strong rural pride in its activities as a provincial centre.

Commercial Centres Lying between Contrasting Regions

The commercial/market functions may be especially well-developed in towns which have particular locational advantages. The following have prospered mainly on account of their situation in relation to contrasting regions and the trade between the regions, which has been stimulated by their diversity. Many ports, as we shall see, derive advantage from the same kind of situation.

Kano. Situated in the dry savannah region of northern Nigeria and lying between the equatorial coast of West Africa and the Mediterranean lands, Kano has long functioned as an entrepôt. For centuries the city collected and distributed the produce which arrived by desert caravan from the north or by porterage from the south. Spices, oils, and salt, still come in from the north and across the Sudan, and Arabs from Tripoli and Berbers from Gadames still operate great camel caravans, which return with local cloth, leather goods, or kola nuts from the Guinea Coast. In addition to long-distance trading, Kano acts as a market for the savannahs of northern Nigeria, collecting groundnuts and hides to despatch southward, millet for local consumption, and cotton and wool for local industries.

The settlement grew up around a rocky promontory, an acropolis, standing above a small stream. The old city still consists chiefly of mud houses, with flat adobe roofs, and the open spaces are pock-marked with borrow pits, several hundred feet across and often over twenty feet deep, from which comes the material to build or repair. The small stream was inadequate as a source of drinking water, which has come, instead, from wells two or three metres deep.

As the settlement grew in importance the walls were extended to include, not only additional dwellings, but also large areas for pasturage in troubled times. However, with growing security and the decline of slave labour, more than twenty kilometres of wall has partly crumbled to form embankments, now used as footpaths. After the British occupation in 1903, a settlement was established beyond the old walls

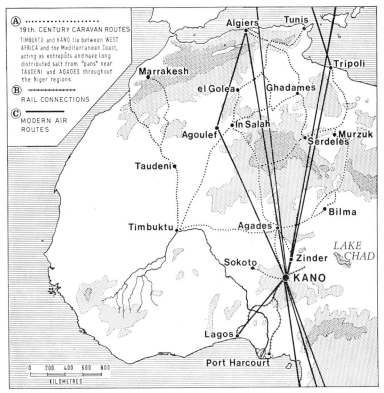

Fig. 53. THE LOCATION OF KANO.

of the city to act as an administrative and garrison town. Today, Kano has a total population of 300 000. Stable conditions allowed rapid growth during the years of British administration, when the Emir of Kano continued to exercise control through headmen, each in charge of a ward, and to direct the operation of the great central market and its eight satellites.

Apart from the roads and railway communicating with southern Nigeria and the coast, Kano has an international airport, and is an important focal point for aircraft travelling between Europe and southern Africa.

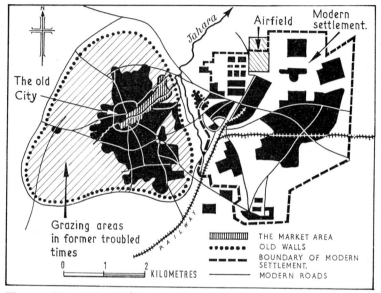

Fig. 54. *Kano—The Old City established when Kano was an important route centre for animal transport, and the New City after Kano had become a major centre for modern air routes.*

Halab (Aleppo). Halab (550 000) acts, as it has always done, as distributor and collector of produce from four distinct geographical regions, which has made it a supremely-important regional centre.

To the north lies the hill country of Asia Minor; to the south-west the oases of Hama, Homs, and Damascus, and the Lebanon beyond. Its trade has always been closely connected with the Mediterranean ports, which include Tripoli and Beirut, and, overland, the dry steppes lead across the Fertile Crescent to Iraq and Iran.

Through the ages the pastures of the Syrian Desert have provided livestock for its markets, and from the further steppes have come livestock, wool, and hides; oases have provided cereals and fruits; and from Asia Minor have come wood and metals. Manufactured goods arrive from the ports and larger towns. For centuries the city has controlled trade in these commodities and housed numerous small craftsmen, skilled in the use of these materials. Here are metal and leather workers, and those who now provide skilled labour for the present flourishing textile industry.

Its functions and its general appearance have changed little with modern times, and its present role as a railway junction follows directly from its earlier control of caravan routes.

Like most towns of the Middle East it has accumulated power and wealth which are in startling contrast to the poverty found in the rural areas, and the landowners tend to live in the relative comforts of the

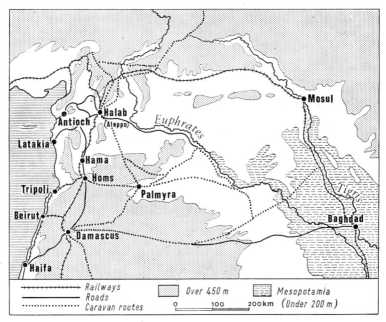

Fig. 55.   HALAB (ALEPPO) AND MIDDLE EAST COMMUNICATIONS.

town. (Compare the relations between town and village, in these circumstances, with those between settlements in the Yangtse Delta.)

That a town of this size should grow up on this particular site is mainly due to the presence of water, readily available in quantity sufficient to maintain a large population; it lies at the centre of a small basin. Nearby salt-marshes also provide a commodity of great value in a region where the rapid rate of evaporation causes a large loss of salt from the body.

Summary.   Such settlements flourish because:

(i) There is a mutual desire for trade between contrasting regions.

(ii) The site itself lies on the continuation of an easy line of communication within either region—thus bringing trade to it, rather than elsewhere.

(iii) It possesses local advantages of site (*e.g.* water-supply, defensive position) and can draw on an agricultural region for food for the urban population.

Commercial Centres—Ports.—These, too, are towns which lie along a line of contact between different, and often contrasting, regions; the actual contact is between land and water, but as the water gives access to all those lands which surround it the port is, in fact, virtually situated between one land region and another.

The functions of a port naturally vary with its location; but the chief function is to maintain a flow of goods to and from its hinterland and to enter into entrepôt trade where required. In addition, the port may house industries based upon imported raw materials, or connected with shipping, and, of course, carry on those functions which may be performed by any large town.

The fortunes of ports may fluctuate greatly and be affected by political and technological developments, which are not necessarily easy to predict. Yet, for a modern port to flourish in competition with others, the ability of port authorities to predict, plan for the future, and make developments in advance of assured custom is very important indeed.

This is especially so now that port areas are often extended to provide facilities for bulk deliveries, and for the industrial growth which often goes with the receipt of commodities—such as oil (petro-chemical industries) and iron ore (steelworks and ancillary industries). The authorities may develop the "infra-structure"—that is allocate and reclaim land, dredge approaches, and prepare services to sites before the individual firms acquire them; the firms will later develop the superstructures in the form of loading and unloading appliances, factory, and plant.

This combined development is well-illustrated by the port of Antwerp, where an infrastructure of reclaimed land and deep-water docks has been developed since World War II along the Scheldt, to extend virtually to the Netherlands border. Now an industrial complex, with specialised terminals, extends for many miles north of the pre-war limits of the port.

Ports of the Netherlands

(*a*) *Amsterdam.* The modern city, with about 900 000 people, covers some ninety islands, and many of the individual foundations are on piles. Planned development has been in evidence throughout most of its history, for concerted action has frequently been necessary in the face of unpromising physical conditions. Most of the marshy soil on which the city is built was originally below sea level, so that drainage and control of the waters have always been vital problems; although extension of the actual docks has been aided by the ease with which material can be excavated.

Originally a small settlement around a dam across the Amstel, it expanded gradually, and in medieval times became an enclosed and fortified city. A great increase in prosperity occurred during the late sixteenth century, when it took much of the trade which had formerly passed through Antwerp. In 1612 the city authorities began to execute a planned extension of the boundaries, which included a remarkable layout based on a semi-circular system of three canals (Plate XXIII). The prosperity within was reflected by the richly-decorated houses of the merchants.

The early nineteenth century saw a decline in trade, but also an increase in population, and a consequent haphazard growth of mean housing took place. The widespread use of larger trading vessels, for which the Zuider Zee was too shallow, was partly responsible for the decline in trade. But in 1876 the North Sea Canal was opened and a trade revival followed. In mid-century there was also a return to planning when a public works authority brought new housing under control.

For centuries the city has dealt with the imports and exports for the Netherlands, and with an entrepôt trade in tropical produce, mainly from the former Dutch East Indies. Industries grew up which were based upon this trade, sugar refining, chocolate making, margarine manufacturing, and with diamond cutting as a highly-specialised craft.

Changes in world conditions, and also technical achievements, have caused notable alterations in the functions of the port. With the completion of the Merwede Canal in 1892 it became connected to the main Rhine, and a canal capable of taking the largest Rhine craft was completed in 1952, joining the city with the Lek and Waal. It has in consequence developed a large transit trade with the lands served by the Rhine. Much of the internal trade is carried by waterways, although the railways converging on the port carry a great deal of traffic.

World War II brought a decline in the diamond cutting industry, for South Africa was forced to cut most of her stones at home; but other industries have prospered and now include shipbuilding, metallurgical and engineering industries, aircraft factories, and a large arsenal. It is the main port importing for the Netherlands home market.

(b) *Rotterdam-Europort.* The town of Rotterdam developed on
the site of a thirteenth-century settlement north of the Nieuwe Maas,
which leads to the Lek. It slowly assumed a triangular shape, spreading along the tributary Rotte and over reclaimed land in the Rotte Delta,
where it was cut by many canals. As a fortified town it remained
within these limits until the nineteenth century, when a rapid increase in

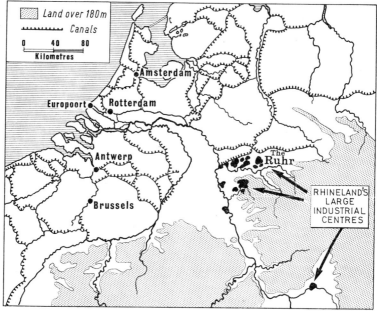

Fig. 56. THE GREAT PORTS AND WATERWAYS OF THE LOW COUNTRIES.
*Through this extensive system of natural and artificial waterways, Europoort,
Rotterdam, Amsterdam, and Antwerp are able to deal with goods passing to and
from the industrial regions of North-West Europe. Canal links extend the water
transport system along the North European Plain, via the Saône-Rhône Valley
to the Mediterranean, and connect the Danube and Rhine by way of the Main valley.*

trade and population caused serious congestion. Further living space
was obtained by covering in many of the canals in the old town, and by
expansion to the south bank.

In modern times it has grown as a major world port—an illustration
of the importance of *position*, in relation to the Rhine axis and its great
European hinterland, as opposed to *site*, which in this case was hardly
a favourable one. Apart from the constructional difficulties, as far as
the city was concerned, there was so much silting downstream that a
deep, tidal channel had to be built (between 1836 and 1872) to give a

minimum draught of 39 ft. Today the waterway carries the shipping serving a complex of storages and industries between Rotterdam and the sea. A flow of water deflected eastward, as part of the development aims of the great Delta Plan, will help to maintain this vital deep-water channel.

Since 1872 the port has so expanded that now only New York handles more traffic. Like so many large cities there has been great outward residential growth from the commercial heart of the city. With its surrounding districts, the population is about 750 000.

The functions which Rotterdam performs are many. Its principal activities are:

(i) A transit port for goods from the Rhine and its vast hinterland, which includes the Ruhr, southern Germany, Austria, eastern France, and Switzerland. (ii) A trading centre for the Netherlands; the bulk of the traffic moves by water. (iii) Shipbuilding. (iv) Petroleum refining. (v) Marine and general engineering. (vi) Vegetable oil production. (vii) Production of a wide range of consumer goods.

In recent years docks have been built down-stream to serve oil refineries, petro-chemical, and synthetic rubber plants. But as the waterway allows only a 39 ft draught a further extension, *Europoort*, has been created at the mouth of the river, south of the new waterway. This super-tanker terminal is linked by pipeline to refineries at Rotterdam and the Ruhr, and its ore-handling plant, blast furnaces, and steelworks are part of a large industrial complex which is to be extended still further seawards by reclamation. Tankers of up to 300 000 tons may use the terminal, though vessels above this capacity may find the approaches along the north European coastline difficult.

Rotterdam naturally enters into competition for the Rhine trade with Antwerp, Ghent, and Amsterdam; and as we have seen, such competition and the steps taken to anticipate economic developments obviously have great influence upon the fortunes and growth of a port.

Hong Kong

In contrast to these ports of the Netherlands, Hong Kong has acted almost entirely as an entrepôt port and transhipment centre, and as such depends very much upon its strategic position, political security, and free trade. Although there are many industries on the island and fishing remains an important occupation, these do not rival commerce as a main function.

Its advantage is one of position. It is situated in the inlet leading to Kwangchow, the communication and commercial focus of southern China. It lies midway between Singapore and Yokohama and near to the direct sea and air routes between them, and also across the routes from south-east Asia to the China coast.   Its natural deep-water harbour is, therefore, of singular importance, as is its international airport, with a helicopter service to and from an island terminal.   A tunnel has been constructed to link the island with the mainland.

The banishment of foreigners from Canton gave rise to the original British settlement and to a transfer of British commercial concerns to the island.   Over three million people live in the cities of Victoria and Kowloon, which lie on the island and the mainland, respectively.   The bulk of the population is Chinese, their numbers periodically swollen

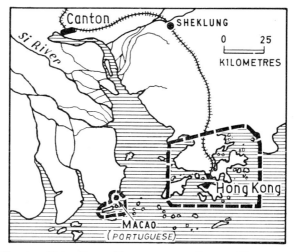

Fig. 57.   HONG KONG, MACAO, AND THE CHINESE MAINLAND.

The two settlements, established by Europeans, hold a unique position in relation to China proper, being the last remaining European trading stations with territory on the mainland—and are of great economic and strategic importance in the Far East.   Canton is now known as Kwangchow.

by disturbances on the mainland.   Much of its trade has been with China, and before World War II this accounted for 40 per cent. of the total trade;   with the mainland Communist coup this volume fell sharply.

The concentration of population and the urban spread on the island are controlled to some extent by relief.   Water supply has been an increasing problem as the population has grown.   The granite rocks cause rapid run-off, and the bold relief makes catchment difficult. Almost half the drinking water comes from Kowloon by undersea pipes, and at times the shortage becomes acute.

PLATE XIX

Above: St Croix de Lotbiniere, St Lawrence River. The strip pattern of cultivation with long villages strung out along the river bank is typical of the French "seigneuries" (see also Fig. 32). (*Central Pacific Railway.*)

Below: Iowa—rectangular pattern of settlement, with "strip" cultivation (here in alternate blocks) with different crops maturing at different times. Incipient gulley erosion shows the need for these measures. [*Fairchild Aerial Surveys, Inc. (through USIS*).]

PLATE XX

Above: Wind erosion. A "Dust Bowl" scene in the U.S.A., with the wind removing the drought-loosened top soil. (*USIS.*)

Below: Gully erosion near Brownsville, Ohio. Unchecked water erosion has formed a veined pattern, ruining acres of farm land and producing deep gullies. Ploughing *down* the slope means that in storms each furrow turns into a water course. (*USIS.*)

The use of the local rock in building, and the fact that the island lies beyond the earthquake zone, yet suffers from typhoons, has given the settlement a much more solid appearance than have most Chinese cities; lack of ground space has made for high-rise building, and a large proportion of the population lives in flats.

Montreal

This large port lies nearly one thousand miles from the Atlantic, deep in Canadian territory, a fact which has proved to be an advantage from the earliest days, when it acted as an outfitting centre for fur-traders and explorers moving into the interior of Canada. Jacques Cartier looked upon its site in 1535, but the first settlement was a Catholic mission station, set up there in 1642. For over a century the French made increasing use of this site as a base, despite fierce opposition from the Iroquois Indians.

The full advantages of the site were more apparent, when, with the British in control in Canada, and the United States of America established in the south, the settlement became the focus of trade routes, by land and water. It is reached from New York by a journey through the gap between the Adirondacks and the mountains of New England, via Lake Champlain and the Richelieu Valley, and it also lies immediately below the confluence of the Ottawa and St Lawrence rivers. The river channel has been deepened between Montreal and Quebec, and, after 1825, the obstacle of the Lachine rapids, immediately up-river, was by-passed by a canal which linked Montreal with the Great Lakes.

As the railroads pushed further and further to the west, grain began to pour into the holds of ocean-going vessels docked at Montreal, and the city became the headquarters of both the Canadian Pacific and the Canadian National Railways.

The completion of the St Lawrence Seaway project in 1959 created a deep-water routeway to Lake Ontario, and Montreal became a port lying between Thunder Bay, 2 260 miles inland, and the Atlantic.

Power from huge hydro-electric stations associated with this scheme, like those at Beauharnois and Cornwall, supplies the metallurgical works near Montreal and the city's many industries, including a large oil complex at the eastern end of the island on which the main part of the city is located. Some of its industries are connected with the country's agricultural produce, such as flour-milling and leather manufacturing; others use imported commodities—sugar refining, tobacco manufacturing, and petro-chemical production.

Within the city are the headquarters of many industrial, commercial, and transportation organisations, and the head offices of some of the country's main banks. There are two universities within the city.

The C.B.D. lies directly behind the docks and some of the older, preserved streets.   Here buildings of the early part of the century were replaced by the skyscrapers of the 'twenties and 'thirties; but so expensive is the land here, that multi-storied high-rise buildings now tower over these earlier stores and offices, and extend almost to the wooded slopes of Mount Royal itself—the prominence in the centre of the island which gave the city its name.

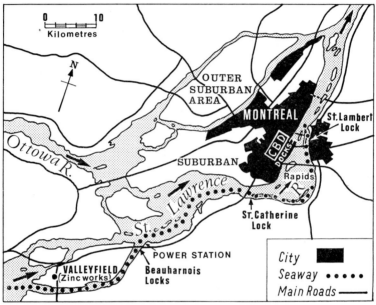

Fig. 58.   The Site of Montreal and the Entrance to the St Lawrence
Seaway.

This continual renewal at the centre, and the outward spread of the suburbs, are typical features of most large American cities.

The port is closed by ice from December to April, which is undeniably a disadvantage, and its overseas trade is transferred to Halifax and St John, and to Boston and New York; but yet it remains Canada's biggest city, chief manufacturing centre, and the port with the greatest volume of trade.   That the growth of population is not yet at an end is suggested by these figures:

Year	1871	1901	1921	1941	1961	1971
Population ('000)	107	268	619	903	2156	2500

Summary

For these ports, as with all settlements, nature offers a site and man makes use of it, as he wills or is permitted.

As we have seen, the sites of Rotterdam and Amsterdam would appear unfavourable for the development of a large city, and yet, with the prospect of a ready flow of commerce, they have prospered and expanded. Hong Kong, on the other hand, despite congestion on the island, is well sited and has an excellent harbour; but its future may well be imperilled by political insecurity in the Far East. Except for the effects of the winter climate, the situation of Montreal, in relation to its expanding hinterland, is favourable and greatly enhanced by the construction of the Seaway.

For a port to flourish, above all the other factors, there appears to be two essential requirements:—

(1) The possession of a productive and populous hinterland.

(2) A position which facilitates a flow of goods to and from the hinterland.

Individual ports may have special, or additional, functions, among the most common being:—

(i) They may act as an entrepôt for ports within range of small coastal vessels, or break down cargoes for onward delivery to other ports by larger vessels.

(ii) Industries may develop which are based upon imported raw materials, for example, chocolate and tobacco at Bristol, and oil refining at Marseilles.

(iii) Industries may grow up under the influence of nearby manu-facturing regions, from which materials may be obtained, in the way that shipbuilding on Clydeside draws upon the heavy industries of the Central Valley. Glasgow, incidentally, has the advantage of having been turned into a deep-water port, close to the heart of a populous industrial region.

(iv) They may act as naval bases, or as trading stations not associated with an immediate hinterland (Hong Kong).

(v) They may possess a fishing fleet. (This may be associated with the main function, as at Aberdeen or St John, Newfoundland; or it may be incidental, as with the multi-functional port of Hull.)

(vi) They may have those functions which may be performed by any town, depending on its status. (Administrative, retail, etc.)

Certain changes may occur which will cause a port to decline in importance:—

(i) A loss of trade to new ports which may be better equipped in some respects. Containerisation is a factor here.

(ii) A change in economy of the hinterland.

(iii) Technical developments in ship construction, which may leave the port too small for modern vessels, or may have other effects—as when the change from coal-burning to oil-burning vessels adversely affected the exports of steam coal from the South Wales ports.

(iv) Silting can seriously affect a port, though the larger ones can usually be kept clear—at a cost.

(v) Political changes may separate a port from its former hinterland—as in the case of Trieste (page 196).

Tides have a considerable effect upon the location, form and use of a port. A large rise or fall of tide makes loading or off-loading of goods difficult at certain times. In such cases sailing and berthing must await high tide, when the water at the approaches is at its maximum depth. Most large ports have docks, which are artificially protected by entrance through locks from the effects of tide. Southampton is particularly favoured as a port, having four high tides daily.

On the other hand tides help to clear silt away from the mouth of large rivers, so that a lack of tide may make it impracticable to operate a large harbour actually at the mouth. Coastal currents usually carry the silt to one side of the river mouth, and ports are generally established on the side free from heavy deposition—as in the Mediterranean, where Marseilles and Alexandria lie many kilometres up-current of the Rhône and the Nile, respectively.

Mining Towns.—Of all minerals, coal has had the greatest influence on urban growth. On many coalfields, the individual mining towns have acquired manufacturing functions, and often an industrial agglomeration develops on or along the line of the field. Such are the conurbations of the Ruhr and those closely associated with the major British coalfields.

The history of a mining settlement is often spectacular, and is apt to terminate abruptly as the mineral deposits become exhausted, particularly in isolated locations from which minerals are transported to distant industrial regions. Where a mining region has developed industrially as a whole, the mining town is more likely to acquire a wide range of activities and consequent stability.

In the Rockies and the Australian outback are many "ghost towns", once flourishing settlements, but deserted almost overnight. On the other hand, there are cities which owe their all to mining, such as Johannesburg. There are also towns such as Ballarat, in Victoria, which began as a mining camp and, though no longer dependent on the mines, are still developing as agricultural or regional centres.

The following representative towns include the old in decline, the old and prosperous, and the young and developing:—

Butte (Montana)

This town, high in the Rocky Mountain system was once described as "the greatest mining camp ever known"; "built on the richest hill on earth"; "a mile high and a mile deep". There are thousands of kilometres of shafts and tunnels beneath the town which have delivered many million pounds worth of copper since the latter half of the last century.

Like many another mining town its aspect is one of slag heaps, vegetation poisoned by fumes from the smelting processes, and dingy streets. In these surroundings thousands have found employment, and helped to create what was a flourishing, if at times flamboyant, community.

As it passed its peak thousands of houses, hotels, and offices became empty. There are still thousands of people directly connected with the mining industry, but, with its source of wealth seriously depleted, the only prospect of maintaining a thriving community lies in the retention of its role as a service centre for the widely-scattered population of this part of Montana.

Johannesburg

Here is a great city, the principal economic centre of South Africa, which has grown to maturity on the once barren land of the high veld. The presence of gold, naturally, provided the incentive for folk to settle on the Rand; but there are the additional advantages of an invigorating plateau climate and a ready water-supply from the Vaal and from beds of dolomite beneath the surface.

Original settlement, following the discovery of gold in 1886, was in the form of temporary camps for outspan wagons, and the foremost of these became the forerunner of Johannesburg. Today the city has more than a million inhabitants, and, although gold remains the chief source of wealth, Johannesburg is the most industrialised city in the country.

In the early days many fortunes were made by those who supplied the needs of mines and miners, and industries producing such articles as engineering tools, drills, and pipes, and a variety of food and clothing grew up along with the mines themselves. Fortunately coal is readily available from the field at Witbank, about 130 km north-east of Johannesburg.

The city is a great regional centre and is now part of a conurbation stretching from Randfontein to Springs. The central Rand has engineering and clothing industries, but also manufactures for the demands of the local markets and mining industries. Johannesburg is the headquarters of the national railways and an international airport.

Within the city there are several zones of occupation. In the centre, the high land-values have resulted in an upward growth of office buildings. The white population mostly lives in well-spaced suburbs but many Africans live in over-crowded outer reservations, and though planned outer suburbs have replaced many "shanty towns", improvements have been hampered to some degree by the

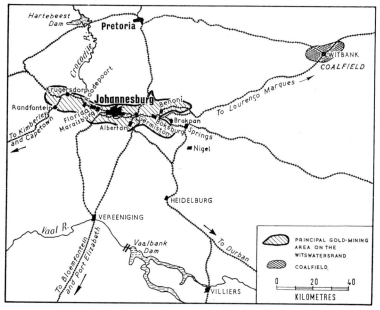

Fig. 59.   THE POSITION OF JOHANNESBURG.
Water for the population and industry on the Rand comes from the Vaalbank reservoir, and coal from Witbank.

fact that many mine workers are on contract for a certain period and afterwards return to their distant families; consequently, large numbers have no permanent attachments or family life in the city.

The contrast between the form of urban development on the mining area in Montana, and that on the eighty kilometre stretch of the Rand, indicates that the mere presence, and availability, of metal is not *alone* sufficient to give rise to a great city.

Lubumbashi (*Elisabethville*)

This is the main settlement on the savannah grasslands of the Haut Zaïre region of Zaïre Republic (Congo), at an altitude of about 1 000 metres.   It is the next most important town to Kinshasa (Leopoldville) in the country.

The tents and shacks of the first European mining community were set up in 1910 in virgin country near to the small native village of Lubumbashi.   African peoples had long mined small quantities of copper in the neighbourhood, exchanging the metal with Arab traders, who carried it to the coast.   Soon copper was being produced on a large scale, chiefly from the famous L'Étoile (Star of the Congo) mine.

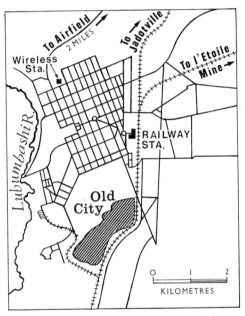

Fig. 60.   LUBUMBASHI (ELISABETHVILLE).

The layout of the centre of a city in the heart of Africa—far from industrial Europe, but flourishing upon the rich mineral deposits of Haut Zaïre which supply the great industrial nations of Europe.   The heart of the old city is shaded black.

The township rapidly developed beyond the shack stage, and African workers came in from all parts of central Africa, especially from the former German province of Ruanda-Urundi.   The copper belt, which extends into Zambia, proved to be extensive and to contain high-grade ore, sufficient in itself to make Haut Zaïre a region of great industrial and commercial prospects.   Its distance from the ocean makes the problem of transport a vital one, and in 1931 the Benguela railway was completed.   This enabled most of the copper to be sent through the Portuguese-owned west coast port of Lobito, a much more direct route to Europe than that formerly available via the Rhodesian railways and another Portuguese-owned port, Beira, on the east coast.

Copper is not, however, the only mineral produced in these rich fields, and gold, tin, cobalt, diamonds, tungsten, radium, and uranium, are among the minerals mined from this great outcrop of ancient rocks. The centre of copper mining has moved to Kambove, about 150 kilometres north-west of Lubumbashi, and many other important mines are being worked within a similar radius of the town, including the deep, galleried mine at Kipushi, thirty kilometres to the south-west. This adds to the significance of Lubumbashi, for, far from being purely a mining town, it has become a regional and commercial centre, with a large airfield, wireless station, hospitals, hotels, banks, and schools. Its population is over a quarter of a million and growing rapidly.

There are two other factors which favoured its development as a regional centre. Firstly, the growth of local industries. The climate suited resident Europeans who could bring their technical experience to the development of the region as a whole. The mean monthly temperatures range from 24°C in October to about 15°C in June and July. Secondly, plentiful and regular rainfall (about 1 200 mm a year) allows the reasonably fertile soils to be used for agriculture, so that, with political stability, Haut Zaïre could thrive on the twin assets of agricultural and mineral wealth.

Smelting furnaces in the town enable crude copper to be exported instead of ore, thereby lowering the cost of transport. Coal production, which has been small as yet, is capable of expansion. Hydro-electric stations already provide power for the whole copper belt and the output of electric power has recently been increased, and new projects are planned, for there are many potential sources of water-power in this part of central Africa.

Mining has thus brought about a big concentration of population in the heart of equatorial Africa, and there is the likelihood of further urban development in this region which, at the beginning of the century, was virtually virgin country.

Mining, then, can influence the form and pattern of existing settlement and establish new and often advanced forms of urban development in remote places. Thus amid the ordered settlements of south-west France, a completely new city, Mourenx-la-Neuve, was built to house workers in industries primarily based on the exploitation of natural gas reserves at Lacq and of the chemicals extracted from the gas.

On the other hand, at Kambalda, in Western Australia, in virgin semi-arid country on the edge of the great salt flats of Lake Lefroy, two townships were established within three years of the first exploitation of nickel ores. Here are air-conditioned homes, modern shopping centres, sports fields, surfaced roads, hotels, swimming pools, and gardens where in 1967 was desolate bush. Such amenities are essential if skilled labour and families are to be attracted to an isolated mining settlement in such a harsh environment. In fact, there are two towns, East and West Kambalda, the latter being built subsequently, six kilometres away, when it became obvious that urban expansion might clash with new mining developments.

Industrial Towns

Most towns are "industrial" to some extent. Some, such as those which developed on the coalfields during the nineteenth century tend to have one or two major industrial occupations and a host of minor ones. Other older settlements, on the other hand, have gradually acquired industries which, in time, have taken priority, in numbers employed, over the former non-industrial functions of the town: witness the growth of small industries at Bedford, which has turned an English Midland market and educational centre into what is now primarily an industrial town.

Power being essential for industrial production, the coalfields had a great attraction for manufacturing industries following the Industrial Revolution, and one can trace a concentration of manufacturing towns across northern Europe, based on the coalfields of the English Midlands, north-eastern France, the Sambre-Meuse coalfield, the Ruhr, and Silesia.

But the electric grid-systems, based first on coal-burning stations, but now linked to coal- and oil-burning, hydro- and nuclear power sources, have allowed a wider distribution of industries. Networks of pipelines carrying oil and natural gas are now established across much of Europe and North America, and are able to feed inland power stations and widely-dispersed industries.

We have already seen examples of industrial growth about centres of raw materials—heavy chemical industries, as at the I.C.I. complex in Cheshire, based on the salt obtained from the underlying evaporite deposits, and of iron and steel industries developed originally on the blackband iron ores of the coalfields, as at Sheffield and in central Scotland.

Other industrial growth occurs at or near ports, where imported raw materials are processed, or used in industries conveniently located at bulk-break points. Some industries are located there by their specific requirements; shipbuilding, for instance.

Industries also tend to group together, in close association, such as component factories near large vehicle manufacturing works, as in the west Midlands, or subsidiary chemical industries and plastics manufacturers close to petro-chemical plant.

Agricultural productivity has often led to local packing and processing industries—fruit canneries, as at Shepparton in the irrigated land of the Goulburn Valley in Victoria, Australia. Here the town remains a regional commercial centre with rural industries. Sometimes, however, the centre of a rich agricultural region becomes the chief commercial, banking, and administrative town, and later develops other industrial functions. Where local power resources are developed, such towns soon acquire a variety of industries to cater for the needs of the growing population of the whole region. São Paulo, Brazil, is a good example of a settlement which has expanded in this manner and which has diversified its industries to meet the demands of a rapidly-expanding population.

From such a variety of what may be termed "industrial towns", we will look at two urban areas which have developed into some of the largest population clusters in the world, but which have different origins and many contrasts in form and development—the Ruhr conurbation in West Germany and the rapidly expanding city of São Paulo in eastern Brazil.

The Ruhr—A Coalfield "Conurbation"

The River Ruhr flows along the outcropping edge of a coalfield. Coal workings began in the early eighteenth century and developed rapidly when, at the end of the century, the river was made navigable down to the Rhine. Local supplies of iron ore were tapped, and in the nineteenth century a string of towns grew up between Duisburg and Dortmund (Fig. 61). With power, raw materials and markets readily available, there was a rapid growth of heavy industries. A similar group of towns grew up to the south, on the Wupper Valley, iron ore with Düsseldorf as a river port.

Rapid expansion continued as additional iron ore was imported, and trade increased along the channels of the Rhine and Ems Canal, stimulated, in the second half of the century, by widening markets at home and abroad, and by the acquisition of Lorraine iron ore in 1871, and the development in 1880 of a means of conversion of the ore into steel—hitherto impossible, for technical reasons (page 193). The individual towns spread and overlapped, so that on either side of Essen in the north, and Wuppertal in the south, there extended a continuous industrial area, based on heavy iron and steel industries, and now oil refining.

Despite the devastation of the war years, the Ruhr grew rapidly, and in fifteen years—from 1950–64—had added a million to its population. The reconstituted industrial conurbation contained nearly six million people by 1965. A slight recession followed, but, despite pit closures, and the rise of other West German heavy industrial centres and manufacturing regions, to which some of the work force migrated, the population has continued to rise.

New industrial functions are providing a necessary diversification of industry. Science-based industries and miscellaneous light manufacturing are helping to cushion the effects of a declining coal industry.

São Paulo

Founded by Jesuits in the sixteenth century, the climate attracted Portuguese and Spanish immigrants. A century ago it was still a

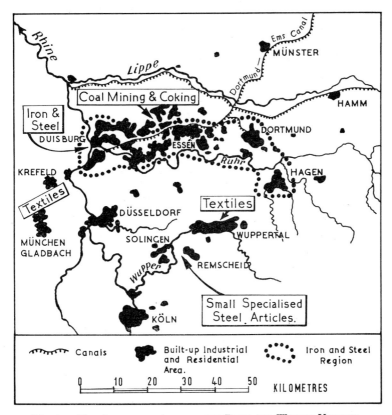

Fig. 61. THE INDUSTRIAL AREAS OF THE RUHR AND WUPPER VALLEYS.

The small towns, which once lay along the old trade route through Dortmund and Duisburg, have lost their medieval character amid the factories and residential suburbs of modern industrialisation. Duisburg, Essen, Bochum, and Dortmund each became a focus of industrial development, and are now part of a continuous built-up area which houses some five million people.

The whole industrial area of the Ruhr (excluding Düsseldorf, Wuppertal, and the southern cities) contains over seven million inhabitants.

small colonial village, but by 1920 its population had grown to
500 000, to two million by 1950, and to nearly four million by 1960.
The extremely rapid growth is also reflected in its income, which more

Fig. 62.   Sᴀ̃ᴏ Pᴀᴜʟᴏ ᴀɴᴅ Sᴀɴᴛᴏs.

(Adapted from Tɪᴍᴇ *map by R. M. Chaplin, Jr.;* Tɪᴍᴇ *copyright, 1952.)*

than trebled between 1940 and 1950, and is still rising rapidly as its
population reaches five million.

It is the centre of a state of great agricultural wealth, notably in
coffee and cotton.   The earliest roads radiated from the walled triangle
of the city into the surrounding countryside of the plateau about 800 m

above sea-level.   Today both roads and railways have a similar radial pattern, as they connect São Paulo with a semi-circle of growing towns, each the centre of a productive district.   It benefits from its situation between the port of Santos and the main productive areas of the hinterland.

São Paulo began its urban growth as the state income grew with the development of large-scale coffee growing, and later developed textile production and several huge meat-packing plants.   Abundant hydro-electric power is generated, within 50 kilometres of the city.   Its industries have become increasingly diversified.   Many thousands of industrial plants turn out a wide range of goods which include textiles, chemicals, steel, tyres, aluminium pistons, and electric lifts.   An even greater expansion seems likely, as its newer products are required by an expanding internal market, and its textiles are finding a place in world trade.   A development plan has helped avoid much of the squalor characteristic of many European industrial regions.   But like so many South American cities, it acquires an outer zone of squatters drawn from an impoverished rural population.   Most of these are eventually absorbed into city life and industrial expansion helps to create new fields of employment.

Administrative Cities.—National administration is but one of many functions of the older capital cities, like London, Paris, or Stockholm; in each case the intimate relation of these cities with the growth of the state has made them the focus of the nation's sentiment, so that, to the people, they represent national unity.

Where a capital must be chosen for a new state or federal group, it would seem advantageous to choose a city, or create one, central to the main areas of population, with good communication with the rest of the country; but there is much to be said for keeping the main administrative centre separate from the industrial areas.   However, the nature and position of the administrative centre is usually influenced by internal politics and in some cases the capital has been sited to be independent of the individual units of a federation.   Thus Washington, Canberra, and Brasilia, each originally built to plan, lie within territory separate from the individual states.   Brasilia's location was chosen partly to focus attention on the relatively empty but potentially rich agricultural lands of the "sertoes".   In each of the following towns their administrative function has been emphasised by the isolation and carefully planned layout of the government buildings:—

Delhi

The city lies on the west bank of the Jumna, where the last ridge of the Aravallis approaches the river.   Its strategic value is

immense, as indicated by the nearby ruins of seven former cities and
the fact that so many decisive battles have been fought in the vicinity,
as armies defended the narrowed gap between the Aravallis and the
Himalayas. Early Moslem and Mogul rulers set up court at Delhi
near the sites of earlier Hindu settlements, and the present city of Old
Delhi, a closely built walled settlement, was commenced by Shah Jahan
in 1638. Descendants of the Moguls remained there until the Mutiny,
in 1857, but after the British occupation the centre of government was
transferred to the trade centre of Calcutta, an outlet for the increasing
volume of raw materials destined for Britain.

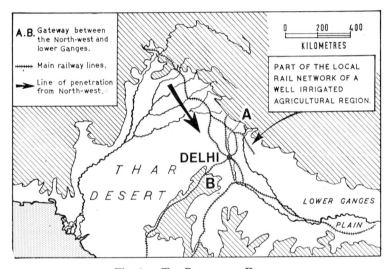

Fig. 63. THE POSITION OF DELHI.

    At the great Durbar of 1911, Delhi was once more restored as
capital, and a New Delhi was planned. This was symmetrically built
and now stands to the south of the Old City. It contains the government house, the parliamentary and administrative buildings, a modern
shopping centre, and official residences. Its function is purely that of
governing India.
    Delhi remains, in view of its central position on the Indo-Gangetic
Plains, an important railway and market centre (Fig. 63), with the
sprawling outer suburbs and fringe of squatter settlements common to
most Indian cities. Besides the old handicraft trades and small
industries of leather, silver, and ivory working, there are large cotton
mills, light engineering chemical works, and food processing industries.
New Delhi stands apart from these areas as virtually a separate city.

Chandigarh

India built Chandigarh as a planned capital for the Punjab, to replace Lahore (now in Pakistan), at a site near the road from Ambala to Simla. In a state of twenty million people, it was expected to house 500 000. Now with the Punjab sub-divided into Hariana and the Sikh Punjab, it acts, precariously, as a joint capital and its future is less assured.

It is designed in some twenty rectangular sectors, each self-contained, with its own schools, community buildings, and bazaar street. Green spaces are incorporated in each sector, and through the whole city an erosion valley forms a park. An industrial area, in the south-east, draws power from a regional hydro-electric scheme, while all around the city a five-mile belt was planned, to be restricted to its original agricultural use. (See also page 32).

Apart from its political ambiguities, Chandigarh has experienced a number of difficulties inherent in its original layout. There have been distinct differences between social districts, with higher-paid individuals able to keep up gardens and the conditions of housing and amenities to a high standard, while the less well-off have been less able to maintain the quality of the urban residences and adjacent amenities. The distance from residential districts to the C.B.D. and the industrial area is also a drawback to the many who must cycle to work, while some of the planned and developed highways remain virtually unused.

Canberra

It was originally proposed to create an Australian federal capital in the state of New South Wales. Because of inter-state rivalry, however, it was finally decided to set up a capital in independent territory, about 250 km south-west of Sydney. A position was chosen close to the route linking Sydney with Melbourne, 580 m above sea-level. Here, despite a low rainfall, adequate water was available from the drainage basin of a higher plateau.

The city was designed as a series of independent "cobwebs", partly separated by small hills which rise above the plain, and the civic and political units are separate. The street plan is devised to maintain this pattern as the population expands. Again, the space between the various clusters leads to a waste of travelling time. Like New Delhi, its function was to be purely that of government, but there are university and government research units, and a growing number of service industries.

The first real growth was in 1927 when the Commonwealth departments began to be transferred to the city (though the Commonwealth territory had been acquired in 1911). In recent years Canberra has grown very rapidly. Increases in diplomatic staff, the presence of the Australian National University, the location of offices controlling national commerce and manufactures, and the advent of more and more scientific units has seen the population rise from 18 000 in 1948 to 120 000 in 1970.

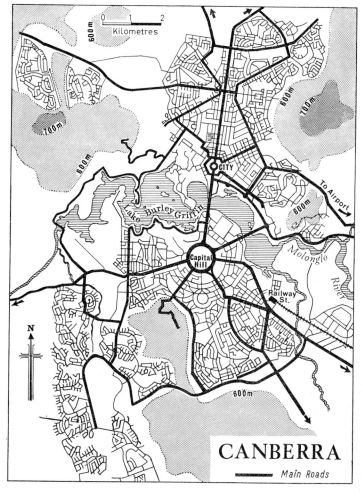

Fig. 64.   Canberra—A Planned Capital City.

The pattern of the roads show the "cobweb" layout of the city and the way in which it conforms to local relief features.   The administrative area is separated from the commercial and residential parts of the city, and allows room for expansion.   Artificial Lake Burley Griffin now separates these two halves of the city.

Resorts.—Many settlements exist with the prime object of providing recreational facilities—a specialised but important function. The basic attraction is the provision of a contrast in environment from everyday life. Millions are involved in the great seasonal migrations to the coast, mountains, and foreign climes.

The effects on settlement patterns in many parts of the world have been dramatic. Parts of the Mediterranean coastlands in southern France, the Spanish Costa Brava, the Italian Riviera have become almost continuous strips of hotels and artificially-improved beaches and coastlines; the new roads, shops, new local housing, and airport improvements are all part of the superstructure of an immense industry—tourism. The effects go far beyond these centres of tourism, and affect the producers of vegetables, meat, fish, and the other daily requirements of the large, changing population. They affect road construction and highway amenities designed to give comfortable access from hundreds of miles away.

The tourist industry is having similar effects on potentially attractive locations in all parts of the world, from Pacific islands to Andean towns, from the Caribbean to northern Norway.

Movements are now international and on a large scale. But within countries themselves there are resort towns, for which the holiday industry is the main function.

Brighton, with its adjacent urban districts, has a population of over a quarter of a million. In 1760 its population was only about 2 000, but by 1860 had risen to over 77 000, and from a small fishing town it had become a fashionable resort. Eighteenth century medical advice stressed the importance of sea-water in "diseases of the glands", and in 1770 Dr Richard Russell, resident in Brighton, produced a widely-read dissertation to this effect, so that patients thronged to the town. Members of the royal family became frequent visitors, and in 1787 a Royal Pavilion was completed as a seaside resort for the Prince of Wales. Lesser buildings sprang up on all sides. In 1846 it became connected to London by rail, and immediately the "one-day rush" to the sea began. By 1880 the population of Brighton was over 100 000 (excluding Hove).

Its assets are accessibility to the large London and Midlands populations, the former particularly; a south-facing sunny aspect; the summer attractions of the sea and beach; the ancillary attractions of amusements, shows, museums (the Royal Pavilion), etc., which have been developed to attract and entertain. This growth of secondary attractions usually follows the establishment of a resort, initially dependent on local climatic and topographic advantages, no matter where it is.

To-day Brighton functions as a residential town, a pleasure resort, an industrial town, as a dormitory for London, and a regional centre for south-east England. Its visitors, staying one night or more, total over four million annually.

Summary.—The towns selected, although varying in size, function, and regional setting, represent only a few of the many types which actually exist. In fact, towns rarely conform rigidly to a "type". Each town requires a separate study in the light of its location, relation to its surrounding natural region, and the particular circumstances of man's occupation of that site, and subsequent residential and economic development about that site.

Such a study should aim at providing answers to such questions as:—

Why does a particular town occupy its present position? What are the reasons for its present form and size? How are its present functions related to its geographical environment? Is it flourishing, or in decay; and what are the reasons for this?

Often, as the examples given above, there is no single clear-cut answer to these questions, and in some cases it may appear that a town might have grown up equally well in an alternative location, or have prospered on some alternative site.

Certain sites, however, seem to have been particularly favourable for initial settlement; for instance, well-drained river terraces, land within a protective loop, or high ground between the confluence of streams. But whereas such sites may be well-suited to early settlement, they may turn out to be less suitable as expansion takes place. In Oxford, the old residential districts were well-sited upon high gravel terraces to the north of the city; but as the city expanded during the nineteenth century, smaller and poorer houses spread over the lower terraces and clay, which are much less suitable for housing because of the tendency to flooding (see Fig. 51).

In any case, the settlement is hardly likely to prosper unless its situation and site relate to those economic assets which can provide for the inhabitants and allow the settlement as a whole to face competition from other places: such assets may be due to agricultural or mineral resources, or to the presence of potential customers.

In a group of similar settlements, the well-sited probably have the best chance of development; but a shift of economic factors, the building of a road, the discovery of minerals, or the whim of a potentate, may be sufficient to change the fortunes of a town or village. Thus, Tehran was not the capital of Persia until 1788; cities to the south-west being preferred instead. But the growth in economic importance of the northern provinces, and the growing strength of Russia, caused a shift of the political centre to the north. Human waywardness can affect the fortunes of any settlement, and it is certainly the human element that distinguishes one place from another, and gives to each occupied region its own particular character.

World Food Supply and Urbanisation

We have seen that, in the world as a whole, city life was not the norm until quite recently. Townsfolk must be supported by surplus agricultural produce from rural areas, and the limits of urban population are fixed by the food-producing capacity of the rural population, and by their means of transporting the surplus to the towns.

In modern times, technological developments, following the opening-up of new lands for cultivation, have created a much larger surplus, capable of supporting larger urban populations. This is still not universal, however, and in underdeveloped countries, as in the Indian sub-continent, a very large majority of the people live in small rural settlements, supported by agriculture, and with little, if any, surplus food production; it is estimated that at the beginning of the century this applied to nine-tenths of the population. For most of them the form of land transport is the slow-moving bullock cart.

Nevertheless, the great increases in food supply since the early nineteenth century has made it possible for countries of the western world, such as Britain, to support their rapid growth of population by supplementing home production by imports paid for by earnings from industrial productivity. In this way great concentrations of population can be supported, and urbanisation has proceeded rapidly in western Europe and various industrial regions overseas, like that developed in the U.S.A. between New England and Philadelphia—which today contains some forty million people.

Trends Towards Urbanisation

There are many concentrating factors which have made for urbanisation; 1-4, particularly, affected nineteenth century urbanisation in Britain, and those discussed in 5-8 have universal significance today.

(1) As industrial mechanised production replaced manual work, and often craft workmanship, labour became concentrated about the factories, rather than scattered in small rural centres or small urban workshops.

(2) As food imports were obtained to supply urban populations, many indigenous small-holders and farm labourers were unable to make a living, or became redundant, and were drawn into the towns for employment. Farm mechanisation increased the trend.

(3) The dependence on coal as a source of power tended to cause concentration of manufacturing on the coalfields, or where coal could be easily supplied, usually at a waterside location. Once industrialisation was established the advantages of clustering for many industries, supplying component parts or using materials produced by other manufacturers, made for the development of really large industrial towns.

(4) Improved transport, and a fixed network of railways and canals, also tended to be locating factors. In some areas with specific advantages, nodality or local raw materials, such modern transport boosted industrial production and urban growth by allowing a ready distribution of products—and import of other necessary materials.

(5) The numbers of people employed in a service capacity, as opposed to industrial production, increased enormously as the towns grew. Outside the factories men could now earn a living by marketing what was produced, transporting it, working in retail shops, in professions, public transport, entertainment, catering, and, of course, in many forms of administration and social services. As a great many of the latter functions were centralised, towns acted as service centres.

As the standard of living rises there is generally an increase in the number who render services—more doctors, more teachers, more taxi-drivers, more entertainers, and so on.

(6) The urban area itself is a large potential market, and so there is a tendency for factories to be established close to this large number of consumers, which results in a "snowball effect".

(7) With centralised services the town becomes increasingly attractive because of its social amenities. There are not only opportunities for employment, but also for various gregarious activities. The larger the centre, generally, the more opportunities and the better the facilities.

(8) As education becomes widespread, more people have a personal ambition to secure what they regard as a better job in the city, or to take part in urban cultural activities.

Rural Depopulation in Britain and Reversals of the Trend

In Britain there was such movement to the towns and cities during the nineteenth century that many of the villages lost a large proportion of their population, and this applied also to the smaller market towns, which tended to lose people to the larger centres.

But in recent times, with relative freedom of movement by car, and the advent of "two-car families", people may live in villages some way away from urban centres and travel in to work and shop, or to take children to school. As a result, many of the villages have increased in size. The strong trend towards outward movement, especially from the inner urban areas, continues. The character of the village and of village life has, of course, changed—being half-way between rural and urban in outlook.

Once again we may note the tendency for the inner parts of towns and cities to lose residential population, and for the residences to be replaced by commercial, light industrial, planned entertainment, and amenity areas. The population moves to suburban estates or out of the urban area.

Rural/Urban Movements in Other Countries

Much the same has occurred in other countries in western Europe and in eastern U.S.A. Movements to the cities by peoples in the underdeveloped lands have other propelling influences, however. Here there is often rural overpopulation, and lack of rural development; with little industrial dispersion, and few opportunities for local employment, the poor migrate from the countryside to the large cities in the often vain hope of finding work.

In India, the overcrowding, the squatter settlements, and the hopelessness of the unemployed is manifest in the great cities of Calcutta and Bombay, the former particularly. The local market town usually has insufficient functions to offer employment, and the peasant farmer moves from village to town, and then on again to swell the numbers in the city—where, in any case, the population grows rapidly by natural increase.

In Central and South American countries with a large indigenous peasant population, there are usually numerous squatter dwellings on the fringes of the larger cities. Here people who have migrated from the hardships of life in the high mountains, or forest, or drought-stricken savannah lands, live in makeshift conditions and seek employment, too often of a scavenging nature. In the expanding cities like Rio de Janeiro and São Paulo, many are absorbed into the city proper, moving into better houses as they are employed.

The Distribution of Large Cities and Conurbations

In some countries the proportion living in large urban areas is very high indeed. In England some twenty millions live in the great conurbations. In Australia, about half the population lives in the metropolitan areas of five cities, Sydney, Melbourne, Brisbane, Adelaide, and Perth, and less than a third in rural or mining communities.

The proportion of that population living in agglomerations of over a million inhabitants is growing at a particularly fast rate.   The figure "one million" is, of course, an arbitrary one, and not easy to apply so as to indicate a particular phenomenon—a "million city": this is mainly because definition of "city" and "urban area" differ from country to country; sometimes this means "city proper", within

CITY SIZE (Millions)

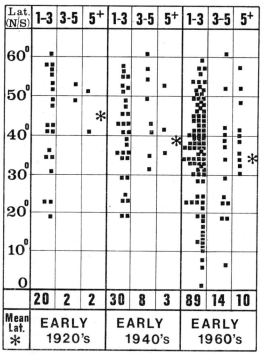

Lat. (N/S)	1-3	3-5	5⁺	1-3	3-5	5⁺	1-3	3-5	5⁺
	20	2	2	30	8	3	89	14	10
Mean Lat. *	EARLY 1920's			EARLY 1940's			EARLY 1960's		

Fig. 65.   *The Numbers and Distribution of "million cities", showing the shift in their medium latitude.*

(Based on statistics given by A. B. Mountjoy, *Geography* 53 p. 365.)

well-defined boundaries, sometimes an agglomeration, including a suburban fringe and the adjacent closely-settled territory.

The relationship between industrialisation and the growth of large cities seemed clear as recently as 1940, when of 41 cities of a million people and over, only seven were located between latitude 30 degrees and the equator.   Most were in the temperate, developed countries. But in recent decades there has been a great increase in the number of "million" cities (five-fold from 1920-60), and especially in the low

latitude countries.   In the early 1960's, of 113 "million" cities, 30 were
in the zone from the 30th parallels to the equator, and 52 of them lay
between the 35th parallels and the equator.

Fig. 65 shows the distribution of the "million" cities in the 1920's,
1940's, and 1960's, and emphasises the rate of increase in the low
latitudes, though it should be remembered that the rural population
in these latitudes is very large, and has also increased at a great rate,
so that the ratio of urban to rural population has not increased to such
an extent.

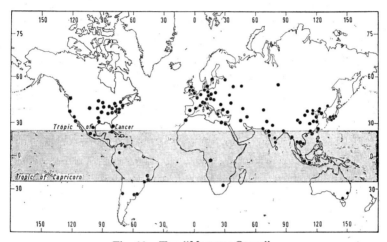

Fig. 66.   The "Million Cities".

*Note carefully the location and general distribution of the great cities, and also
observe those parts of the world where there are no cities of this class.   Remember,
however, that "one million" is an arbitrary figure and that many large towns
approaching this figure are part of urban agglomerations of over a million, but
actual conurbations are not shown as such.*

What is striking, however, is the rate of growth of many of these
cities over these thirty years, when Caracas, Tehran, Seoul, and
Karachi increased their populations some seven or eight times.
Twelve other cities in the low latitudes increased their population
more than four times.

In the underdeveloped countries, the housing, hospitals, education
facilities and other amenities are better developed in the towns than
in the country; and the cost of providing adequate facilities in rural
areas with rapidly-growing populations means that development in the
countryside remains inadequate.   For this reason alone there is a
powerful attraction towards the urban areas.

In developed countries where the interior lands are used for extensive farming or for mineral production, there is usually a startling contrast between life in the small places which serve the dispersed rural population and that in the mammoth cities. The latter generally have strong maritime connections and were established in the early days of settlement, such as the five mainland state capitals of Australia, and Montreal, Quebec, Vancouver, Buenos Aires, Cape Town, and Durban. Nevertheless, hierarchies of central places may develop inland, with large regional cities at the apex—as in the North American Mid-West (page 134).

An indication of the relationship between the large cities and smaller central places, which may suggest whether or not an urban hierarchy does exist, may be obtained by applying the "rank-size rule".

The Rank-Size Rule: Order and Functions of Settlements

A concept used in urban studies in recent years is that of a rank-size regularity of urban centres. This maintains that when a system of urban places is maturely developed, the population of the nth settlement will be $1/n$th times the size of the largest city.

In some countries, notably the U.S.A., this seems to be very much the case. In most countries, however, the largest city is greater than the rule suggests that it should be.

In Australia, where there were separate nuclei of colonial development, there seems to be little regularity. The second city, Melbourne, is much bigger than the rule indicates. If the states are considered separately the second city is between a tenth and a twentieth the size of the capital city (Fig. 67).

Generally, where a city far outranks the next in size it is called a "primate city", and may be seen as having in it an unusual concentration of commercial wealth and industrial development, and often political strength as well. Such cities attract a far larger proportion of the population and economic activities than the other urban places.

Turning to Australia once more, we may see here a reflection of the nature of the agricultural "outback". The small places have few functions, other than to serve the immediate needs of the dispersed farming population, and so do not increase in size with time to any extent. With the advantages of modern communications, the local people from time to time make use of the commercial firms and amenities of the large cities, and so tend to by-pass the intermediate market centres for a number of functions. Hence there are a very large number of small places, relatively few intermediate ones, and a few very large ones.

Where a more regular hierarchy exists, there tends to be grouping of settlements with roughly the same number of functions and functional units, and thus with approximately the same population. (A service garage represents a function and two service garages two functional units.) Another grouping should be apparent among settlements of the next higher order, with more functions and hence a greater population; this should produce a "stepped" effect on the rank-size plot, and may, or may not, be apparent for individual

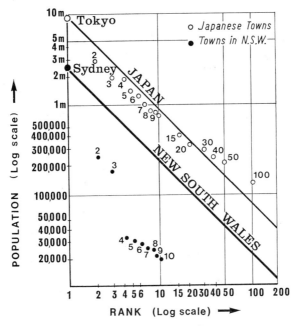

Fig. 67. THE RANK SIZE RULE.

The population of Tokyo is that of the administrative area. The hypothetical readings given by the rank-size rule may be read from the graph ($y = x^{-n}$) in each case. The Japanese towns follow the general slope of the graph, but in this industrialised country there are many low-ranking towns with a population greater than the rule postulates.

In the case of New South Wales (as in other Australian states), the state capital stands out as the primate city. The industrial-residential coastal cities of New-castle (2) and Woollongong (3) also stand apart from the inland centres, which from 5 (Wagga Wagga) downwards function as rural market-service centres. Fourth is Broken Hill with mining its main function.

countries or regions. Where, for instance, there are many manu-facturing centres of recent growth, or populous resorts, or dormitory towns (with few functions), they may blur the pattern, and produce a smooth, rather than stepped, curve. If functions are plotted against population (Fig. 26), such places are usually shown clearly isolated from the others.

Despite the anomalies, the rank-size concept is a valuable one for a study of settlement distribution; like all theoretical models, it helps us to think clearly about the observed patterns, and the apparent anomalies, and to seek reasons for them.

Land-use Competition

The outward movement of dwellings and industries, away from the old town centres, brings a real threat to the countryside, so that urban development comes into direct competition with agriculture. Besides the houses themselves, there are factories, playing fields, airfields, mines, and military training areas which all made considerable inroads into agricultural land. In a country like Britain the loss of such land is keenly felt, both on account of the loss of agricultural land (although Britain does not aim at complete self-sufficiency) and because of the destruction of more and more of the country's unique form of rural beauty.

Planners attempt to preserve whole areas from being overrun, by creating green belts, and by controlling the siting of industries (page 127); but, with many conflicting interests, their problems are never easily solved. Several different and legitimate interests may lay equally powerful claims to the same land. Large populations need local food supplies, and even if their grain and meat come from abroad, market gardening is usually established near the large cities. But unless gravel, which is essential to the building industry, is obtained from pits close to the towns, its cost is considerably raised (a twenty kilometre carry may double the cost). Moreover, gravel often lies beneath that well-drained soil which is eminently suitable for market gardening. Thus there develops a competition for land-use.

Sometimes expansion involves proposals for the demolition of rural or urban features of great historic or aesthetic value. The merits have to be carefully balanced and decisions made in the public interest, one way or the other. In fact, the absolute rate of urban expansion is less than many imagine, in terms of rural landscape "consumed", and effective channelling of such expansion may preserve much of Britain's countryside. It is direct threats to local features which are more likely to prove serious as urban expansion proceeds.

Pollution, in one form or another, is often the greatest threat: ruined beaches, "dead" rivers, and the like. Again, the threat may come both from urban sources and from rural developments: hedge destruction, which upsets the balance of wild-life, especially of bird species and the insects they feed on, or the misuse of pesticides or fertilisers.

CHAPTER VIII

THE POLITICAL UNIT AND ITS FRONTIERS

We have briefly considered how men settle in a region and form clusters of habitations, connected by various forms of communication. Small tribal groups may come together for protection, or to exploit and share the agricultural and mineral wealth of a region. Larger political groupings develop; and as they become associated with a given area, so they define their territorial limits. A sovereign state comes into being when some form of government is acknowledged, which administers the area as a whole, exercises some control over the resources of the territory, and looks to its security.

A modern political atlas describes world states as they exist *at the time of its publication*, yet people tend to accept the pattern shown in their atlas as a "normal" one, in the way that every child accepts the idea of his own country as occupying quite naturally, and by right, a specific area of the earth's surface. But the geographer, as well as the historian, is likely to be concerned with:—

(*a*) Why there are separate states.

(*b*) How each has developed.

(*c*) How long each has occupied its present territory.

(*d*) Why each state does, in fact, occupy its own particular area.

(*e*) The present political and economic stability, or instability, of each state.

A geographical study of the development of any state must then take into consideration (i) the kind of people who live within its bounds, (ii) the territory itself—its dimensions, natural regions, and resources, (iii) the situation of this territory in relation to neighbouring states, (iv) the economic relationships between this and other states.

THE PEOPLE

The "geography of a country" is too often taken simply to mean the facts of its situation, relief, climate, and vegetation, a description of its products and trade, and the size and distribution of its population. These facts are apt to be presented as statistics which reveal little of the individual characteristics of inhabitants, who come to be considered as being "all of a kind": those who live in France being "Frenchmen", and those of the U.S.A. "Americans", or, possibly, "white Americans" and "black Americans". Such terms conjure up for most people a composite picture, a private caricature of the natives of those lands.

/ The population, however, is rarely homogeneous in respect of race, religion, or language, although this latter is more likely to be a common factor. Few political units have been fully peopled as a result of a single migration, and there is usually continual movement into and out of the area subsequent to the original occupation. Thus, although normally there is a dominant racial group, most countries contain a mixture of racial types, speaking different languages or dialects./

It is essential, therefore, to know something of the racial, tribal, and historical background of the people before considering their relations with their geographical environment and fellowmen.

Use of the Term " Race "

The geographer must, naturally, be aware of the distribution of the major races, and must know something of men's racial characteristics. But he must also realise that unfortunately the word "race" has several meanings and is often loosely used. Too often it is used to describe a national or political group, in a phrase such as "the French race" or "the German race". It is better that the geographer use, in the political sense, "people" or "nation" instead of "race".

The Classification of Mankind: Criteria to be Used?—The geographer may look on members of a particular race as people characterised by the possession of certain inherited physical features, such as size and shape of parts of the body or skeleton, hair colour, or blood group. Certain sections of mankind have obvious features in common; the crinkly black hair, thick lips, and broad nose of black Africans; the straight black hair, prominent cheek bones, and short stature of Chinese. It appears obvious that a Chinaman and a native of West Africa are of two different races, and this may suggest that the races of mankind can be classified in a simple manner. But so numerous are the different clusters of mankind, each with their own distinct physical characteristics, that no universally accepted classification has yet been put forward. Are the Ethiopians, with frizzy hair, narrow nose, and some with reddish-brown skin, to be classified with other black Africans? Are the Lapps, with brown hair, deep-set eyes, and broad cheek bones, racially kin to the Chinese, or to the so-called "Caucasians", which includes most European peoples? Authorities disagree not only about the classification of these two peoples, but about the true kinship of many others. This is only to be expected, where intermarriage between groups of different racial origin must have occurred during the course of tribal wanderings and subsequent

segregation in distant parts of the earth: also, different criteria may be employed by individual scientists.

Physical Characteristics: Effect of Environment.—The following are among the more important criteria employed as a basis for classification:—

(*a*) The percentage ratio of the breadth of the head to its length (cephalic index).

(*b*) Percentage ratio of the breadth of the nose to its height (nasal index).

(*c*) Skin colour.

Before similarities in these characteristics can be used as evidence of racial kinship it must be quite certain that they are indeed purely hereditary traits; and it must also be established that the effects of environment on one generation cannot be handed down to the next. Most scientists are of the opinion that physical changes caused by environment cannot be transmitted *directly* from one generation to the next: but, on the other hand, by a process of natural selection, men most likely to survive, and hand down their personal features, are those with a type of skin, bone structure, and constitution most suited to the environment in which they live. Thus, in the stock as a whole certain physical characteristics may become prominent.

The following observations, when related to the criteria outlined above, give some idea how difficult it is to make hard and fast rules about racial characteristics:—

(*a*) From measurements of cephalic index it has been claimed that the children of Jews who have settled in the U.S.A., and of Japanese who have settled in Hawaii, show marked deviations from the head type of their parents. But a long time must elapse, and observations cover several generations, before this can be attributed to a change in environment.

(*b*) The broad nose of the negro, and the narrow nose of the Eskimo, *could* be due to the operation of natural selection, for the human body needs warm moist air, which the negro can readily obtain through wide nostrils, while for the Eskimo the air is warmed and moistened as it passes through a narrow aperture. It is possible that adaptation to environmental conditions has occurred by means of natural selection, but could well be that groups already possessing those characteristics have come to occupy regions to which they are physically suited, and have not survived in others to which they are unsuited.

(*c*) As a general observation, the majority of the people living in low latitudes appear to have darker skins than those living outside the tropics, and, while there is not a regular gradation in colour, there is evidence of a close association between pigmentation and latitude. Here too it is possible that natural selection has taken place, and the darker skins, which shield the body from harmful effects of strong sunlight, are a form of adaptation to environment.

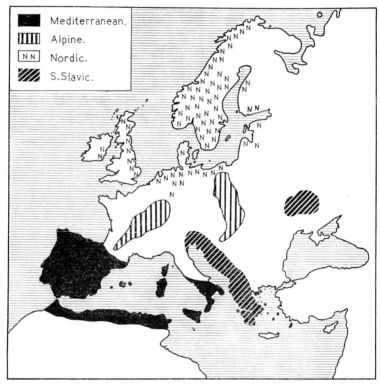

Fig. 68.   AREAS WHERE CERTAIN HEAD TYPES CLEARLY PREDOMINATE.

Based upon a distribution map by van Valkenburg, this includes his classification " South Slavic" for related groups of broad-headed folk, who are closer to each other than to the other (Alpine) broad heads.

For clarity, many small areas have been omitted—for instance, areas of predominantly long-headed folk in " Mediterranean France" and in Lombardy.

Even though it seems probable that human characteristics may be modified considerably by a process of natural selection, it does not mean to say that all the different types of mankind are the result of long series of selection from one given stock.   Even at a very primitive stage there is evidence of markedly different "racial" characteristics among men, who have migrated from source areas to become diffused over most of the land surface of the earth.

The Major Races.—Small groups, perhaps only families, seem to have moved outwards from various source regions in southern Asia and central Africa. The general direction of movement of peoples can be deduced from human remains and artifacts, and from the present distribution of mankind.

There is no absolute agreement as to the physical characteristics of a pure race. A number of broad classifications have been put forward by different authorities, using a variety of terms, as shown by two of them (I and II).

| I | Caucasian (including Mediterranean). Mongoloid. Negroes and Negritoes. Australoid. | II | Alpine and Mongoloid. Mediterranean. Australoid. Negro. Negrito. |

In each of the major races large groups have acquired distinguishing physical characteristics which are so marked that the group may be termed a "sub-race". The existence of such groups is probably due to isolation from the main stock, and the processes of natural selection or inbreeding over a long period of time. Thus the Mediterranean type of people are sometimes classified as a subdivision of the Caucasian race (see below), though regarded by other authorities as a pure racial type.

To describe the characteristics of each of the racial types is beyond the scope of this book. It is doubtful whether there are now any peoples of "pure" race, although the few Veddas in Sri Lanka may be unmixed. Certainly there is no such thing as an "English race", a "German race", or a "Chinese race".

Similarities in language or culture do not, of course, imply any racial kinship, although such terms as "Aryan", or "Dravidian", strictly linguistic, are often thus misused.

A BACKGROUND TO THE STUDY OF A NATION STATE—FRANCE

The Peoples of Europe.—The continents are inhabited by people in whom the racial elements have become fused. Different racial proportions "crystallise out" in various localities—here markedly Mongoloid, there Caucasian.

In Europe the white or "Caucasian" race has three important subdivisions: (a) the Nordic people; (b) the Mediterranean people; (c) the Alpine people.

(a) *The Nordic people* are tall and have fair hair, blue eyes, fair complexion, and long skulls. They are found chiefly in north-west Europe, Denmark, Holland, north Germany, Scandinavia, and Britain.

(*b*) *The Mediterranean people* also have long skulls, a medium stature, slim build, dark wavy hair, olive complexion, straight nose, and dark eyes. They are found in all the countries bordering the Mediterranean Sea, and in western Ireland and western Scotland.

(*c*) *The Alpine people* have broad skulls, brown or dark hair, grey or dark brown eyes, and are often thick-set. They are found chiefly in the mountainous areas of eastern and central Europe.

These sub-races have intermingled and interbred, particularly in the lands of western Europe.

Fig. 69.   PARTS OF FRANCE WITH A HIGH PROPORTION OF BROAD HEADS IN THE LOCAL POPULATION.

This present-day distribution of broad-headed peoples is an indication of the early movements of such folk along the highlands of East and Central France.

Tribal Wanderings and Eventual Settlement.—In France the population is descended from immigrants of Mediterranean, Alpine, and Nordic types. There has been considerable fusion, although each sub-race predominates in certain areas; for instance, the broad heads of the Alpine type in the mountains of the Pyrenees, the central Massif, and the Savoy Alps (Fig. 69).

The line of inroad of the early immigrants was very much in accordance with the topography. The Rhône Valley gave easy access to movement from the Mediterranean and the north-east; the Alpine people moved centrally through the uplands from Lorraine to the Pyrenees; and the Nordic type of peoples moved along the North European Plain, although the last major group came with the invasion of the Scandinavian Norsemen in the ninth century.

The facts that France with Iberia is a peninsula, and that the Pyrenees are a formidable barrier, meant the end of the westward movement for the many wandering tribes, who thus had the option of settling or retracing their steps.

Western Unification Under the Roman Empire.—Nation states as we know them had no existence before the creation of the Roman Empire. Tribes occupied areas favourable to their particular form of civilisation, but there was little unity, beyond fluctuating tribal federations.

The Romans established political control of the lands around the Mediterranean, and occupied such territory as would secure a strategic frontier at a convenient distance from the Mediterranean Basin. Gradually, therefore, the lands south of the Danube and west of the Rhine achieved a sense of unity, and prospered under the military protection, and through the technical achievements, of the Romans.

Fortifications were established at points along the eastern limits of the Empire, where otherwise there would be relatively easy access for barbarian tribes, who might be tempted to advance on the more attractive and fertile areas within the Empire. Protective walls, auxiliary stone fortresses, and fully-fortified towns, were sited, according to the terrain, to guard the easier routeways. Thus, while the marshes of the lower Rhine afforded some natural protection, the open stretches of the north European Plain and the tributary valleys of the middle Rhine, the Neckar, and Main were fortified in depth.

A frontier zone thus became fixed upon the ground, but, as yet, there was no sign of the pattern of nation states which was to cover western Europe. Only after the decline of Roman power did a few relatively stable settlements, established after centuries of westward folk movements, form the seed of future European states.

The Barbarian Invasions.—Even at the height of power of the Roman Empire there were almost continual skirmishes with the tribes beyond the north-eastern frontiers. With the decline of Roman power, strong confederations of tribes moved to the south and west along the general lines of advance indicated in Fig. 70. This was in no sense a coordinated movement, but followed the breaking down of the frontier zone in the third and fourth centuries A.D. The paths of the tribes lay along the geographical lines of least resistance. The Goths, for instance, made use of one of the old amber trade routes, which ran from east of the estuary of the Vistula, the source of amber, outflanking the

Carpathians, and, skirting the Pripet Marshes, to the Black Sea. Here after some degree of settlement north of the Black Sea, the pressure of the Huns from the east led to further migration.

There were probably several reasons for the successive movements of tribes westward through central Europe:—

(a) Further east peoples such as the Huns and Magyars were on the move, away from arid conditions prevailing on the steppe-lands.

(b) It is likely that the homelands of the Germans, along the north coast, eastward from the Rhine, had, rather earlier, experienced a wet climatic period, which extended the forest and bogland. Certainly

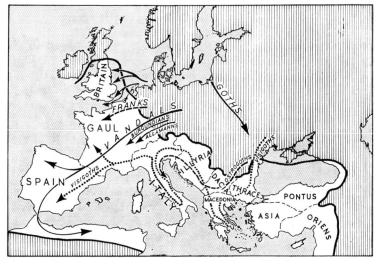

Fig. 70. THE LATER ROMAN EMPIRE (unshaded) WITH AN INDICATION OF THE ROUTES TAKEN BY BARBARIAN INVADERS.

many tribes had moved southward and eastward during the second century A.D.   The German tribes in central Europe were thus increasing in numbers, so that pressure of population became a strong motive for invasion of the Empire.

(c) The attraction of better soils, more favourable climatic conditions, and the prospect of plunder, to be found in the west.

The Fate of Gaul.—A branch of the Franks, the Salians, moved into the low countries, from the lower Rhine, as early as the third century.   Other branches firmly occupied the lower Rhine plain, and faced the Romans along the middle Rhine.   In the fifth century they advanced, separately, into Gaul, and in 486 Clovis, the king of the Salian Franks, defeated the Romans, who were holding out in the Paris Basin. The Frankish branches united and faced another group of peoples, the Visigoths, along the line of the Loire. These latter had advanced into south Gaul, and into Aquitaine, before moving northward to the Loire; while in the south they crossed the Pyrenees, and spread into almost the whole of Spain (Fig. 70).

The Franks succeeded in overthrowing the Visigothic kingdom, and not only ruled their wide territory from their headquarters in the

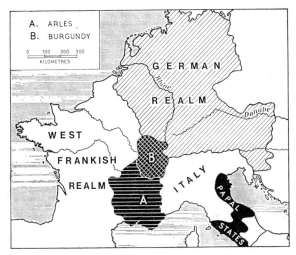

Fig. 71. The Second Division of the Empire of Charles the Great—
The Treaty of Mersen (888).

The boundaries indicated represent a division by agreement into Frankish and German realms, neither of which were then nations, as such, but were territories which in the distant future were to correspond, roughly, with the French and German states. The Rhine, as yet, played no part as a boundary, and, of course, the frontiers agreed on were not actually demarcated.

Paris Basin, but established firm settlements in the conquered lands. They gradually adopted a Romance language instead of their own Germanic tongue, although the German tongue remained the language of the peoples to the east of Gaul. A state was thus established which was rather more extensive than that of present-day France, for the tribal areas of the Allamanns and the Burgundians, who had made incursions into Roman Gaul, were also absorbed into the Frankish territory. But, unfortunately, on the death of Clovis, the Germanic practice of dividing land equally between male heirs resulted in a succession of partitions, and there was little real political unification until the eighth century.

At the end of the eighth century, Charles the Great united the Frankish inheritance and extended his power to create an Empire. But, largely owing to the poor communications of the time, this proved unwieldy and difficult to administrate.   During his son's reign it was accordingly partitioned between three heirs, and in 843 a division between the western Romance-speaking territory and the Germanic territory to the east was established for the first time.   Between them a middle kingdom, Lotharingia, was created, which stretched southwards from the low countries and included the Maas and lower Rhine, the Rhône Valley, the Plain of Lombardy, and the northern part of the Italian peninsula—formerly the kingdom of Italy, within the Empire of Charlemagne.   But this proved unmanageable and a further treaty of 888 divided it, in the north, between the Frankish and German kingdoms; while in the south Italy became separate, as did several feudal territories, including Burgundy and Provence, which were placed under an east Frankish king.

The Growth of the French State.   In 987 Hugh Capet became king of a France which was far from being a single political unit.   The royal estates formed the geographical nucleus of the French state, but beyond this Capet and his successors had only nominal overlordship over a number of powerful lords.   However, the Capetian kings succeeded in extending their royal territory, by methods varying from marriage to war.   From this time, by slow historic growth, France developed into a coherent nation state.

The domain of Hugh Capet was approximately that of the region known as the Ile de France.   Although Capet favoured Orleans more than Paris, the latter undoubtedly occupied a dominant position at the focus of the Seine tributaries, where the earliest settlement was on a protected island in mid-river.

The ultimate course of national growth could not have been foreseen, for apart from the feudal control in central France, the Vikings, or Northmen, had occupied Normandy; Aquitaine, soon to be a fiefdom of the English king, had long been a separate duchy; Brittany and its Celtic people remained apart with a regional aloofness that has persisted to the present day.   In addition, Mediterranean France, although eventually subordinated to the north, had many independent characteristics: the climate and the natural products, including the olive; the fact of its thorough "Romanisation"; its early association with Spain; its occupation by the Moors; and a characteristic Romance tongue—Provençal—are all features which differentiated the Midi from northern France.

The strong regional consciousness of the Frenchman, apparent in the wealth of local customs and dialects, has its roots in the early development of these distinct cultural regions, which antedated by many centuries the nation state we know as France. The main features of relief have had much to do with this. The Central Massif helps to define, and maintain, the unique qualities of the basins of the lower Rhône, the Garonne, and the Loire; Brittany, in its rocky peninsula, lies apart from the north European Plain; while the series of "rims", the escarpments of the saucer-shaped Paris Basin, used from time to time as strategic lines in defence of the capital, help to distinguish it as a separate region within which lie rich, broad, plains.

In spite of the existence of a strong regional consciousness in many distinct territories, the French state grew, by a process of accretion, around the nucleus of the Paris Basin. It may well be that the very existence of such numerous and diverse regions in western Europe helped to make possible the development of the nation state. As small feudal groups existed, each fairly well integrated with its natural environment, their incorporation into the growing state did not upset its stability.

There is no space to follow the details of the expansion of the Royal domain in France, but Figs. 72 and 73 show broadly how political unification took place. With it came national awakening, although regional loyalties remain strong, particularly in Brittany, Normandy, and the Midi. Statesmen now began to review the national boundaries, and in the seventeenth and eighteenth centuries there arose a demand for the state to expand to its "natural limits", namely the Pyrenees, the Alps, and the Rhine. The desire to use the mountain regions as boundaries may seem to have had some justification, but to include Alsace within the state on the grounds of "natural" grouping was to include a region belonging to the Rhine Basin, rather than to the Paris Basin or Lorraine Plateau. Nevertheless, both Alsace and Lorraine were incorporated in the seventeenth and eighteenth centuries. More recent territorial changes are discussed below, together with some of the problems of France's eastern frontier (page 193).

The Formation of Other States

France is an example of a state created slowly from a blend of peoples, and covers an area which includes many contrasting physical regions. Despite such diversities, the slow historic growth has resulted in national strength, and in much the same way the English state acquired stability, later to be extended to a United Kingdom.

The gradual process of unification around a core area is but one way in which a state may be established. States, have been created in quite different ways: through subdivision—by treaty, or by decay or by the absorption of smaller political groups; by deliberate colonisation, or conquest, or unification after freedom from colonisation.

The extent to which geographical facts are bound up with the state's development is revealed only by a close study of the individual circumstances, in which historian and geographer should combine. Even when the boundaries appear to be well-adjusted to natural features, a host of internal problems may arise if minority groups exist in the state. Historical, linguistic, or religious differences may

Fig. 72.   France—The Expansion of the Royal Domain.

(After Pounds.)

adversely affect the national well-being, and these, amongst other problems, come to light in the following sections, which deal with matters related to the fixing of boundaries.

INTERNATIONAL BOUNDARIES

The earliest boundaries were usually zones, rather than lines— border marches, which might be waste ground separating areas of settlement. As the countryside around the original settlements became peopled, the zones narrowed, until finally they disappeared, leaving a line of contact between the two occupied areas.

The Treaty of Verdun laid down limits for the territories of Carolingia, Lotharingia, and the German kingdom, but this was far from creating boundaries, as we know them today. Certainly no boundary line was marked out on the ground (a process usually referred to as *demarcation*).

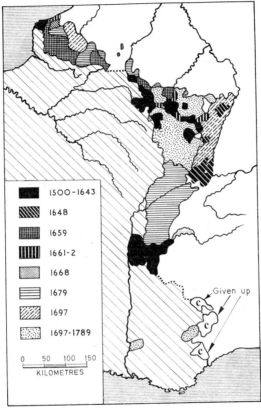

Fig. 73. THE ADVANCES OF THE FRENCH STATE TOWARDS THE RHINE.
(After Pounds.)

With the growth of nationalism in Europe, international boundaries have not only become rigidly fixed, but are almost always clearly demarcated. When a nation state is firmly established, its inhabitants come to look upon their country as occupying a part of the earth's surface "by right". Sometimes a given physical region comes to be regarded as the natural inheritance of the state. Consequently, if a state does not entirely occupy such a region, demands are made that the boundaries be extended until it does.

The main functions of a boundary are to separate the peoples on opposite sides, and give a measure of protection to each group. In the early days, the march, or vacant land, gave protection in that, in view of the long approach which had to be made, a surprise attack was difficult to achieve. Modern boundaries can protect the state in the sense that guaranteed external aid may be forthcoming should the agreed frontier be violated.

The functions of most modern boundaries are concerned with peacetime rather than with wartime, and in considering whether a boundary is good or bad, one must consider conditions as they are in time of peace. For example, how far does the nature of the boundary allow the state to exercise the control over the free intermingling of people and goods, which may be desirable, for economic, health, or security reasons?

Natural Barriers as Boundaries or Protective Zones

The transition from one natural region to the next is usually gradual, and natural linear boundaries are rare. It is reasonable, however, that states should wish their perimeter to be protected by strong natural barriers, or to have frontier regions which can be made secure by well-sited fortifications, and some natural features are more suited to this purpose than others.

The Sea. The boundary between land and sea is usually clearly defined, although there is a fluctuating zone which is land or water according to whether the tide is low or high. Territorial waters normally stretch for an agreed distance from the coast and their limit runs parallel to it. The presence of rich fishing grounds may make some coastal waters attractive to the fleets of many nations, so that it is desirable to demarcate the limits of territorial waters very accurately; complications occur where the coast is greatly indented. Some countries, like Iceland, Peru, and Britain, in relation to E.E.C. commitments, have particular interests in protecting their inshore fisheries.

By restricting trade and passenger traffic to specific ports of entry the sea boundary is made a barrier. The length of the coastline and the possibility of surprise attack lessens its effectiveness as a means of protection against an armed enemy.

Deserts. For centuries the Sahara was the southern limit of European civilisation. The difficulties of replenishing food supplies and fodder, and the slow rate of camel transport, made crossing by an army impracticable, although ancient trade routes, making use of oases, are still followed. Modern armies have proved that battles may be fought under desert conditions. Aircraft, roads, and railways cross them, but nevertheless, deserts are effective barrier zones.

Even in desert land the boundary must be carefully defined, and at some points demarcated, for mineral wealth may be discovered close to the frontier. This is borne out in the Sahara, where great reserves of petroleum, natural gas, and iron ore are among the minerals discovered. Purely astronomical (straight line) boundaries (page 190) are therefore not always the best, and, though they may be convenient in the absence of well-defined physical features, may disrupt trade-routes or divide oases tapping the same water reserves.

Mountains. Mountains act as a barrier by virtue of their rugged-ness, and because of the low temperatures and scarcity of oxygen at

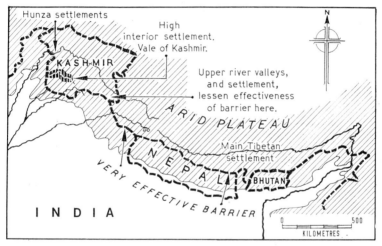

Fig. 74. BOUNDARIES IN THE HIMALAYA.

high altitudes. These circumstances may combine to limit the possibility of settlement, and, as with deserts, their emptiness becomes a virtue if they are to serve as boundaries.

The differences of climate and natural vegetation which often occur between two sides of a range may mean that it separates, quite naturally, communities with different cultural backgrounds. Thus the high Himalayas are followed by the boundaries between several states (Fig. 74), and almost cut off the people of Tibet from those of the Indo-Gangetic Plain. The same is true of the Andes between Chile and Argentina; though further north the high central plateaux of the Andes are relatively favourable to settlement.

Few of the great mountain ranges consist of a single high, well-defined ridge. They are rather zones of separation, which may contain high plateaux, densely-populated basins, and valuable mining districts, as in Peru and Bolivia, closely-occupied agricultural and pastoral valleys like the Vale of Kashmir.   In hot countries the mountains may sometimes provide a relatively comfortable climate for man.

Fig. 75.   National Boundaries of the Middle Andes.

Because of the width of the high plateaux, the extensive settlement in the upland basins and valleys leading to irrigated coastlands and to the Oriente, the mountains of the Middle Andes are not barriers in themselves, and the highlands contain no boundary between east and west.

Such populated districts and their communications weaken the barrier presented by that part of the mountain system.

Series of parallel ranges are usually more effective barriers than are single ranges.   The relatively low Appalachians, difficult to cross except through the river gaps, limited settlement for a long time to the eastern seaboard of the "New World".

It is not always easy to decide the actual line of demarcation along a mountain range. In 1898, Britain agreed to arbitrate in the dispute which arose between Chile and Argentina over the demarcation of their 3 000 mile boundary. It was required by existing treaty to be fixed along "the highest crests which may divide the waters". Argentina claimed the line of the highest crests, and Chile claimed the line of the watershed. In fact, considerable areas east of the main heights were found to drain to the Pacific. The award, announced in 1902, was based on a compromise, and accepted by both countries. The prevention of possible conflict, by means of arbitration, was subsequently commemorated by a great monument known as the "Christ of the Andes", erected in the Uspallata Pass.

Forests. Forests, in themselves, have little value as barriers or as boundaries. But in combination with mountain ridges, as in Burma and Malaya, they help to form very formidable obstacles. Areas of dense virgin jungle are difficult to penetrate, except along waterways; but even they have economic value, perhaps hardwood or natural rubber, and may contain settlements in clearings. The softwood forests are so much in demand for modern industries that they are subject to extensive clearance.

Swamps. Swamps in their natural state are, like forests, difficult to cross—the Pripet Marshes long formed a satisfactory "waste zone" on Poland's eastern frontier—but it is possible to drain them, so that they lose their efficacy as a barrier. Some drained marshes with rich alluvial soil, such as the English Fenland, become productive and densely peopled.

Rivers. Rivers can usually do little more than impose a momentary check on an invader. They have, however, the advantage of being easily recognisable as a boundary, especially desirable for primitive communities.

There are, however, other considerations which affect the value of a river as a boundary. If its function is to divide, a river would indeed be an obvious and efficient boundary if it separated people of contrasting race, language, religion, or occupation. On the other hand, many rivers flow through a basin in which the people have similar racial and social characteristics, speak the same language, and are very often engaged in similar occupations. If the river is navigable and used for commerce, there may be a concentration of people along the riverside, particularly in the neighbourhood of river ports. Roads and railways follow the easy gradients of a river valley, and may cross and recross the stream itself. In these circumstances the river may be an efficient indicator of a political boundary, and common interests may make for stability among the peoples involved.

On the other hand its use as a boundary must tend to disrupt the unity of the region. The Rhine frontier between the Vosges and Black Forest illustrates some of the problems. The boundary *is* divisive, and the folk on either side owe allegiance to different states; but similarities in culture and land-use within the valley were sufficient to provide an excuse for a policy of German "unification" of the valley by acquiring Alsace.

Fig. 76.   DISTRIBUTION OF WATER FROM THE COLORADO RIVER.

The river flows mostly through arid territory, crossing state frontiers and acting as the boundary between other states. Water has been made available for irrigation through the construction of great dams, and is distributed in accordance with agreements between the states concerned.

To the east the Rio Grande acts as a boundary between Mexico and the U.S.A.

Where a river valley is shared by different states, vital problems may arise over the use of the water, irrigation, navigation, and regulation of flow. The problem may occur either where the boundary cuts across the valley, as in the dispute between Egypt and the Sudan over the control of the Nile waters, or where states lie on either side of the river, as do the U.S.A. and Mexico on the Rio Grande.

Where the boundary is internal, as along the Colorado River, U.S.A., agreement on river usage may be made within the federal constitution of the nation.   Thus, in 1922, roughly half of the volume of the Colorado's flow was assigned to Wyoming, Colorado, Utah, and New Mexico, while the lower basin states of California, Nevada, and Arizona, were to receive a certain proportion of the remainder. Arizona stood out against this compact for twenty-two years, and even attempted to halt, by force, the construction of the Boulder Dam (now known as the Hoover Dam), for fear of the loss of more precious water to California.   If the struggle for water can be sufficiently bitter to bring internal strife to the members of a single nation, the dangers which may arise in international bargaining for irrigation rights are obvious.

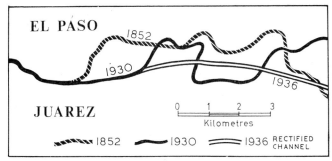

Fig. 77.   Meanders and Changes of Course of the Rio Grande—
U.S.A./Mexico Frontier.

The changes of course in the vicinity of El Paso were such that frequent adjust-
ment of the boundary was necessary.   In 1936 a channel was constructed to
regulate the flow and thus to avoid meanders.

(*After Boggs.*)

Further complications arise where a river meanders.   The changes in course of the Rio Grande, due to meandering, have frequently called for adjustment of territory between Mexico and the U.S.A.   Between 1907 and 1933, near El Paso, the course became so erratic, due to silting, that it had to be straightened, which reduced 155 miles of waterway to 86 miles, and necessitated the exchange of numerous portions of land between the two countries.   The changes were accomplished peacefully, but the need for them underlines the drawbacks which may result from choosing a river as a boundary merely because it is easy to identify on the map and see on the ground.

Artificial Boundaries

All boundaries are "artificial" in the sense that they are man-made. Apart from using obvious physical features, man has adopted other means of delimiting territory. Thus the Great Wall of China, Hadrian's Wall, or Offa's Dyke were built to demarcate the line chosen to separate peoples of different cultural backgrounds. These artificial barriers tended to follow existing features of relief. Other boundaries may be chosen to follow tribal, linguistic, or religious divisions, in the way that the line separating Hungary from Austria was chosen to divide Magyars from Austrians. In some cases boundaries are set up in positions of compromise, or along a line of military deadlock; after World War II, the 38th parallel in Korea, and the boundary between the Russian and Western occupying powers in Germany, bore close relation to established military positions.

Boundaries of the astronomical or geometrical types are more obviously artificial.

Astronomical Boundaries. Such boundaries are fixed with reference to lines of latitude and longitude. Among the best known is the 49th parallel between Canada and the U.S.A. They are common in lands of European colonisation and were often drawn previous to actual occupation by white settlers. Many of them reflect geographical ignorance at the time of their determination, bisecting, for instance, the drainage areas of rivers, and intersecting mineral deposits or potential grazing land. On the other hand, there is not the confusion which may occur when boundaries are defined in terms of watersheds or other physical features which may not easily be identified on the ground. Astronomical boundaries can be fixed precisely; but, because of the detailed survey required, are usually most expensive to demarcate.

The fact that a boundary is fixed before extensive settlement occurs may, in fact, contribute towards its success; for folk respect it as something established, adapt themselves to it, and usually view the enclosed territory with patriotic feelings. On the other hand, when a boundary is superimposed on a densely-populated region, the fact that it must cut across farms, tribal areas, villages, or even towns, inevitably causes hardships and grievances.

Geometrical Boundaries. Some boundaries follow geometrical lines which are related to specified points or natural features on the earth's surface. In this way the original boundary of the zone of the Panama Canal followed a series of arcs of circles of five-mile radius from points on the axis of the canal. In the Gambia the north and south boundaries of the state are constructed so that they run parallel to the river and at an agreed distance from it.

Geometrical methods are often necessary in the detailed demarcation of a boundary which follows a natural feature, such as a river, lake, or coast. It is not always easy to decide the exact course of this type of boundary owing to the difficulty of choosing an exact line of reference. A boundary which is required to run through a lake or an estuary could be constructed to follow the shore-line, or else a median line, or perhaps a navigable channel. It is necessary to agree how the line will change course on encountering such features as tributaries, wide inlets, or islands at varying distances from the shore, and to decide whether the shore-line itself is that exposed at high-water or at low-water, and, finally, to agree upon the appropriate geometrical methods to be employed.

To establish the international boundary through Lake Erie, an agreement was first reached as to the allocation of the islands at the

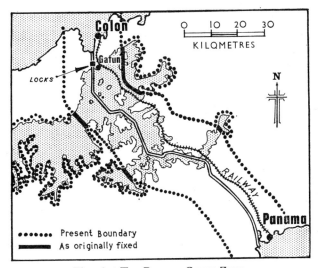

Fig. 78. THE PANAMA CANAL ZONE.

west end of the lake. A great number of points were then plotted, which were equidistant from the nearest points on either shore, and lastly a median line was constructed between the islands assigned to Canada and those of the U.S.A.

Boundary Problems in Closely-Settled Lands

If boundaries are to function satisfactorily in closely-settled territory, as in Europe, their alignment must be carefully related to existing differences of race, language, religion, and culture. But peoples of various ethnic and cultural origins had intermingled before the rise of the nation states, so that it is unlikely that any division will separate populations which are entirely homogeneous in these respects.

The result is that nations have always contained minority groups, often of alien culture, who have cherished hopes of reunion with those of kindred race, language, or religion, beyond the national frontier.

The occupation of Czechoslovakia by Germany in 1938 was undertaken after an alleged plea of the German-speaking peoples of north-west Bohemia for a return to the German Fatherland. After World War II, large minority groups were exchanged between certain nations; Czechoslovakia and Hungary, and Turkey and the U.S.S.R., all exchanged sections of their population, in an attempt to prevent internal dissention by "foreign" elements. The exchanges between India and Pakistan, in 1947, involved millions of people, and unfortunately, a heavy loss of life.

Whether such policies are good or bad in themselves depends on the circumstances under which the people are transferred. There are great dangers to human liberty under the system of mass transfer. Such transfers may be advocated on other grounds, even when no *exchange* of populations is intended. It can be argued that culturally backward people, unable to make full use of the natural resources of their environment, should not be allowed to occupy, and perhaps misuse, land which could be better developed by others. Such an argument could have been used to justify the replacement of Palestinian Arabs by Jews who, by determination and financial backing, were in a better position to develop the country agriculturally. If such arguments are allowed as valid, the threat of invasions on the plea of fully exploiting the possibilities of this or that region would be great.

Mineral deposits located near national frontiers are frequently a bone of contention in boundary disputes, and the political division of a mineral-producing region is extremely likely to cause international disagreement. Such areas are sometimes densely populated, and the economic administration may be integrated throughout the region, so that political division disrupts an industrial area which is already functioning as a single economic unit. Such disruptions attended the long sequence of border disputes between France and Germany, described below. Tariff-free movement of industrial raw materials made possible by E.E.C. agreements, and the whole climate of international common economic policies, act to lessen such tensions and to alter the concept of frontiers as such.

Some Troubled Frontier Regions

Consideration of a few selected frontier disputes may help to stress some of the causes of dispute which arise where artificial lines of division prevent peoples from freely associating with each other; where small ethnic and cultural differences become exaggerated;

PLATE XXI

Above: Soil conservation. Here, in Texas, the soil is protected from erosion by contour ploughing, terracing, strip cropping, and by outlet control—note the long, stepped channel (middle left). (*USIS.*)

Below: The All-American Canal. The irrigated land in the background contrasts distinctly with the desert conditions to the left of the canal.

PLATE XXII

Above: Naarden, Holland. Planned fortifications built to counter improved forms of artillery. The wide double moat, starlike bastions, and salients kept the town beyond range and allowed all-round defence from emplacements on the spearheads.

Below: Durham—the Cathedral and Castle of the old city lie on the land contained by an incised meander of the River Wear. The only land approach is barred by the Castle. (*Aerofilms.*)

and where, because customs barriers separate differing economic systems, geographical regions are partitioned.

The Franco-German Border.—The frontier zone from Switzerland to the borders of Luxembourg contains, on the French side, the provinces of Alsace and Lorraine. While Lorraine is the extreme eastern part of the Paris Basin, Alsace lies to the east of the Vosges Mountains, turning away from France, and is a part of the Rhine Valley. There is, therefore, no valid geographical reason for regarding "Alsace-Lorraine" as a single unit.

Historical claims are often double-edged. When, after World War I, the French claimed Alsace and Lorraine as part of France, seized by Prussia in 1871, the Germans countered with reminders that these provinces were annexed by the French during the seventeenth and eighteenth centuries, after many previous centuries of Germanic rule.

After 1871, Germany attempted to make German language and culture compulsory in these provinces, with the result that many French-speaking inhabitants migrated. Later the French attempted to reverse this process, but compromised, in the face of opposition, by accepting bi-lingualism. Today the majority of the people of Alsace speak German, although this does not necessarily imply sympathy with the German state.

Much of the attitude of the French and German populations toward the frontier has been emotional. The French were led to regard the Rhine as the "natural frontier", and Marshal Foch considered the control of the left bank of the Rhine essential for the protection of France. This and similar attitudes fixed themselves in the minds of the French people, so that the river-line has had keen emotional associations. The emotional appeal which was awakened in Germany in the mid-nineteenth century found expression in German poems of the time, one of the most fervent being the famous *Watch on the Rhine*.

Immediately after the German annexations of 1871 came the invention of the basic process whereby the phosphoric iron ores of Lorraine could be converted into steel. The boundary had been drawn so that a large part of these beds were included in the German state; later, however, they were found to be more extensive than had been thought, and about one-half of the ore remained on the French side of the new boundary.

Lorraine ore was brought to the Ruhr coalfield, and an enormous industrial expansion took place in Germany. France made use of the ore of western Lorraine, but, even after regaining the whole of Alsace and Lorraine in 1919, remained dependent on high-grade coal from the Ruhr; while Lorraine ore continued to contribute to the heavy industries of Westphalia.

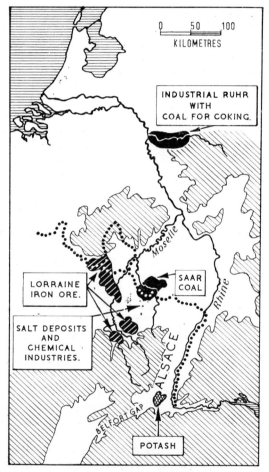

Fig. 79.   THE FRANCO-GERMAN BORDERLAND AND ITS INDUSTRIAL RAW MATERIALS.

Many of the raw materials required by heavy industries lie uncomfortably close to the boundary between the French and German states (dotted line).

The location of such extensive mineral beds so close to the border has been a strategic disadvantage, and this applies also to the location of French coal and potash deposits.   The principal coalfield, that of the Nord department, lies close to, and extends across, the Franco-

Belgian frontier. The smaller but important Saar coalfield is crossed by the Franco-German frontier in Lorraine. The greater part of this coalfield is in that part of Germany which was formed in 1919 into the Saar territory. The mines of this territory were leased to France from 1920 to 1935, when the territory was returned to Germany after a plebiscite. In 1945 the French again gained a position of special privilege in the Saar region. Since 1957, however, the Saar has been part of the German Federal Republic, though France has temporarily retained direct economic control of various concerns in which French capital is tied up.

The deposits of potash lie in Alsace to the north of Mulhouse. Here the rich valley slopes and the flood-plain between the Vosges and the Rhine are in themselves great assets. Vines have long been established on the slopes, and old villages lie among fruit trees and hop-lines, above the fields of cereals, which are the principal crops.

Finally, there is the river itself. Although along part of its course it hampers east-west communications, within a united Europe it could be a unifying element, fulfilling, even to a greater degree than at present, its role as a channel of communication between northern and southern Europe. This aim will be furthered by the completion of the deep-water Rhône-Rhine Canal, via the Belfort Gap, for much of the heavy transport of the Common Market countries is by water.

The Italian-Yugoslav Border.—The following are some of the geographical facts which have formed a background to disputes between Italy and Yugoslavia, and which influenced boundary settlements between the two countries:—

(*a*) About 70 per cent. of Yugoslav territory drains towards the Danube, and the country as a whole looks to the Danube Basin. The other large river system, of the Vardar, drains to the Aegean.

(*b*) The parallel folds of the Dinaric Alps are of limestone, which produces a broken, arid countryside, forming a most effective barrier between the narrow Adriatic littoral and the interior of Yugoslavia.

(*c*) The limestone regions continue northward to the Julian Alps and the main Alpine system, so that communications between the Adriatic coast and the Danube Basin or the Balkans are restricted to a few passes.

(*d*) The narrow coastal areas have a Mediterranean climate, vegetation, and forms of land-use familiar to many Italians, but less so to most Yugoslavs.

(*e*) The islands formed by the concordant Dalmatian coastline provide deep, sheltered anchorages and hide-outs for small vessels.

Both nations have become politically unified only relatively recently. The first union of Italy dates only from 1860; in 1866 Venetia was secured from the Austrians, with Prussian aid; and in 1871 the government transferred itself from Florence to the recently-acquired city of Rome. In 1919 the Trentino and upper Adige were gained from Austria.

The new kingdom of Yugoslavia was proclaimed in Belgrade in 1918, following the break-up of the Austro-Hungarian Empire. Serbs, Croats, and Slovenes, all Slav peoples, with a variety of political,

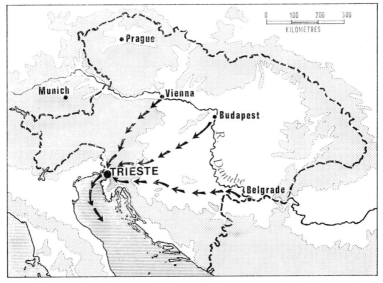

Fig. 80.   Trieste as the Southern Outlet of Austria-Hungary.

From 1867-1918 the hinterland of the port included the whole of Austria-Hungary, and therefore most of the Danube Basin, with three of the four great cities of the Empire.

religious, and social traditions, united in forming a federation, in which the Serbs were the dominant members. At the peace conference, frontiers were settled with Austria, Hungary, Roumania, Bulgaria, Greece, and Albania; but there was much disagreement on the subject of the Italian frontier.

There had been "Italian" (*i.e.* Venetian) settlements on the littoral of the eastern Adriatic since medieval times. Aided by the sea power of Venice, the ports of Split, Kotor, and Dubrovnik, which had been developed by "Italians", conducted a considerable trade throughout the Mediterranean. They possessed no real hinterland, but looked seawards towards Italy, so that, with Zara, Trieste, and Fiume (now Rijeka), they came to contain a great number of Italians; although in the suburbs and the surrounding countryside the population was mainly Slav (Croat or Slovene).

Italy, having joined the victors of World War I, pressed for these ports on historical grounds, claiming the whole Dalmatian coast, including not only Trieste but Fiume also. Italy also wished to control the islands, and thus lessen the danger of their being used as submarine bases (as they had been during the war), and looked with mistrust upon the creation of a new kingdom which might control the whole of the eastern Adriatic shore.

Trieste had been the chief port of the Austro-Hungarian Empire, connected with Vienna, via the Semmering and Piedicolle passes and through the Slovene centre of Ljubliana. The severing of this connection by the Italian occupation of Istria might mean that the port would lose much of the trade from the middle Danube regions and from Austria. Italy was awarded Trieste, the whole of the Istrian Peninsula, and, although denied the complete length of the Dalmatian coast, occupied Zara, several islands in the north, and some in the south, including Lagosta. Fiume, declared a "free city", was annexed by Italy in 1924, and although the Yugoslavs retained the smaller port of Susak, the Adriatic virtually became an "Italian Lake".

Ethnically this was an unsatisfactory arrangement, for, as Fig. 81 shows, most of Istria and the Julian Alps, outside the towns and their immediate neighbourhood, was overwhelmingly Slav.

In 1947 the Treaty of Paris ended Italian occupation of Dalmatian territory and of the islands, and readjusted the boundary to give to Yugoslavia most of the predominantly Slovene and Croat areas, including the Italian-speaking towns. Italy gave up the whole of Istria, but in 1954 was allowed to re-occupy the northern part of a small international-controlled area which included Trieste. By mutual agreement the city has now become Italian, and Yugoslavia has occupied the southern part of the former international area.

The task of fairly dividing this area between Italy and Yugoslavia was complex and difficult enough, but made worse by the position of Trieste itself, which is by location best fitted to serve as port *neither* for Italy *nor* for Yugoslavia but for Austria and central Europe, as it did under the Hapsburgs. Not only are ethnic and economic considerations involved, but also strategic and sentimental ones. There were emotional attachments for both peoples, for the Yugoslavs considered its possession as signifying the unification of the southern Slavs; while the Italians, besides recognising past cultural influences within the city, were taught by Mussolini to regard it as symbolic of Italian strength in the north-east. As with most boundary problems, possible

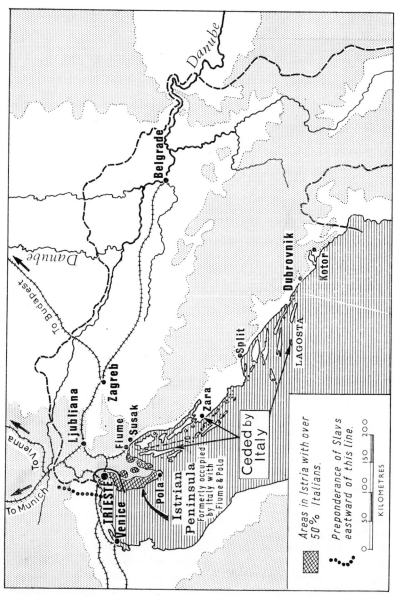

Fig. 81.   Trieste and Yugoslav Territory as Established at the End of World War II.

solutions cannot be based upon considerations of natural regions and their resources alone, but must take into consideration a host of other facts related to the prejudices and aspirations of peoples themselves.

India and West Pakistan (the Punjab Boundary).—In the case of India and Pakistan, boundaries have been created to divide peoples whose differences, due largely to religion and past history, were unlikely to be reconciled or even mutually tolerated. In 1947, British India was divided into two states—India and Pakistan, the latter consisting of two separate parts, West and East Pakistan.

The Indian sub-continent contains a mixture of peoples from all the main human races. From very early times small tribal units entered through the Himalayan passes, generally migrating southward under the pressure of subsequent immigrants and invaders. From as early as the fourth millenium B.C. the invaders brought cults, epics, and hymns, which, mingled with later religious philosophies, became part of Hinduism, which is both a religion and a social system. Hinduism was adopted in various modified forms by tribes of the most diverse cultures. The bulk of the population became styled Hindu, but converted tribes retained many of their primitive beliefs and practices, and found their own level in a most complicated caste system. There were many religious minorities, but up to the arrival in strength of the Moslem invaders these did not form any considerable proportion of the population. Although Gautama was born in northern India, and the first tenets of Buddhism imparted to his disciples in Banaras, Buddhism attained its greatest strength beyond the borders of India.

In A.D. 711 Sind was conquered by Arabs, and by the tenth century, Moslem tribes started to pour through the north-west passes. For centuries successions of Moslem bands entered the country, and there was frequent bloodshed along the northern plains, not only between Moslem and Hindu, but also between various Moslem factions. Eventually a fairly stable rule was established under the Mogul emperors, who more or less dominated all but the extreme south of India. This rule declined during the eighteenth century, when, by treaty, trade, and occasional conflict, the country came under British control.

The majority of the Moslems settled in the north-west, chiefly along the Indus Valley and in the land of the five rivers—the Punjab. But Hindus and Moslems intermingled throughout the fertile northern plains, and in east Bengal the large number of converts to Islam placed the Moslems in a clear majority.

When, in 1947, it became clear that a separate Moslem state must come into being, plans were made for the creation of an eastern and a western branch of the state. However, when it came to determine the actual boundaries between what were to be parts of India and Pakistan, many serious problems arose.

In the east the main difficulty was that a line based on existing majorities of Hindu or Moslem population would give India the industries of Calcutta and Hooghlyside, while Pakistan would have a very crowded agrarian state with little industry, yet growing the jute needed by the Calcutta factories.   The natural delta region has, in fact, been divided, but it has been said that "if geographers were kings there would have been no partition in Bengal at all".

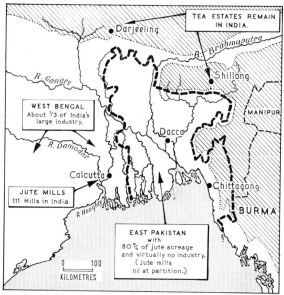

Fig. 82.   THE BOUNDARIES OF EAST PAKISTAN, AND THE INDUSTRIAL SITUATION
AT THE TIME OF PARTITION.

The line of the frontier was based on the inclusion in Pakistan of those districts with over 50 per cent. Moslems—except in the south-west (Khulna District 49.3 per cent.).   There were also minor adjustments in the extreme west.

Most of the existing industry lay in India; but Pakistan later built many jute and paper mills (using bamboo), and developed Chittagong as a major port.

For West Pakistan the choice of a suitable boundary was complicated in the extreme, and the following were among the many facts which had to be considered:—

(a) The great canal irrigation system of the Punjab had brought together a dense population of both major religions, most of whom were small holders or tenant farmers.

(*b*) There existed a large Sikh minority (some two million), many of whom were among the biggest landlords, and often the most progressive. A large number held small grants of land for past military services, while much of the original irrigation was for the benefit of the Sikhs displaced after the Sikh wars.

(*c*) The trade and industry in the central Punjab was largely in the hands of Hindus, even where, as in Lahore city, there was a large Moslem majority.

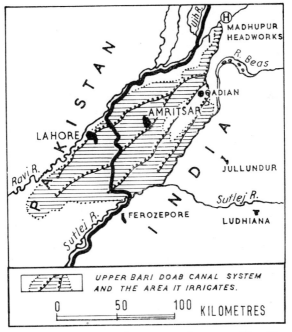

Fig. 83.   THE PUNJAB BOUNDARY BETWEEN INDIA AND WEST PAKISTAN AT THE TIME OF PARTITION (heavy black line).

This shows the Upper Bari Doab Irrigation System and the area supplied with water. Disputes over the distribution of water have already occurred.

(*d*) The existence of Holy Places throughout the Punjab, revered respectively by Hindu, Moslem, or Sikh. Amritsar is the Sikh holy city, but their sacred centre of Nankana Sahib lay in a predominantly Moslem area. On the other hand, Qadian, holy centre of a big Moslem community, was entirely surrounded by Hindu majority districts.

(*e*) Water is everything to the Punjab. The integrated irrigation system is impossible to divide without disruption, for while each river supplies its own system of canals, excess water from one river-canal system is frequently conducted to a neighbouring river across the doab—*i.e.* the land lying between adjacent rivers.

(*f*) It was inevitable, on all proposed schemes of division, that the area supplied by the hydro-electric station at Mandi would be split.

After the claims of the various parties had been investigated, a boundary commission made the award of a line which cut across the upper Bari doab, between Lahore and Amritsar, but otherwise largely followed the courses of the upper Ravi and the middle Sutlej (Fig. 83).

The widely-dispersed Sikh community suffered badly, as their holdings were divided; many joined the four million refugees who crossed the border shortly after partition, and they were heavily involved in the communal strife which attended the move.

The fact that parts of the boundary follow rivers is significant only in so far as these were used where they approximated to boundaries already decided on the grounds of communal distribution or other reasons. The rivers have some advantages as boundaries, in that there is little or no navigation, a negative zone of sandy waste or coarse vegetation along their immediate flood-plain, and few major crossings. Their disadvantages include the facts that their courses may change from season to season, they can be forded at many points, and they are used for irrigation, and for timber rafting.

One other important issue was involved—the future of Kashmir. This must be considered as a problem in itself, but it is relevant to the Punjab boundary problem both strategically and because the hydro-electric potential of the north-west is mainly in Kashmir and those parts of the Punjab allotted to India. Furthermore, the upper Jhelum which flows through the broad mountain basin of Kashmir, directs a large volume of snow-melt towards the plains. The war of 1971 again brought Kashmir's problems to the fore. The internal struggles in East Pakistan stem from the division of the state of Pakistan, the difficulties of unified control, and economic imbalance. But Kashmir remains a zone of confrontation and the lack of a final solution as far as the claims of India and Pakistan are concerned make it a flash-point in any major conflict between the states.

PART II

CHAPTER IX

WORLD POPULATION AND LIVING STANDARDS

We are living in a period of unparalleled population growth. In 1970 the estimated world population was more than 3 500 million and apparently increasing by over 8 000 each hour; *every day* there are an *additional* 200 000 mouths to be fed. With such a rate of increase the peoples of the world may find it impossible to raise their production of food and other necessary raw materials at sufficient rate to maintain, let alone to improve, living standards.

The difficulties of accurate census-taking in some of the more heavily-populated countries, such as China, means that statistics can be regarded only as fairly accurate estimates; nevertheless, the following table gives a clear indication of recent trends:—

WORLD POPULATION (millions)
(estimates in italics)

	1800	1850	1900	1950	1970	*2000*
Europe ..	187	266	401	559	692	*947*
Asia ..	602	749	937	1 295	2 060	*3 870*
Africa ..	90	95	120	198	378	*517*
America ..	25	59	144	321	510	*904*
Oceania ..	2	2	6	13	20	*29*
Total ..	906	1 171	1 608	2 386	3 660	*6 267*

It is essential that we understand the nature of the acceleration of population growth which is occurring. This is emphasised by considering the time taken to add to the world population each 1 000 million human beings—the figure first reached in 1830 A.D.:—

Date	Time Interval (years)	Population $\times 10^9$
1830	—	1
1930	100	2
1960	30	3
1975	15	4
1987	12	5
1995	8	6
2000	5	7

Thus, in the five years between 1995 A.D. and 2000 A.D. it is estimated that the world's population will increase by another 1 000 million.

The Predictions of Malthus

The seriousness of the situation was first brought to public notice by the publication in 1798 of a book by Robert Malthus, entitled *Essay on the Principle of Population*, and was later emphasised in 1803, by a second edition, which was virtually a new book.

Malthus pointed out the contrast between the rapid growth of population and the relatively slow increase of food supplies. He suggested a mathematical comparison based on the assumption that whereas food would increase in arithmetical progression, the population would increase in geometrical progression. Thus if food supply is assumed to increase by a constant amount every twenty-five years, after 200 years the *food supply* would be greater by *nine times*, whereas, as the following table shows, the *population* would multiply *256 times*:—

Years	0	25	50	75	100	125	150	175	200
Unit of population	1	2	4	8	16	32	64	128	256
Unit of food	1	2	3	4	5	6	7	8	9

Such figures indicate a fall in the amount of food available per head of population, until such drastic checks as famine, disease, and possibly war, reduced the number of extra mouths to be fed.

Malthus did suggest some remedies, including the voluntary limitation of families, which at that time was hardly likely to prove effective. That the catastrophes predicted did not befall Britain was largely due to events that he was not able to foresee, for the great increase in productivity, and the accompanying social benefits, which were to result from the developments in transport and from the new techniques in agriculture and industry, were only beginning to take shape. In fact, though the population of the country rose from ten million in 1801 to thirty-seven million in 1901, the general standard of living also rose considerably. This was due largely, however, to the fact that industrial Britain was obtaining huge quantities of food and raw materials from abroad in exchange for manufactured goods, under trade conditions very much of her own making, and to her own advantage.

The great increase in productivity which accompanied the rapid growth of population in nineteenth-century Britain does not necessarily occur in other lands or at other times. Millions of people live under conditions like those Malthus knew. The future of peoples in south-east Asia and Central America, for instance, with low living standards, relatively backward methods of agriculture and industry, and a high rate of population growth, can only be contemplated with anxiety.

Population Trends

There is a considerable variation in population trends in different parts of the world; the birth-rate and death-rate, and consequently,

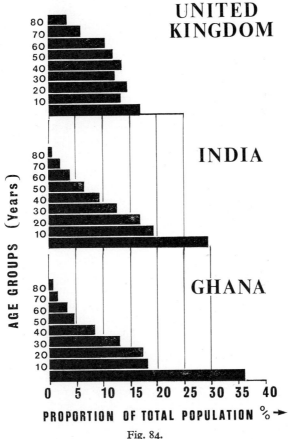

Fig. 84.

the annual rate of increase of population, varies from country to country, and from region to region within a country. It is important to appreciate the situation in each country, for the population trends have considerable bearing on economic and political matters, and *vice versa*. For each state the size of the population and its rate of increase have a particular significance. For instance, a large and growing population may be an important industrial and military asset, and where home resources are adequate is likely to be a source of great power; on the other hand, in a land of limited agricultural potential, little developed industrially, a population similar in size and rate of growth may press hard upon the land, and create problems of food supply, or lead to political discontent.

It is also necessary to consider whether the annual rate of population growth is itself increasing or decreasing; in other words, whether an acceleration or deceleration is taking place, and to assess the reasons for this. A rapid acceleration may be due to a fall in the death-rate, following, perhaps, the introduction of better methods of hygiene or food production and distribution. A decreasing rate of population growth may be due to the introduction and acceptance of methods of birth-control; or it may be that in countries with a high standard of living, parents are trying to provide themselves and their children with more and more material "benefits", and so set a limit to the number in the family, that each may acquire a larger share. Religious beliefs also influence men's views regarding each of these circumstances, and so have a bearing upon the rate of growth of population.

Changes in the rate of growth of population affect not only the absolute numbers but also the age-structure of a community. Even a slight decline may change the balance between the numbers of young and able workers and men of retiring age; despite the increasing use of automation, this could be a serious matter for an industrial nation.

Fig. 84 shows the contrasts in age and structure between countries in Europe, Asia, and Africa. The continuing high rates of increase in many African, Asian, and South American countries has led to a situation where a high proportion of the population is really young, and with large numbers of young people, reproducing at a relatively early age, the absolute increases of population continue to be very large indeed.

This surge of young people must be fed, clothed, housed, and educated. The problems of providing sufficient schools and trained teachers are real, and a large pupil/teacher ratio means less effective education, despite the increasing use of mass media for educational purposes.

Fig. 85 shows, diagrammatically, population statistics for various countries. It emphasises the considerable differences in their rates of growth, and stresses that the greatest absolute increases are taking place in countries like China and India, where the population is already very great.

The overall population density for each country is shown in Fig. 85, but this in itself tells us relatively little, for, as the next section indicates, it does not reveal the true pressure of the population on the land and its resources. Fig. 85 also demonstrates the position in a country like South Africa, where the white and coloured populations are not only of very different size but are increasing at different rates—two important political factors.

The Meaning of " Over-Population "

Most maps showing the distribution of world population tend to give a misleading impression of the extent of the pressure of people

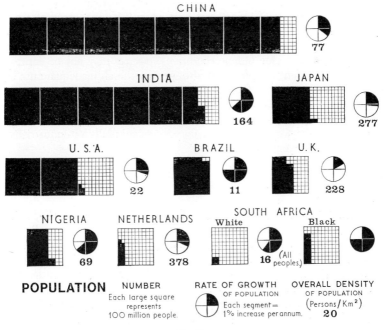

Fig. 85.

upon the land and its resources. To consider extremes: a large desert region can contain oases which are grossly over-populated and yet be represented by its overall density of, say, two persons to the square kilometre. On the other hand, Bengal has an average population density of about three hundred per square kilometre, and yet large areas, the Sunderbans for instance, are only sparsely populated. A more accurate picture of the agrarian situation would be given by plotting the population per unit cultivated area.

Before drawing conclusions from figures of population density, we should certainly take into account the degree of industrialisation. Whereas people in a London suburb may live comfortably with a density of two thousand per square kilometre, the population of those districts in the Ganges delta with an average figure of some four hundred per square kilometre, press hard upon the land they farm for their bare survival.

Thus it is impossible to say whether a region is over-populated or not without some terms of reference. Industry can indirectly support a far higher density of population than horticulture, and horticulture than farming. What may appear as overcrowding to one section of the population may appear quite normal to another. People have different standards of living, and, just as in Britain, some prefer the simple amenities of the countryside and others the organised attractions of the city. Though it is true that certain areas are overcrowded to the point of inducing famine conditions, poverty may not be entirely due to "too many people", but also, perhaps, to an inadequate use of natural resources—inefficient farming or failure to develop local industries. Thus, it is difficult to express an ideal size of population for a geographical region without considering the capabilities of the occupants, the way they are organised, agriculturally or industrially, as well as the economic resources.

POSSIBLE REMEDIES

Anticipating the Problem.—In theory, governments should be able to estimate likely population increases and plan accordingly. But, in fact, official estimates can be well wide of the mark, even over short periods. In India the population was expected to grow from 362 million in 1951 to 408 million in 1961. By the mid-fifties the estimate was increased to 431 million, but in March, 1961, the figure was 438 million, 30 million more than anticipated. The rate of growth figure confidently published as 1·3 in 1958 was then revised to 2·2. In 1970 it was stated to be 2·5—with a population of 550 million.

Even if the problem *is* anticipated, to educate the predominantly rural peoples of Asia to impose a voluntary check on the size of families is an enormous task, for the peasant marries early, and knowing that the mortality rate is high, deliberately raises a large family; religious considerations are involved: the Hindu, for instance, wishes to be sure that a son will survive, to perform for him the last rites, and, in a country where the average expectation of life, at birth, is still only about thirty years, finds assurance in being father to many sons. The

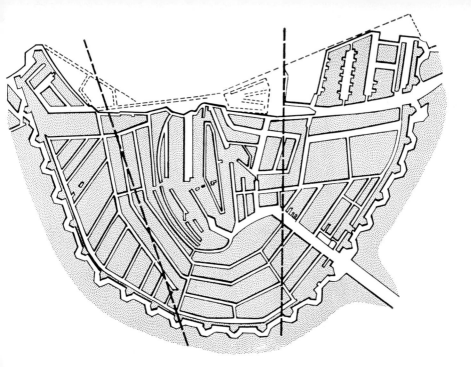

PLATE XXIII

Above: Seventeenth-century Amsterdam and (*Below*) the part within the broken lines, showing that the basic pattern remained virtually unchanged into the twentieth century. (*KLM—Aerofilms.*)

PLATE XXIV

Above: Hereford in 1650. The walled and moated city is already a well-established regional capital, market centre, and route town. Compare this with Norwich (Plate XVII). [*Hereford City Art Gallery and Museum (model by L. J. Starkey*).]

Below: Iwerne Minster. Study its position on the Ordnance Survey Sheet 178 and identify features on the map with those in the photograph. Consider the significance of its location (pp. 285-9). (*Aerofilms.*)

normal Indian family has more than six persons, and the average is higher in rural areas. Nevertheless, there has been considerable success for a widespread campaign aimed at the adoption of means of family planning and birth control among the rural populations.

Emigration.—One country at least, Ireland, has relieved the pressure of population by emigration; but it is doubtful whether this offers any real solution to the population problems of Asia. The Indian population is increasing by nearly fifteen millions per annum, so that, even to *maintain* the present population in India, at least this number would have to be resettled each year. Even were such a feat of organisation possible, there is no indication that sufficient voluntary emigrants would be forthcoming.

In fact, voluntary emigrants from overcrowded regions have tended to be those who have some resources and usually some education. The desperately poor and deprived may not have the knowledge or drive to move to a distant land where enterprise may be required to see them established. This was very much the case in the mass migration from Italy during the early twentieth century, when so many went to the developing cities of the New World.

In most countries today, the technician, or the prospective farmer with some capital, is more welcome as an immigrant than the poor peasant or labourer.

At present few countries open their doors to immigrants of any and every nationality, and may require the prospective immigrant to possess a specified amount of capital.

The Development of Resources

Agricultural Possibilities. A more positive approach is to attempt to increase world agricultural and industrial output, and to formulate acceptable economic conditions under which the resources may be distributed as freely and equably as possible. Increased production and better distribution are two quite different things. It is important, however, to realise that only a very small proportion of the world production of cereals enters international trade, and that most of the world's supply of food is consumed in the country in which it is produced. There is, therefore, a great need to make sure that production is made as efficient as possible through organisation of labour, land distribution, soil conservation, and carefully chosen and managed crops and stock.

On the other hand, agricultural production can be increased by opening up new land as well as by obtaining a higher yield from that already occupied. The total land area of the world is some 13 400 million hectares. It is estimated that only about 11 000 million hectares are "climatically suited" to crop growth, but of this only about 4 000 million hectares are at present cultivated. Much of the remainder is inaccessible, far from existing centres of population, and, though bearing adequate natural vegetation, is difficult to bring under cultivation without a tremendous outlay on plant, equipment, and engineering projects.

There are still possibilities of increasing the total area under crops by extending cultivation into marginal lands. The U.S.S.R. and Canada have made use of faster growing and earlier ripening varieties

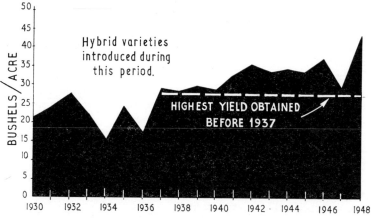

Fig. 86. MAIZE YIELDS PER ACRE IN THE U.S.A., 1930-48.

The introduction and improvement of scientific techniques applied to plant cultivation are important methods of increasing food production. The effect of introducing hybrid maize seed in the U.S.A. is strikingly illustrated by this graph.

of grain, and of the process of vernalisation, to extend cereal production northward. The Russians have crossed wheat with a perennial grass which provides a permanent grass cover and gives an annual yield of grain. But it is unlikely that such regions can support a large number of people, either locally or by exporting grain or animal produce. In Canada such extensions as the Peace River settlement area, near 58°N, are very limited.

Irrigation has brought thousands of square miles into agricultural use in south-central Russia (page 232), western Peru, North Africa, Pakistan, and elsewhere. Much desert and semi-desert can still be made productive in this way, but the enormous cost of development means that the capital outlay must be carefully weighed against the ultimate return.

There are very large areas in low latitudes which appear cultivable, yet are lacking population. Many parts of the Amazon Basin and New Guinea can still be classed as "pioneer areas", and could conceivably become important producers of tropical produce. Yet, here again, a scheme of technical development coordinated with planned immigration would require enormous initial expenditure. Brazil is embarking on a great road-building programme to open up her interior forests and savannah woodlands for pioneer settlement. But experiences in Africa, in particular, have made pioneers of tropical farming cautious of disturbing the plant/soil balance, especially in areas not farmed by native peoples. Nevertheless, development seems possible in many tropical lands, and those planned extensions of ranching and agriculture on the Brazilian highlands, and large-scale ranching in the interior of Guyana may support many people in a continent of rapidly-increasing populations.

Of these two possibilities, the more immediate target would seem to be an increase in yield from land at present occupied. This applies to the lands of extensive farming as well as the small-holdings of the millions of peasant peoples.

For many years the great tracts of temperate grassland have produced large quantities of cereals and meat for export. It is proving possible to increase yields without a serious decrease in soil fertility, through the use of rotation systems, fertilisers, selective breeding of crops and animals, and mass methods of pest control; all of which helps to swell the volume of food and raw materials produced. But these countries, too, have growing populations. Natural increase and immigration are not now adding significantly to the agricultural labour force, but mean more mouths to be fed; so that production must be substantially increased in order to maintain the volume of food exports while providing for those at home. The problem is not a straightforward one, however, for all the extensive producing lands are apt to experience times of high yields and glut, and times of low yields; the present systems and economic organisation and controlled distribution also make for fluctuating demands. Both Canada and Australia have experienced the ups and downs caused by China's need for large quantities of grain imports in some years and virtually none in others.

It is even more necessary greatly to increase the yield per acre in the densely-peopled peasant lands. India, for instance, grows and consumes great quantities of grain but still has to rely also on imports and external loans. Here, and elsewhere in the world, small holdings could be made to yield more: experimental farms in India commonly gather in twice the yield that neighbouring peasants obtain from similar land. Much depends, therefore, on the outlook and efficiency of the small farmer. The need for education and for suitable stock and equipment must be met by some central planning organisation, whether national or supra-national. The Indian government has promoted many Community Projects, in which groups of several hundred villages are served by government workers and voluntary helpers who attempt to create an overall improvement in agriculture, housing, health, and social services. So far the results have been encouraging, but the size of India's tasks is gargantuan. A little ground is won each year as the nation tries to lift itself out of poverty by its own efforts, but financial and economic assistance from the developed countries is still absolutely essential.

Industrial Development in Underdeveloped Countries. In the peasant lands of Asia, where most people depend on the land for a livelihood, there are already more people than are needed for efficient cultivation, so there is an urgent need for industries to provide productive employment for the large numbers of under-employed. Cottage industries are already widespread in India and are receiving a great deal of encouragement under the present series of plans; but large-scale industrial production is also needed. Such projects may combine agrarian improvements and industrial development—irrigation with hydro-electric power production, the setting up of new factories to process agricultural produce, to make agricultural machinery, or manufacture fertilisers.

Many countries in southern Asia have derived great benefits from the Colombo Plan, drawn up in 1950 to provide equipment, funds, expert advice and training, and to help to marry agricultural and industrial development. Australia, Britain, Canada, New Zealand, Japan, and the U.S.A. have provided hundreds of million pounds' worth of aid. Quite apart from this, the U.S.A. has provided huge amounts in grants, loans, and supplies to the underdeveloped countries, and in recent years Russia has provided much financial and technological help in the Indian sub-continent. In India the dams on the Damodar River in Bihar, designed to open up the richest mineral basin in the country and provide water for irrigation, have been built with help through the Colombo Plan. One factory at Sindri, constructed under this scheme, turns out hundreds of thousands of tons of fertiliser a year. Pakistan at the time of Partition had practically no large-scale industries, and so has spent a large proportion of the funds allotted under the Colombo Plan on industrial development, while at the same time constructing dams in the north-west and improving water control in the lower Indus valley to increase the home production of foodstuffs and raw materials.

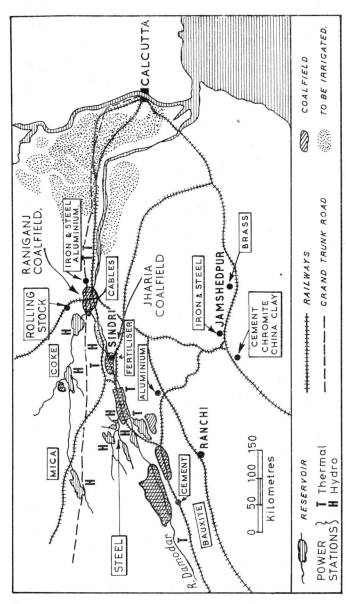

Fig. 87. THE DAMODAR RIVER VALLEY, WHERE THERE HAS BEEN PROGRESSIVE DEVELOPMENT OVER A NUMBER OF YEARS.

A "Valley Project" which aims at a fuller development of the richest mineral basin in India. Some of the industries which received immediate benefits are shown in the diagram. Power is provided from water held in reservoirs behind dams, which also supply a network of irrigation channels, of particular value in the drier areas of the east. Thermal power is also available, of course, and many nations have given aid towards industrial developments in the region as a whole.

Industrial development in western Europe was followed by a phase of accelerated population growth before the rate of increase of population declined. Japan, too, passed through this stage, and though her population is still increasing rapidly the rate of increase has sharply declined. In south-east Asia there are compelling reasons for developing industries to a greater degree than at present; but it is not at all certain that, in these vast areas of poor peasantry, industrialisation will assume the form it has in Britain, Japan, or the U.S.A., and it is likely to be a very long time before the standard of living of the "working classes" of the industrial nations of western Europe is attained, and before social circumstances of the kind which tend to retard the rate of growth of population can operate. In China, too, the pattern of industry and the rate of population growth is difficult to foresee; much depends on the policies and pressures exerted by the Communist Government. Despite early intentions of creating small, but numerous and widespread, metal-producing and manufacturing industries, priority has had to be given to the planned use of labour for the production of grain and other foodstuffs. Despite technological achievements in the nuclear field, in smaller industrial, constructional, and agricultural projects it may well be more efficient to make as full use as possible of the individual manpower available in such a populous country.

Stress has been placed upon the problems of Asia because there the food situation is acute, and examples have been taken from India, rather than China, because details of population and food production are more readily available for the former.

Other Possible Remedies

There is little agreement between experts on the real seriousness of the population/food supply problem or concerning the most effective remedies. Most people would agree that the present rate of growth of world population is alarmingly high; but as to whether the numbers will soon outstrip resources of food and raw materials predictions vary between the depressing and the wildly optimistic. A frequently stressed possibility is the greater use of ocean produce, with a much wider use of "fish farming", or perhaps the direct use of plankton for human consumption. The use of atomic energy might well help to develop arid areas of the world through the use of sea-water, by providing power for distillation plants and for the actual supply to inland deserts. Another serious suggestion has been the use of such energy to melt parts of the polar ice caps, not only to make clear-ways for navigation, but to cause changes in the climatic conditions in polar and temperate regions. Obviously these are large-scale and long-term projects, but they indicate that there are possible ways of increasing the productivity of lands and oceans which only a few years ago would have seemed quite fantastic. But can they increase production sufficiently, and in time? Certainly the problem is serious enough to warrant the most careful surveys, planning, and cooperation at international level.

Economic Cooperation—Problems of Distribution

However much men may talk of extending the area of cultivation and of increasing crop yields throughout the world, a general rise in living standards can only become a reality if all nations are willing to cooperate with one another to share the results of their experience and the fruits of their labour.

Unfortunately, the actual position in the world today is very different. Political, social, and economic barriers prevent the effective use of many potentially productive lands for the general welfare of the peoples of the earth. The U.S.S.R. and U.S.A., with great internal development of resources, stand apart politically, while economic barriers and problems of monetary exchange add to the difficulties of a ready distribution of agricultural produce through the rest of the world. America, for instance, produces surplus food and raw materials and yet cannot release all her excess produce to a hungry world without causing an upheaval in her own agricultural economy and probably that of other countries as well. At times American farmers have had to make cuts in acreage, instead of producing more; great surpluses of food and textile raw materials have had to be disposed of within the country, and sometimes destroyed (practices by no means confined to America). Meanwhile, tariff restrictions have prevented the U.S.A. from purchasing those foreign products which would give other nations the currency needed to obtain American surplus stock.

The stultifying effect of these man-made barriers on the ready distribution of agricultural produce is a problem which, in a world where millions live on the borders of starvation, is as urgent as that of inefficient use of the land. The crux of the problem is the unequal distribution of the world's mineral and agricultural resources, and the widening gaps in the economies of the developed and under-developed countries make the need for more equable distribution ever more pressing.

An equally distressing lack of agreement exists in the field of population limitation and voluntary birth control.

The Urgency of the Problem of Population Increase

The situation is more urgent than it may appear when one considers possible solutions. A general rise in living standards seems difficult to achieve as each million extra mouths clamour for food, and each extra million means that the gap between the "haves" and "have-nots" becomes more difficult, if not impossible, to close.   At present, the advanced nations are consuming natural resources at a per capita rate which is perhaps some 25-30 times that of the others.   A general rise in standards will tend greatly to increase the overall consumption of natural resources.

There is as yet little sign that the rates of population growth are being slowed down to replacement level.   At the present rate of increase, in five centuries there *could* be 400 000 000 million people (literally shoulder to shoulder)—though, obviously, a calamity situation will arise well before that time.   Even calamities of a magnitude now regarded as a "world-scale disaster" scarcely affect the problem.   The half million destroyed by the Bengal tidal wave of 1970 were replaced by Pakistan's own population growth in *just over a month*!   This is the urgency of the problem.   There are possible ways of avoiding this extreme state of over-population, but immediate and universal actions are required.

CHAPTER X

SOIL EXHAUSTION, EROSION AND CONSERVATION

If a balance is to be achieved between an increasing world population and the natural resources available, all land under cultivation must be carefully conserved and maintained in a state of fertility; for even the most fertile soil will degenerate if exploited without enrichment or protection.

On any soil capable of supporting growth a balance is achieved between the natural plant community and the organic and inorganic components of the soil; but as soon as human occupation takes place the balance is upset. If men are wise, their careful husbandry produces a new and equally stable plant/soil biological relationship, though even then they must beware lest a long succession of crops result in the eventual loss of soil fertility through exhaustion of mineral substances essential for plant growth.

Should the soil become exhausted or unduly exposed to the elements, and its condition go unheeded, not only will the active plant life degenerate, but the natural agents of erosion will soon remove the upper layers with what humus remains, scatter the loosened particles of the sub-soil, and may eventually reach bed-rock.

Natural Protection by Vegetation

The maintenance of a good plant cover is of prime importance in preventing the loss of soil. Plant growth helps to check erosion in a number of different ways:—

(a) The roots of living plants help to hold together the soil particles.

(b) The leafy covering checks the force of heavy rain, which might not only remove particles, but also close openings in the soil surface, thus reducing percolation and increasing run-off.

(c) Plant cover breaks the wind force at ground level, thus preventing both transportation of particles and rapid evaporation which would dry and loosen the soil.

(d) A stable soil is usually porous, and yet its particles are cohesive. Humus in the soil helps to bind the soil particles together and at the same time maintain the porosity of the soil. The humus layers have a high water-holding capacity, and water is retained by capillary action in the very small openings, called micropores, forming what is termed a "soil reservoir".

Forms of Harmful Erosion and Their Causes

Human mismanagement allows wind and water, the two greatest natural agents of soil erosion, to remove the topmost layers of the soil; for any process which interferes with natural plant protection is likely to cause accelerated erosion, especially on steep slopes or where strong winds or heavy summer rain are encountered.

As a soil loses its porosity and cohesion, the rain water, which was formerly absorbed, runs off the surface in a series of small rivulets, and carries soil particles with it. The removal of a thin upper layer may not be noticed, but this *sheet erosion* may soon give rise to *gully erosion*, as the abrasive power of the water in the rivulets is strengthened by increased run-off, so that small channels rapidly become deep scars. Gully erosion can be spectacular, the countryside often being torn into great chasms, but sheet erosion can be less apparent and dangerously insidious for it removes first the principal water-holding layers of the soil (see Plates XX and XXI). In periods of torrential rain sheet-wash may carry a large load of top soil down-slope, especially under previously dry conditions; this is both more obvious and more harmful.

As run-off is accelerated a greater volume of water enters surface streams, carrying an extra load which, on deposition may raise the level of river beds, cause flooding, or block reservoirs

Wind erosion chiefly occurs over broad, flat, areas, where the soil is dry and unprotected. It is especially likely where the soil is of low fertility and crumbly texture, and under these conditions, thousands of tons of earth particles can be removed by a severe wind storm.

Forms of Mismanagement

Common forms of human malpractice include:—

(*a*) Overcropping, which brings about a loss of fertility, depletes the stores of humus in the soil, making it less cohesive, and so affects the permeability.

(*b*) Ploughing up soil which is unsuited to lengthy cultivation, or is in an unduly exposed condition. [In North Dakota there is a statue to an anonymous North American Indian who viewed the ploughing of the prairie land (later to suffer destructive wind erosion) and grunted his typically terse comment, "Wrong side up!"].

(c) Overgrazing, which quickly removes protective vegetation.

(d) Deforestation.

The World's Eroded Areas

The effects of erosion on lands which have been misused, or neglected for one reason or another, are amply illustrated by present-day conditions in Libya, Israel, Iraq, and parts of central Asia. Libya once contained rich corn-growing land, but, like Palestine, suffered centuries of neglect after the decline of Roman power. Terraces and irrigation channels fell into disuse, and cultivation was replaced by the grazing of sheep and goats. In Israel, reclamation schemes have already brought much waste land back under cultivation. Parts of desert Iraq were once among the most densely-populated in the world; and early Chinese civilisation embraced cultures nurtured by peoples living in what is now part of the Gobi Desert and in the loess lands of the north-west.

It is impossible to list, let alone describe, all the regions where erosion is threatening man's supplies of food and raw materials, but the following summary gives some idea of the seriousness of the problem.

The U.S.A. It is estimated that over half the land area has been affected to a noticeable degree by soil erosion, and that already about an eighth of the cropped acreage of the country has been rendered useless, and much of it abandoned. This has occurred not only in the semi-arid lands, but in some of the most productive regions, such as the Black Belt of Mississippi and Alabama. Some areas have been particularly severely devastated, notably the "Dust Bowl" of the south and central prairie lands, and eastern Tennessee, which is described more fully below. Texas and Oklahoma were very badly hit by the great drought of 1935; in the latter state three counties are thought to have lost some fifty million tons of soil, blown away, *in a single day*; while in Texas, north of Amarillo, there are still houses which lie buried beneath the black top soil of the western farms. It is estimated that parts of the Missouri river basin lost, on an average, 200 mm of top soil in twenty-five years. It is extremely significant that the Mississippi, which draws its water from twenty-eight states, deposits a load of over 400 million tons in the Gulf of Mexico every year.

East Africa. The former policy of restricting native agriculture to reserved areas, and curtailment of the old practice of shifting cultivation, resulted in much over-working of the soil. Though the practice of shifting cultivation left partly exhausted land to the mercy of the weather, it has at least the merit of allowing the soil a rest period for consolidation. Under such a system of land distribution there was often insufficient cultivable soil available to allow a long rest period.

Initially, little was done to prevent the loss of top soil, though there were attempts at primitive conservation, by placing logs across the slopes and constructing rough stone walling. In Kenya large areas of the reserves deteriorated through over-stocking and in the mid-1930s had to be closed to grazing.

The lands acquired by the Europeans had the most fertile soil; yet by the early 'thirties areas ploughed up for maize and wheat in the 'twenties were showing serious soil losses and, where treated, the consequent scars took as long as twenty years to grass over. Unfortunately, many white farmers had insufficient experience to check the damage. Now, more enlightened farming is usual; since 1940 a Soil Conservation Service has worked to construct protective walls and terraces. Though a great deal remains to be done, the principles of contour ploughing and careful rotation have been widely adopted: farmers in the Kericho district have a particularly high standard of agriculture, and it is hoped that in the more fertile districts the new owners of redistributed land will benefit from past experiences.

South Africa. Here the menace is such that Field-Marshal Smuts once pointed to soil erosion as the greatest problem facing the country, greater in the long run than present political troubles.

It is unfortunate that over most of the country the majority of the scanty rainfall occurs in the summer months, and falls in heavy convectional storms, which have considerable erosive power, especially following drought conditions which leaves the soil desiccated and crumbling. Erosion has been particularly serious in the reserves of the south-east, where the short rivers of Pondoland and the Transkei bear torrents of muddy water to the sea; for the summer storms sweep the precious soil down the gulleys, or dongas, and into the short steep, tributary streams.

New Zealand. New Zealand provides many examples of the ways in which animals may upset the plant/soil balance.

In less than a century, after initial settlement, three-fifths of the native "bush", or forest, had been destroyed (Fig. 22). Trees were felled to clear land for the plough or for grazing, and by those who traded in kauri, totara, and other initially plentiful timber. Sheep were often pastured on the tussock land above the bush and as their numbers increased the condition of the flocks deteriorated. In an effort to increase the supply of young succulent grass, the farmers burnt the hillside, so that new growth appeared—and was duly eaten.

The heavy rains removed the unprotected soil from the slopes, and erosion has become a major problem.

Originally, New Zealand had no grazing or browsing animals; but the farmers, the homesick, and the sportsmen, introduced many species, including goats and deer. Without natural enemies, and in an environment that suited them, the deer rapidly multiplied and soon began to upset the delicate balance between soil and vegetation. Hooves pounded the ground and removed the undergrowth, so that in summer the ground became drier and harder, with less water available for scrub and forest growth; bush fires also increased. Deer ate the bush itself, concentrating on favourite species, and destroyed many trees through ring-barking with their antlers.

The decrease of berry bearing trees caused a reduction in the bird population. Also, stoats, weasels, and ferrets were brought to destroy rabbits which had been introduced earlier; but while having little effect on the rabbits, they killed large numbers of unsuspecting birds. With a marked drop in the number of birds, their ability to aid seed dispersal and pollination also declined, being a direct loss to the forest and scrub, and an indirect cause of widespread erosion.

It is estimated that almost a quarter of the entire country has already been affected by soil erosion.

Indonesia. Here, as in other tropical countries, agricultural output is smaller than it might be. In Java, the population increased five-fold in the century 1860-1960, leading to an average density of population of about 500 per square kilometre (excluding forest reservations and high mountain areas). The size of peasant holdings became progressively reduced, making for inefficient farming and soil depletion. Despite the fact that the steeper slopes have been covered by protective forest, and that an excellent system of terracing for rice cultivation has long been maintained, about two-fifths of the land is showing erosion. This was partly accelerated by the removal of much forest cover during the Japanese occupation, and partly by lack of care in the dry-farming lands.

Elsewhere in the Indonesian Archipelago, shifting cultivation, unrestricted grazing, and uncontrolled burning of grassland and forests are constant dangers to soil stability.

The Mediterranean Lands. Centuries of use of exploitive forms of crop and animal husbandry have been practised in these lands of long dry summers, with little integration of crop and livestock management, and therefore little sown pasture or growth of legumes. In many of these lands the goats and sheep still close-crop the dry pastures, most of which are on slopes from which the natural forest has long since vanished.

In Greece, four-fifths of the land is mountainous, and nearly one-half of the agricultural population lives there. About a third of this land has already been ruined beyond reclamation, and roughly the same proportion is fast deteriorating.

Many coastal plains and alluvial flats in various parts of the Mediterranean are closely farmed by intensive methods, and involving the use of irrigation. Many of these now fertile areas have been built up by the deposition of material eroded from the hillsides inland, and it is there that so much damage has been done.

Soil Conservation

The conditions pictured above are far from being confined to these few areas, which, however, illustrate the need for strong action, both by governments and individuals.

There are three main ways of making as much land as possible available for productive cultivation:—

(*a*) Through soil conservation, which aims to preserve the stability, while turning to agricultural use such soils as are climatically suited to cropping. By this means natural soil communities are converted into rich and stable artificial ones—as crops take the place of the natural vegetation.

(*b*) By prevention of erosion; which is a task for the small holder as much as for the sponsors of great schemes.

(*c*) By reclamation of areas which have become unsuitable for cultivation.

None of these processes is new to man, and for thousands of years, in one land or another, care of the soil has been rewarded by the establishment of an area of cultivation, in and around which a civilised community might thrive. In the western Andes, Amer-Indians became adept at preserving and reclaiming the soil. On the high plateaux numbers increased rapidly in the settled areas, which were generally alluvial flats along the deeply-entrenched rivers. Consequently men moved to cultivate the mountain slopes, checking erosion with tiers of terraces, and learning to vary their crops with height. The Indians of the coastal plains brought water from the mountains through *puquios*, flagged irrigation channels, and removed great thicknesses of sand to reach fertile soil beneath. The aqueducts of the Romans, the floating gardens of the Aztecs, the bunds and terraces of the small cultivators of China, Java, or Burma, the dry stone terracing of the primitive Pagans of Nigeria and of the Cypriot farmers, all represent efforts to make conditions suitable for a good yield and to increase the area under cultivation.

The Prevention of Erosion

Where erosion is likely to be rapid special precautions may be taken, and certain modifications introduced into normal farming methods. The soil, to remain cohesive, must be kept as moist as possible throughout the year, and, at the same time, excess water must be carried away without disturbing the upper soil layers. Apart from the many methods of irrigation and the use of fertilisers to improve soil quality, the following measures may be undertaken where appropriate:—

(*a*) *Contour ploughing:* which means that the furrows follow the natural contours. Ploughing at right angles to the slope creates virtually a series of retaining walls to hold the water, and lessens the chances of the furrows being deepened into gullies by the down-rush. Such "walls" also help to check a downward movement of the soil. Where rainfall is intense, and the slope great, it may be necessary to introduce large ditches which also follow the contours and protect the lower slopes, allowing the ditches to be drained through prepared channels (Plate XXI).

(*b*) *Terracing:* here the slope is cut, or built out, into a series of shelves, each with a stretch of level soil and an outer retaining wall. Terracing is particularly suited to rice cultivation, for the succession of ledges can easily be flooded by water, which courses down the hill-side in regulated channels; but dry farming on terraces flanked by stone walling is common throughout southern Europe.

(*c*) *Strip cultivation:* in which alternate strips are left fallow, or different crops planted in parallel strips, so that no large area of the soil is left bare for any length of time. The texture of each strip of soil will be slightly different, which helps to prevent wind erosion. Standing crops also help by providing wind-breaks for the fallow areas, and may increase water absorption, by preventing some of the run-off (see Plate XXI).

A successful "corridor system" introduced by the Belgians, is used in equatorial Africa. Cleared corridors run from east to west, to receive maximum light during the short equatorial days. They are about a hundred metres wide and a thousand metres long, and planted with a rotation of crops for three or four years, and finally with a crop such as cassava or banana which aids the re-establishment of the forest. The strip then reverts to forest, for twelve to fifteen years, before recultivation. The cultivators were persuaded to establish a series of corridors around their village and to plant crops in a recommended rotation. Thus rice or maize can be followed by beans, and then by cassava; tobacco, soya, sugar cane, or groundnuts, may be introduced into the scheme as advised.

(*d*) *The planting of lines of trees, or hedges, to act as windbreaks, or "shelter belts"*. Staggered windbreaks, which separate blocks of arable land, are used in many dry regions where there are strong winds during the hot, dry spell. They are also planted where certain crops need special protection, as in the citrus orchards of California. In the U.S.S.R., agricultural improvements have included the digging of many irrigation canals, coordinated with the planting of thousands of kilometres of tree belts, in the Ukraine and east of the Volga (see page 233.

Reclamation

If badly eroded land is to be reclaimed for cultivation, the soil must first be held in place and then the fertility restored gradually. Brushwood hurdles, or wire netting, are sometimes laid as a first covering on steep slopes, and a coarse grass allowed to take root, while in gullies a species of vine may be established, as a preliminary to shrubs and bushes. Fertilisers are generally unsuitable in the early stages, and the soil must be allowed to regain a natural texture and become richer in humus. Finally, by the use of legumes and a planned rotation system the land may be brought back to productive farming.

Regional Planning

Though individuals may be aware of the causes of erosion, too often they do not possess the capital required to ensure proper maintenance of the land; in any case, where the agents of erosion are vigorous, individual action is usually insufficient. In modern times there have been some outstanding regional plans for the prevention of soil erosion and for reclamation. The regional planning of the Tennessee Valley Authority (T.V.A.), initiated as a Federal scheme in 1933, was one of the first outstanding examples, and its success has provided inspiration for planners in many countries, who have been able to study and profit by its techniques and its mistakes.

T.V.A.

The Tennessee River is about 1 500 km long and its basin, which drains most of Tennessee and portions of six other states, is about four-fifths the area of England and Wales.

The climate is mild and the average annual rainfall is 1 300 mm, although in the mountain areas over twice this amount is occasionally recorded. In summer there are spells of heavy rain which can rapidly remove top soil, especially when exhaustion has set in.

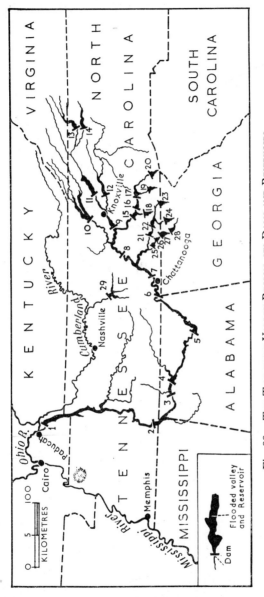

Fig. 88. THE TENNESSEE VALLEY REGION, ITS DAMS AND RESERVOIRS. *The dams are numbered. Three others have been constructed recently, bringing the total to thirty-two. [A profile of those on the main river between Knoxville and the Ohio junction (1—9) is given in Fig. 89.]*

White settlers were firmly established in the valley by 1835, and, as there was land to spare, grew maize until the soil was exhausted, and then moved on. The richer bottom lands eventually passed into the hands of large landowners, so that later settlers turned to the hill slopes. After 1850 the railroad brought a further influx of would-be farmers, and also provided an outlet for produce, so that cotton and tobacco became good money-making crops.   More of the slopes were cleared and the soil worked, and over-worked.   At the same time the forest covering was stripped for timber and the cleared ground was then farmed by many of the former lumber-men.   Yields were poor, so that the mountain sides and upper valleys became occupied by a "poor white" population, rapidly multiplying, primitive in farming methods, and poverty-stricken.

Up to the 1930s there were few industries to serve and provide work for the two-and-a-half million inhabitants, so that the excess population continued to turn to the land.   There was little pasture, no large-scale dairying, and little application of fertiliser.   Soil erosion became rampant, and as the land lost fertility hundreds of thousands of hectares were abandoned.   Sheet erosion was followed by scoring of deep gullies upon the hill slopes.

Before 1933 the surface run-off, aided by the bare slopes and the concentrated flow in the gullies, poured into the Tennessee River via its many tributaries, and caused frequent flooding.   The Tennessee being a tributary to the Ohio, which in turn joins the Mississippi, was therefore in part responsible for the recurrent and severe flooding in the lower Mississippi Basin.

T.V.A. treated soil conservation and reclamation as its major objectives, but aimed at much else besides.   Part of the plans related directly to the river, and part to the economic development of the basin as a whole.

Control of the River.   (*a*) Thirty-two dams have been constructed, nine on the main river; nearly all of them contribute to flood control, navigation, and electric power production.

(*b*) The reservoirs behind the dams store a great volume of water, the controlled release of which helps to avoid irregularities in flow and has the effect of reducing flood heights on the Mississippi by as much as a metre.

(*c*) Before 1933 there was little commercial navigation, but a channel more than 3 m deep now extends for about 1 000 km to the river's junction with the Ohio, sufficient for large quantities of freight to be moved along the river.

(*d*) As new hydro-electric stations made cheap electric power available the pace of the much-needed industrial development was accelerated.   By 1950 the power consumed was over ten times that of 1933, and still not enough. New industries provided alternative employment to agriculture, and farmers benefit from electric pumps, hay-driers, threshers, milking machines, etc. By 1953, 80 per cent. of the homes had electricity compared with 3 per cent. in 1933; now virtually every home is supplied.

(*e*) The reservoirs, which have the appearance of huge natural lakes, provide recreational facilities for millions of tourists, who come to view, camp, fish, or sail, and to make use of the state parks set aside by T.V.A. The swamps of the lower Tennessee have been drained,

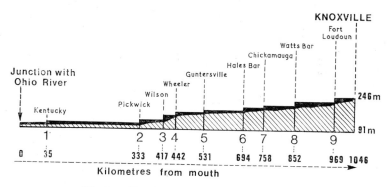

Fig. 89. The Dams on the Tennessee River.

The retention of water by these nine dams enables the authorities to regulate the flow, to control seasonal increases in volume, and to maintain sufficient water for irrigation during dry periods. A constant flow is also available for the adjoining stations.

and malaria, which was a scourge throughout the valley, has been almost eliminated through the instigations of anti-malarial campaigns and by large-scale spraying of insecticide.

Land Improvement. The scheme integrated a number of measures directed at soil improvement:—

(*a*) The old atmospheric nitrogen plant at Muscle Shoals was reopened and other factories built to produce fertilisers for the exhausted land.

(*b*) Gradual reclamation of the eroded areas was undertaken on the lines described above (page 224).

(*c*) Demonstration farms were set up under the T.V.A. to point out the proper use of fertilisers, to demonstrate methods of ploughing and planting, and to suggest a suitable selection of crops.   Each farm presents its own problems, but in this way neighbouring farms can benefit from research carried out in their own district.   As a result of this there is a much wider use of terracing and contour ploughing, a diversified crop production, with a greater use of legumes, and an increase in sown grass and numbers of livestock.   Many cooperatives have also been set up.

Economic Progress.   The effect upon the pattern of occupation and upon the life of the peoples is not confined to the immediate vicinity of the river or the dams, or even to the farms.   In ten years the value of products manufactured in the area rose by 68 per cent., and the wholesale trade increased in volume by 80 per cent.   Small cotton towns have become busy market centres, or river ports; while none has had greater growth or significance than Oak Ridge, Tennessee, where T.V.A. power made possible the creation of a huge atomic plant. Elsewhere factories turn out agricultural machinery specially adapted to the hilly conditions, and forests feed newsprint plant.   Mineral resources have been tapped, particularly sources of aluminium and phosphate.

The outlay for an improvement scheme of this nature is vast, but the financial return due to the revised economy of the region, and the huge sums saved by avoiding flood damage, as well as the improvement in social conditions, is also immense.

Hindrances to Regional Planning

Many river basins would obviously benefit from some form of overall control, but human aims, political and economic, do not always harmonise sufficiently to allow comprehensive planning.   Schemes have been put forward for many great river basins; proposals, for example, to set up Authorities for the Missouri, Danube, and Jordan; but inter-state and international politics have intervened to prevent their full implementation.

The Missouri drains roughly one-sixth of the entire U.S.A., and pursues an erratic course through seven states, carrying with it millions of tons of silt and gravel every year.   It was long appreciated that irrigation from dams in the upper part of its course could bring extensive new land under cultivation; that control of its upper reaches and turbulent tributaries, like the Yellowstone, Cheyenne, and Platte, could help to eliminate disastrous floods and prevent the annual loss of millions of tons of farm soil; and that enough energy could be produced to transform the economy of the whole region, bringing in industry, and greatly improving rural amenities.

It may, therefore, be surprising to find that many human interests opposed control through a M.V.A.; but up-river states, with irrigational problems, and down-river states, with poor navigation, floods, and erosion, viewed the proposed scheme and its possible consequences from different angles; large companies feared a shortage of labour if new industries were developed; and despite the example of T.V.A., many feared the cost, the public reaction to the extra taxes and a possible loss of states' rights. However, though no M.V.A. materialised, more than twenty flood-control dams have been built by the Army Corps of Engineers as part of an integrated system for the whole Mississippi Basin, and some of the artificial lakes are enormous, like the hundred and fifty kilometre long Fort Peck Reservoir in Montana, and the four hundred kilometres of reservoirs in North and South Dakota.

In the case of the Danube similar problems might be solved by regulating the flow, maintaining a deep navigable channel, and supplying power to the industrial areas of the countries which border on the great river. Irrigation is particularly desirable in the middle and lower reaches, and although land between the Danube and the Tisza and east of the Tisza is already under irrigation from river-control schemes, the present political division of the basin means that the indisputable benefits which would result from overall control by a D.V.A. cannot be obtained.

Before the partition of Palestine, proposals had been made to overcome drought conditions in the Jordan Valley, and to reduce the alkalinity of the soil. It was suggested that the valley could be leached by fresh-water flooding, much in the way that areas around the Dead Sea have been reclaimed for olive growing. This would have been accomplished by leading the waters of the upper Jordan, Yarmuk, and Zerya rivers along the slopes of the Jordan Valley by canal, while compensating for the loss of water in the Jordan River by a sea-water canal cut, and tunnelled, through the Plain of Esdraelon. This water would also be a source of power, utilising the long descent to the Dead Sea, while passing through concrete channels to prevent seepage of the saline water to the improved land. There are technical difficulties, but with the possibility of resettling several million people the goal is well worth striving for. The issues between Israel and Jordan have effectively prevented the establishment of a J.V.A., though each country is carrying out part of the scheme; perhaps integration of their separate systems will eventually be possible.

Regional Schemes in Operation

Despite man-made obstacles to regional projects, there are a great number of such schemes in operation throughout the world, and a growing consciousness of the need for coordination in the face of the forces of nature and the ignorance of the individual. A comment by John Gunther on the proposals for a M.V.A., is terse but to the point. "Neither God, nature, the Missouri nor the Tennessee recognises state frontiers."

In the aftermath of World War II important steps were taken to enable countries to implement large-scale land reclamation, rehabilitation and regional planning. Financial help which followed the adoption of the Marshall Plan enabled countries in Europe and North Africa to carry out large-scale projects for the reclamation of land for agriculture. The countries of Italy, Portugal, Greece, the Netherlands, Ireland, Austria, and Turkey all benefited from aid for specific projects.

In Italy the coastal drainage schemes, and widespread and repeated application of pesticides to eradicate malaria, allowed much resettlement of once-fertile land by families from over-crowded hill villages. This has since been extended by long-term planning of the Casa per il Mezzogiorno for the economic development of southern Italy. Here the value of far-seeing schemes may be appreciated.

Besides the reclamation of southern Italy's coastal lowlands and the establishment of new farms and planned villages, capital has been poured in to integrate roads, railways, drainage, and soil stabilisation in an overall plan, which also aims to create new industries. Major industrial developments, including steel complexes and petro-chemical works have been established between Bari, Brindisi, and Taranto, and are viewed as part of the overall plan for the under-developed south. Land reform and large-scale investment in agriculture was the first priority, together with projects to halt rapid soil erosion in the uplands: next the processes of industrialisation to create new social and economic relationships.

Turning once more to water-control projects we see in France the Rhône and Durance River development schemes, comparable in size with the T.V.A. scheme. Many new hydro-electric plants, and dams, reservoirs, and canals are helping to reclaim and settle arid land in Languedoc and Provence.

There are indications of a widespread growth of regional consciousness, and increasing use of multi-purpose development of river basins—as far apart as the Hwang Ho, the Mekong, the Cauca, the Zambezi, and the Rio Grande in Brazil. In Australia the planned development of the country's resources involve inter-state co-operation, illustrated by the joint River Murray Agreement between the Federal Government and the State Governments of New South Wales, Victoria, and South Australia on the control and allocation of the waters of the Murray. Thus the Snowy Mountains Development for water diversion and control, and for hydro-electricity, has been constructed by the Federal Government with cooperation from the States, who also gain in increased production from new land irrigated by the Murray and Murrumbidgee rivers.

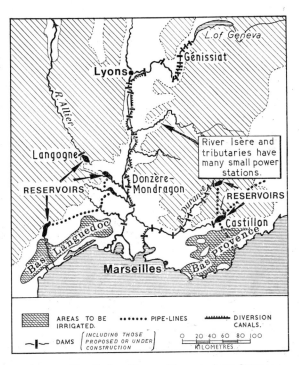

Fig. 90. THE RHÔNE VALLEY DEVELOPMENT SCHEME.

The dams on the main river will harness most of the Rhône's estimated power potential of some 2 million kW, and many other power stations are planned for Durance. The scheme also aims to help navigation along the Rhône, and to control flooding. In addition, nearby dams, such as the Langogne and Castillon, will help to irrigate the dry lands of Bas Languedoc and Bas Provence. A canal will take water from the Rhône above Arles to the eastern Languedoc.

There is still room for bargaining for priorities between these States, however; but it is interesting that regionally conscious groups have been active, and that a league was formed in the Murray Valley "to advance the general welfare of the valley regions from Kosciusco to the coast". They suggested the formation of regions which would ignore inter-state boundaries and called for an authority to "integrate the regions and plan the future development of the whole valley . . . as a regional unit".

Another huge integrated project has been the development plan for all state and collective farms within approximately 200 million hectares of the semi-arid steppe in European Russia.

Fig. 91. THE WATERWAYS, IRRIGATED AREAS, AND MAIN HYDRO-ELECTRIC STATIONS OF THE VOLGA DEVELOPMENT PROJECTS.

The old grain-fallow system has been replaced by a grass-grain rotation, with manuring and the use of selected seed, and at the same time creating extensive irrigation systems and protective forest belts.

The entire course of the River Volga has been transformed into terraces by successive dams, with hydro-electric stations providing much of their output for the electrification of farms, and to help increase agricultural production. Power for this purpose also comes from dams on the lower reaches of the Don, the Dneiper, and the

Volga tributaries, and supplies many factories which process farm produce. The Volga is navigable by large river vessels and a number of the main irrigation canals also serve as important waterways. The Volgograd Canal now connects the Volga and Ural rivers, while the

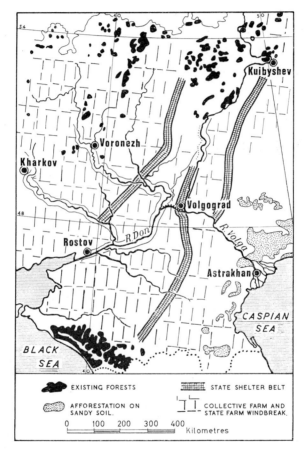

Fig. 92.   SHELTER BELTS, WIND-BREAKS, AND AFFORESTATION ON THE RUSSIAN STEPPELANDS.

Volga-Don Canal is used to take coal, metal, and grain from the Don Basin to the industrial regions of the Volga, and allows wood, chemicals, cars, and tractors, to be shipped to the Don for use in the Black Sea area,

The Volgograd reservoir supplies water to the dry lands as far as the Ural River; the Kuibyshcv Dam also irrigates areas east of the Volga, and scores of smaller reservoirs supply districts to the west of the river. The great stretches of new irrigated land are being farmed for wheat, rice, beet, and cotton, and provide grazing for millions of sheep and cattle.

Afforestation has played a big part in these schemes. Shelter-belts, stretching mostly from north to south, have a total length of nearly 10 000 kilometres. Forests have been planted along ravines and gorges, and in sandy areas; while, in addition, a closer network of wind-breaks is being established on collective and state farms.

Russian scientists have found that where wind-breaks surround unirrigated fields the yield is 20-30 per cent. better for cereals, and 50-75 per cent. better for vegetables, than on unprotected fields under equivalent conditions. Forest strips are said to increase the amount of moisture in the top metre of soil by at least 30 per cent., and forested areas may act to increase humidity and rainfall over small surrounding districts. It is worth noting, however, that because fairly large areas of forest intercept rainwater, absorbing some into plant tissues, and returning much of it to the atmosphere by transpiration, they may in fact cause a reduction in the quantity of water available for neighbouring regions. Only careful local research can determine the actual effect of tree cover in any specific area.

CHAPTER XI

EUROPE AND THE TROPICAL LANDS

A host of geographical facts and conditions surround and underlie the numerous problems which have arisen as a result of European motivation to seek natural resources, trade, or settlement, in tropical or near-tropical lands. The political uncertainties in the relations between European countries and their tropical colonies and former possessions indicate that many of these resulting problems have become acute, and that their solution is a matter of urgency.

The following chapter considers such problems chiefly in relation to Africa, for by the end of the nineteenth century most of the continent was under the control of European nations (Fig. 94); here, too, are large areas suitable for white settlement. Europeans, naturally, did not confine their activities in these latitudes entirely to their own colonies, but came in contact with peoples of many independent tropical countries. Most of the once extensive European possessions and concessions in the Americas, the Far East, southern Asia, and Africa, are to a greater or less extent free from direct European rule or domination and yet retain, through mutual economic and political interests, close relationships with Europeans. In most of eastern and southern Africa, white and coloured peoples remain in close daily contact, and here particularly, the aspirations of each community come into direct conflict.

The Movement of Europeans into the Tropics

The relations between European and tropical countries have always been affected by their respective geographical backgrounds. The natural resources, or lack of resources, of the European country help to determine what it requires of the tropics, and whether or not, in the early days, a tropical region attracted Europeans to settle or trade also depended on its natural resources and their accessibility. Political factors apart, the establishment and maintenance of permanent white settlement depended largely upon the climate.

Initially, however, the overseas ventures of the unified nation states of Europe were not based on any detailed knowledge of the potentialities of the tropical lands. While it is true that the spices and silks of the East, formerly reaching Europe by overland routes, were strong incentives to try to establish a sea route to the Far East, and that the dreams, and rumours, of El Dorado spurred on many a Spaniard to explore the highlands and the forests of South America, many of the early attempts at exploration and colonisation were an expression of the national unity of the European states. Others were in the nature of religious crusades; while the personal drive of men with the pioneering spirit must not be discounted as a force which opened paths for later trade and colonisation within the tropics.

Those powers which had achieved unity were the most vigorous in their overseas activities—Spain, Portugal, and England. Conversely, Italy and Germany, whose unification did not take place until the nineteenth century, played no great part in the early colonisation.

Geographical situation undoubtedly favoured some states rather than others, and in the fifteenth century Spain and Portugal, lying to the extreme west of Europe, were well placed to carry out exploration, and to direct ventures which sent the sailors of these strong sea powers to seek new lands for trade or conquest. Venice, on the other hand, although it controlled much of the Mediterranean trade, and was in an excellent position to receive goods from northern Europe and the East, was scarcely well placed for access to the broad oceans of the world.

The extent to which colonies were established depended on the existing population and on the state of civilisation in the tropical country, as well as on the military and naval strength, the man-power, and the internal politics of the European state. In south-east Asia dense populations already occupied favourable agricultural lands, and many native states had a strong political organisation and a culture of long-standing; facts which led European countries to try to establish trade rather than to attempt to conquer. The Portuguese found that in the East they had to compete with, and guard against, Arabs who had long-established trading connections in the Indian Ocean. On the other hand, the relatively empty lands of Brazil allowed the Portuguese to colonise and set up plantations, which, because of the scarcity of local labour, were mainly worked by imported negro slaves.

The Spaniards, many of whom had experience of living and mining in semi-arid and forbidding territory, sought mineral wealth rather than agricultural settlement, and turned their attention to the acquisition of gold and silver in Mexico and the Andes. Later, however, the lack of industrial development at home, and the shortage of available man-power for colonisation, which in Spain was partly due to the strong allegiances within its many distinct geographical regions, prevented both Spain and Portugal from meeting the full needs of their colonies. The defeat of the Armada foreshadowed the eventual disintegration of the Spanish Empire, and the prolonged survival of the Portuguese Empire was to owe much to an earlier alliance with England.

Until quite modern times, the type of transport and the difficulties of provisioning limited the extent to which colonisation was possible, not only by sea approach but also by land. The Sahara was a much more formidable barrier to European progress into central Africa than was the Atlantic, and the dry lands of Arabia and the Middle East were an effective obstacle between Europe and south-east Asia. Consequently it was the maritime countries of western Europe who, using the oceans of the world, made the more numerous and widespread contacts within the tropics.

The search for known luxuries in tropical lands also disclosed new ones, such as tea and tobacco, which were acceptable to European tastes, and which in turn engendered a stronger desire to control the source of such luxuries. During the seventeenth century, the British and Dutch laid the foundations of their respective economic and political control of India and the East Indies, chiefly by establishing trading stations. The West Indies were settled by Europeans, and, throughout the tropics, England, the Netherlands, and France, strove to increase their wealth and resources by extracting as much as possible from their overseas possessions and trading posts. For some Europeans, persecuted in their native country, the chief incentive to settle abroad was the prospect of religious freedom.

The eighteenth century saw movements by Britain and France towards a systematic imperial policy. These policies strengthened during the century, until the period of the French Revolution was followed by political events and military action which resulted in many colonial possessions changing hands. France ultimately lost most of her Empire, and the Dutch were forced to give up the Cape Colony, Ceylon, and Java—although the latter was restored to them in 1815. After the domination of Spain by Napoleon, the Spanish colonies were no longer administered by the mother country. By 1825 there was little left of the former Spanish, Portuguese, and Dutch Empires.

Meanwhile the British, though losing much of their North American possessions by revolt, had established and extended an Empire in India. This was achieved neither by planned annexations nor as the result of a desire principally for political power, but through the assumption of military protection and control over the widespread business domain of the East India Company; which eventually established Western methods of government in areas divided politically and rent by a continuous series of tribal wars. In the face of attacks by a combination of Indian powers, backed in the south by French agents, British rule was further extended, bringing unity, and a wide

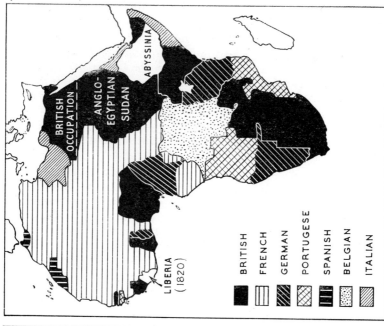

Fig. 94.   1914.

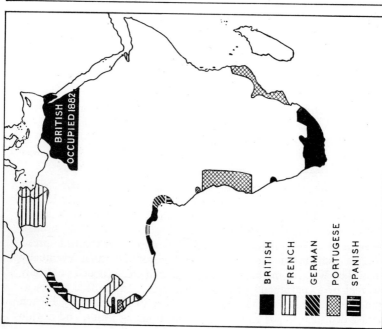

Fig. 93.   1884.

EUROPEAN ACQUISITIONS ON THE AFRICAN MAINLAND (see also Fig. 95, p. 251).

measure of security, to the many conflicting racial and religious groups within the sub-continent.

The eighteenth century saw also the beginning of white settlement in Australia and South Africa, and an increase in the use of coloured labour on white estates in tropical and sub-tropical lands. But it was not until the nineteenth century that the effects of the Industrial Revolution set European countries scrambling for any territory which might conceivably provide raw materials, man-power, or strategic bases from which to protect the routes to their overseas possessions.

The great period of empire building in Africa dates from 1870, although the French had earlier acquired Algeria—and incidentally, gained a foothold in Indo-China—and Britain had sought to enforce her will in South Africa. As new industries developed in Europe, and continental countries each stood behind the protection of trade barriers, nations avidly sought sources of raw materials, new markets, and foodstuffs for their increasing population. Expanding empires meant an increase in the strength and prestige of the homeland, and colonial troops became available for the armed forces, and for the occupation of strategic positions within the tropics. Progress in communications, transport, and medicine, helped to hasten the penetration and seizure of hitherto remote tropical regions, especially in this "dark continent" of Africa.

Britain, France, Belgium, and Germany were foremost in the competitive imperialism (Figs. 93 and 94). Britain was fortunate in having a base in South Africa, from which Rhodes launched the northward movement into what were to become the Rhodesias. Kenya was opened up by the British East Africa Company as a route-way to prosperous native territories in Uganda, and, as Egypt was occupied by British troops, Britain could lay claim to territory stretching north to south almost throughout the entire continent.

France also possessed a valuable base in Senegal, and held a few ports in West Africa, relics of her earlier Empire. From these her explorers and traders moved in to take possession of the great lands which became part of French Equatorial Africa.

Germany, starting virtually from scratch, took possession of south-west Africa, made local alliances on the east coast, and established a formal protectorate—German East Africa (Tanganyika); the Cameroons and Togoland were also appropriated, under the nose of the British. Meanwhile Stanley explored much of the Congo Basin at the expense and to the advantage of the Belgian king, who eventually passed this very rich territory into the hands of the Belgian people.

This rapid opening up of Africa to European influence meant that in a short space of time the four powers mentioned above, together with Portugal and Italy, held sway over economic resources, the extent of which they could not even begin to estimate, and over peoples with cultures far removed from their own, and with whom they had to establish some form of relationship. For a long time the respective home governments exercised little control over the activities of Europeans within their colonies, being content rather to allow them to manage their own affairs and develop their own territories. It is not surprising therefore that serious mistakes were made in social and economic fields, which, however unintentional, have become very difficult to adjust, eradicate, or ignore.

Elsewhere in the world, the older possessions were being consolidated, and degrees of liberalism introduced, as in the Dutch East Indies, where in 1870 labour became free instead of compulsory part-time service. In the Pacific Ocean, groups of islands were partitioned among European powers, and the U.S.A. replaced Spain as the controlling power in Cuba and the Philippines and, shortly afterwards, annexed Hawaii.

Economic Interdependence

From the vast areas of tropical lands come minerals vital to European manufacturing industries: the political stability of the mineralised areas in, for example, Haut Zaïre and Zambia, is on this score alone, of great concern to European nations. The temperate regions also need a great number of vegetable products which cannot be produced in their own latitudes. Some may be classed as "luxury articles"—spices, tea, coffee, cane-sugar—while others are now regarded as necessities by the industrial nations of the world; among these, rubber, fibres, and vegetable oils rank high on the list of "essential" raw materials. For a long while economic plants have been transferred, for cultivation, between various tropical regions, and the agricultural methods by which they are grown and prepared for market have already been discussed in Chapter V.

There is a universal need to increase the tempo of development of these lands as producers of food and industrial essentials; and many of their raw materials are likely to be needed in large quantities by industrial nations. There, obviously, should be stable relations between these consumers and the tropical producers, who justifiably expect to benefit from the wealth obtained from their land, from the economic, quite apart from the humanitarian, point of view. At this stage in the independent development of so many tropical countries, it is tragic if unrest adversely affects local development plans, or prevents the flow of raw materials, on which the ultimate prosperity of *all* depends.

The instability of political affairs in Asia has already brought home to industrial nations the fact that over half of the world's supply of tin and about nine-tenths of the world's output of natural rubber comes from the countries of south-east Asia. But while south-east Asia has long been the major provider of tropical produce, European interest has turned more and more to the potential resources of Africa, where in recent years the upsurge of nationalism changed the political face of the continent.

On the face of it, most African countries have great tracts of open land available for large-scale cultivation. However, besides the human problems involved, the limits of natural soil fertility impose serious restrictions on cultivation, and large-scale agricultural production usually requires a very large capital outlay. Taken as a whole, there are relatively few regions where soil can be directly utilised by African cultivators for the large-scale production of a cash crop; and even where the soil is rich in minerals the humidity may be too low for satisfactory cultivation.

The nature and volume of trade with tropical countries has long been affected by the low standard of living of so many of the peoples, who lack the means to improve their own conditions or to purchase the high-quality goods which European countries have wished to export. It is often difficult for such peoples to escape from their poverty. Much of the "laziness" once attributed to tropical cultivators has had its roots in under-nutrition, and a consequent lack of resistance to cholera, typhus, diseases borne by the mosquito, or tsetse fly, or to hookworms. Many peasant cultivators of Asia are still unable to obtain a regular diet of meat, milk, or fresh vegetables, with which to supplement their main cereal, be it rice, millet, or wheat; and the same is still true for the many Africans for whom millet, maize, or cassava is the staple food in a diet which lacks variety and is mainly starchy. Deficiency diseases are consequently common. Hence, regional improvement schemes should aim to increase the production of local food crops so as to give a balanced diet, as well as organising campaigns against disease. People with a well-balanced diet are likely to be more effective cultivators; and, as in consequence, their standard of living increases, so should their own purchasing power—providing incentives for local industrialisation, and resulting ultimately in more stable economic relationships with other industrial countries.

Human Relations between European and Non-European

The relationships between Europeans and non-Europeans have always varied considerably from one area to another, and have depended not only on the foreign policy of the European power but also on the outlook and behaviour of the individual European. The attitude of, say, a missionary, trader, planter, mining engineer, or permanent settler in close contact with the native peoples, is largely coloured by his occupation. Also relationships naturally vary with the education, degree of technology, and political advancement of the people themselves.

In their early maritime ventures, Europeans made contact with Asiatic peoples who were members of politically advanced states, and found that, providing agreements were respected by both sides, a profitable trade could be carried on. It was not until much later that Europeans assumed control of the major economic regions of southern and south-east Asia.

In Africa, however, the interior was for centuries debarred from European influences by the existence of the great desert in the north, the disease-ridden coastal lowlands, and the difficulty of finding easy access to the plateau, from which the rivers cascaded over forbidding rapids and falls. Nevertheless, many tribes of the interior suffered terribly at the hands of slave raiders, representatives of European desire to use Africa as a human reservoir, from which to draw the labour forces needed in the unpopulated, or depopulated, colonies in the Americas.

When more personal contacts were finally made, the poor health of the Africans, and the lack of cohesion between the tribes, invited the European powers to assume absolute control. A powerful argument for complete control lay in the assumption that only thus could such huge areas be developed for the benefit of mankind as a whole, and for the welfare of the native peoples in particular. In parts of West Africa, Europeans encountered an established and organised economic system. Overland connections with the Mediterranean and Middle Eastern countries had brought Mohammedan culture to northern Nigeria, whose cities also had a flourishing trade with several powerful agricultural centres in the south. As a result the British found it relatively easy to introduce and conduct a policy of Indirect Rule (page 250). It was through the Emirates of northern Nigeria that Lugard demonstrated the value of rule conducted through local notables: a principle of government which was extended as far as possible throughout British Africa.

In the Americas and the Caribbean area, relationships between European and coloured were, and are today, essentially of a different nature. Millions of Africans were brought in as slaves, and their descendants entered upon their official freedom in conditions of peasant poverty, or as poor labourers in an agricultural system dominated by the great plantations. The favourable climate of the islands, lying in the path of the trade winds, allowed a white population of long standing to establish "rights of occupation". The fact that the majority of the people of the West Indies and South American tropics are now of mixed ancestry, lessens the chances of a rigid colour bar, but underlying racial causes have helped to accentuate differences in the social status and ways of life of the "haves" and "have-nots".

Difficulties have often arisen when Europeans and the peoples of the tropics fail to understand each other's way of thinking. The European is sometimes apt to confuse simple living with oppressive poverty, with the result that the most praiseworthy attempt to introduce a style of living more comparable with European standards may do little more than disrupt a settled rural community. The peasant of Asia and Africa often regards his mode of life in a way that the European finds difficult to comprehend. It is interesting to note that there was considerable opposition to the proposed increase of irrigation in the Damodar Valley region of India—from those whose lands would benefit from the extra water. Many of the villagers argued that they would be expected to grow two crops where, formerly, one was sufficient to maintain their simple way of life; and, because they look for little more in the way of worldly possessions, they were not prepared to work twice as hard. The peasant finds it difficult to understand the significance of every additional pound of foodstuff produced to the country as a whole. His attitude to life, and to the many millions of his compatriots, is conditioned by the simplicity of his rural existence, and this attitude must at least be understood by those who seek to provide him with more material advantages.

This does not mean that no effort should be made to raise the standard of living or to urge the peasant to make the most of his land; but rather that innovations should be carefully introduced, so that their impact may not disturb the balance of what is so often a stable, and relatively contented, way of life. In India the government finds that one of the most effective ways of introducing new ideas is to send teams of actors around the countryside to portray the advantages of new agricultural practices in mime; and the radio is being used to bring new ideas and create new standards for villagers throughout the country. But here the problems are now the responsibility of the Indian government, who have enlisted the help of thousands of young, educated volunteers to enlighten the rural population, and no longer hinge on European and non-European relations.

It is in Africa, however, that the problems due to European influence and white settlement are most apparent and pressing; and, though solutions to these problems are far from obvious, geographical facts have the utmost bearing upon them, and an appreciation of such facts is necessary for their ultimate solution.

The Establishment of European Farms and African Reserves

During the nineteenth and early twentieth centuries, Europeans came to the tropics either as settlers to make their home and living in a new country, or else as administrators or technicians, who returned to Europe for periods of leave and eventual retirement.

In Africa, as elsewhere, settlers, naturally, sought rich soil and a climate suitable for themselves and for agricultural occupation. In some cases they took possession of land where Africans had previously enjoyed precisely the same natural conditions, but had obtained from the land only enough food for bare subsistence. In what are now the states of Kenya, Tanzania, Malawi, Zambia, and Rhodesia (as well as in the strictly extra-tropical South Africa), large areas were reserved for African agriculture, though generally the better soils and richer grazing grounds were set aside for large European farms.

The great danger of containing African tribal groups within rigid boundaries was that the area so contained became congested. As, with the advantages of peace and medical aids, numbers increased, the natural shifting cultivation had to give way to a more continuous use of the land, which, in a tropical climate, soon became impoverished. There was relatively little scope for the progressive African farmer; but, as described below, circumstances are rapidly changing. In South African Reserves, even in the well-administered Transkei, each cultivator has only a small holding, which makes efficient cultivation difficult for the enterprising African farmer. In Rhodesia certain land was set aside for purchase by progressive farmers, whether African or European, but there have been severe restrictions on the areas in which Africans might acquire land.

Not all the rural population has lived in Reserves. Many Africans have worked and lived as labourers on large farms, some as permanent hands, others giving service for so many days in return for rights of grazing and cultivation. This "squatter" population has been fairly fluid, returning after a while to tribal areas, or perhaps departing to seek employment in towns or mining camps.

African Urbanisation

Many young Africans have sought opportunities in the towns and mines, denied to those who remain in the villages. There has been a continuous movement of young men from the agricultural lands of eastern and southern Africa into towns, to the copper belt of Zambia, and to the mines of South Africa, though, on the whole pastoral peoples have maintained their numbers and mode of life. So great has been this migration both seasonal and long term, that, besides the disruption of family life, there has frequently been a deterioration in local agriculture, and a resultant reduction in the production of foodstuffs; for, although a family group may retain all its holdings, a wholesale migration of young people is bound to be felt on the land. Many who return to the village find themselves unable to adjust to the routine of rural life and the observance of local customs, thus helping to bring about an unstable condition, which has been termed "detribalisation"—an attitude where loyalty to the tribe is weakened, yet not replaced by other firm allegiances.

In the towns themselves, independence has given greater opportunities for the African to take employment in service industries, and when trained, in technological employment also. This has been possible in East Africa as many Europeans and Asians have left the independent countries; but it has led to a difficult transitional period when so many have lacked experience or are under training. Priority has to be given to increasing the opportunities of general and technological education among the growing numbers of urban Africans.

African Education

Education in various forms has spread far into the bush and the grasslands, awakening ambitions in many Africans, preparing more and more for higher education in schools and colleges. The opportunities for education vary greatly in different parts of Africa—even in single countries with relatively high proportions of educated Africans, like Ghana and Nigeria. But this is a process which must go forward, for ambitions are unsettling if there is little chance of their fulfilment. The coming of independence to so many African countries has created opportunities in administration and business hitherto unavailable, though under-development may cause bottlenecks for young educated Africans. Yet many independent African states need men with education and administrative experience, not necessarily at the top, where many have been to an overseas university, or have legal, administrative or commercial experience, but at local regional levels.

It is not always easy even for a trained African to take over regional administration. Within his own district bonds of family ties and local allegiances can be hampering, while in other districts, apart from the language difficulties, local support may be withheld from what is regarded as a "foreign African"; though, as education spreads, these difficulties should gradually diminish. While the more usual Westernised form of schooling has done much to bridge the gap between the rural African and the administrator, perhaps the greatest need still is for the form of enlightenment which will enable the local farmer to make the most of his land, and to accept those technical innovations, which, like farmers the world over, he treats with conservative suspicion.

White Settlement in the Tropics

Physiological Factors. The popular impression that tropical lands are uniformly and bountifully supplied with warmth, moisture, and all the conditions required for ready plant growth, leads to the assumption that, once home ties are broken, the prospective settler has only to move on to his new land, acquire a supply of local labour—and prosper accordingly.

There are, in fact, relatively few parts of the tropics where Europeans have permanently settled. The effects of a lifetime spent under tropical conditions cannot be accurately assessed until several successive generations have occupied the land, but there is little doubt that the moist low-latitude regions, with high temperature and humidity, and absence of seasonal, and only small diurnal, variations, adversely affect the body. It is doubtful whether even changes of diet or habit will allow whites successfully to acclimatise themselves to permanent settlement in these regions.

Most of the white settlement in the tropics has been on the highlands. The plateaux of East Africa and parts of the Brazilian plateaux represent the largest continuous territories which appear suitable for white occupation. In the East African highlands many areas have average annual temperatures of under 20°C, compared with nearly 27°C at sea-level, and the positive advantages of larger diurnal variations are appreciated by Europeans; it does not appear that the strong sunlight and rarer atmosphere produce any adverse physiological effects, although there are contrary opinions. The best conditions appear to be between 3 500 feet and 6 000 feet above sea-level.

At present the only tropical parts of the world where, on many of the farms, whites are the sole labourers are along the tropical coastlands of Queensland. Here, for several generations, they have performed manual work on sugar, fruit, and cotton crops. Many are of Italian stock, from warm temperate rather than from cool temperate climatic regions, and many of the seasonal labourers spend part of the year in the more temperate south, but certainly not all. The Australian north offers such prospects for future development that a number of large-scale schemes are planned. These include the Ord River development project which will allow the cultivation of areas of proved fertility on the lines of successful pilot schemes run by white farmers; now there is interest in the possible long-term physiological effects of permanent settlement in low-lattitudes.

One of the most frequently cited reasons why whites should avoid tropical areas is alleged susceptibility to the many diseases borne by insect pests. But all settlers run the gauntlet of such tropical disease carriers as the anopheles mosquito and the tsetse fly, and there is little evidence that Europeans are, by nature, more likely to acquire such diseases; indeed, they seem less likely to succumb to them than an indigenous population with an unbalanced diet which may leave them with relatively little resistance. Also the European, technologically better equipped, has usually been successful in finding means of controlling disease-bearing insects—a positive advantage for the whole community.

Pioneer Farming. A settler in the tropics, and particularly a pioneer, must run risks, which are often difficult to foresee. Local conditions frequently set their own particular problems, which may defeat even those with experience of other tropical regions. Many of the original white farmers in Kenya exhausted their capital before they discovered which crops would be sufficiently productive to be worth cultivating for profit; and when, finally, the land was producing and cattle thriving, unexpected diseases would devastate crops or herds. Experience thus hard-won has, however, proved to be of enormous benefit to those farmers, both black and white, who have followed in their footsteps. There still remains threats in the form of gradual soil erosion and exhaustion, and the possibility of world slumps in various crops. Today, however, research institutes and development funds are able to give advice and assistance, and much of the pioneer farming to come will be by African farmers who will have a bank of knowledge for guidance.

Plural Societies. As a result of European colonisation in Africa, one of the most difficult, and yet understandable, of all the problems has been the different social conditions and living standards between white and black. The settler, used to a high standard of living in western Europe, may have found it hard to cope with conditions in a new land, but to the African he has necessarily appeared a favoured individual, one of a minority group, occupying the best land, comfortably housed, and moving in a different social sphere from that of his own experience. Consequently a situation comes to exist where natural envy gives way to political unrest. The African worker has looked for an improvement in living conditions, and the educated African at least a share in governing a country in which black and white are fellow countrymen, or, more probably, a state for black Africans. In Rhodesia many whites, and their fathers, have been born in Africa and regard themselves as Rhodesians—white Africans rather than

Europeans. They and later settlers are outnumbered, and are becoming more so by the disproportionate rates of population increase between blacks and whites. It is realised that a situation of equality of political opportunity, and certainly the realisation of "one man, one vote", will leave them powerless to influence the destiny of a country developed largely through the organisation and economic system established by their white compatriots; many fear at least a decline of their standards of living. Black Africans, on the other hand, are naturally anxious to assume as much responsibility and control as possible. Education and a greater share in land-ownership will increase the numbers who reach the position of being able to contribute in an enlightened way to the political life and management of the country. The time factor is important. White Africans may feel the need to "make haste slowly", black Africans press to accelerate the processes of change.

When a plural society exists, as in Kenya, where many shopkeepers and middlemen of Indian origin formed a class apart from the Africans and Europeans, the aspirations of each racial, or national group, becomes correspondingly more difficult to reconcile. The six million Africans at the time of independence greatly outnumbered the few hundred thousand non-Africans, who nevertheless were given the opportunity of taking up Kenya citizenship. Large numbers of Asians and many Europeans left Kenya, but certainly not all; those who remained, with Kenya citizenship, contributed much to the development of the new state during the transitional period.

In Kenya today, Africans are naturally becoming landowners on a much greater scale than in the past, and are being trained to farm more effectively in a country whose natural economy has depended on European agricultural development. Whether such a transition can be effected smoothly and productively largely depends on the success, or otherwise, of the land-redistribution schemes.

Land redistribution within the African-held lands has already proved a positive step forward, with the consolidation of the many scattered fragments of land into single holdings of equal acreage. The small-holder now has to learn not only how to improve crops and stock, but also how to put back some of his profit into land improvement.

The taking over of some of the large mixed farms involves different problems. Many landless African farm workers are dependent on such farms. The division of big farms into small holdings may well lead to a substitution of peasant subsistence standards for large-scale farm organisation with mechanical aids. This has happened to some extent in Brazil, where some large coffee fazendas have become areas of peasant farming, to the detriment of the land and with an overall decrease in productivity—though it is fair to say that a noted decline in fertility had led in some of the cases to the sale of the estate. To prevent the widespread development of peasant farming on Kenya's better soils it would seem wise for African and European landowners to continue to employ labour, using modern equipment and technical skill; there is, perhaps, four times as much good land to be developed as is at present farmed.

Another step forward has been the growth of cooperatives, which enable more people to have a share in the land without breaking up large farms. Some of these have already had encouraging financial success. But, above all, education is the main need, with the provision of farm training centres. This needs financial assistance and a liberal attitude from the government and from outside; so that much depends on political issues.

Commonwealth Administration

Just as no administrator, colonial or otherwise, can work efficiently without some appreciation of the geographical background of his territory, so no geographer should study the human relations within a region without some knowledge of the existing system of administration and of systems which have prevailed there in the past. Independence has come to many former colonies; but their previous status and form of administration often have much bearing on their present allegiances and methods of government. It is as well, therefore, to touch upon the past and present mechanism of colonial administration within the Commonwealth, with a brief glimpse of French and Belgian policies.

The following are the principal rankings of the non-self-governing territories, and their relations with the British Crown. In the past they have not all had the same status, and in some cases the form of administration varied within the boundaries of the state.

Colonies have been annexed to the British Crown, and the British government is responsible for their external and internal affairs, and for their defence. Their peoples are British subjects.

Protectorates are governed in the same way but have not been annexed, and their peoples are not subjects but protected persons; Uganda's peoples were protected in this way.

Protected States retain their own sovereignty, but their peoples are protected by the British government, in return for certain rights and responsibilities. A treaty of protection was made in this way with the Federated Malay States.

Trust Territories, mostly former colonies of nations defeated in war, were entrusted to Britain by the United Nations to be governed as colonies, but a report on them was to be sent to the United Nations each year. Their peoples are protected persons. Tanganyika, now a part of independent Tanzania, was created a Trust Territory after World War I.

Some, for historical reasons, were created part Colonies and part Protectorates—Kenya, for example.

Throughout the main colonial period, the minister responsible for colonial affairs was the Secretary of State for the Colonies, advised by the staff and experts of the Colonial Office. Colonial policy on any matter communicated to the Governor, who exercised a strong control within the Colony, and had under him an Executive and a Legislative Council.

In the Legislative Council, there was always a majority of "official" members and a certain number of "unofficial" members. In the African Colonies the proportion of Africans serving as unofficial members, and voicing the opinion of the native population, varied according to their proved capabilities, and to whether or not the Colony contained white settlers. In the "settler colonies" the whites were originally dominant in such councils. In 1945 the Gold Coast (a "non-settler" colony) became "the first Colony to achieve a wholly African unofficial majority", and in 1957 achieved full independence as Ghana, the forerunner of the many political changes shown in Fig. 95.

Direct and Indirect Rule

The system of government has been based as far as possible on those native institutions which make for social and economic welfare, and wherever possible the traditional authority of the native chiefs upheld. In Nigeria, for instance, the Emirs retained control of their own treasuries, law courts, and police; though in each Emirate, prior to independence, advice was given by a British Resident and British District Officers.

While the institution of such *Indirect Rule* was a relatively simple matter in this part of West Africa, it was more difficult to achieve in areas where small tribal units had little in common with each other. The task of finding a representative chief, or leader of a council, acceptable to all parties, often proved to be difficult. However, gatherings of tribal fragments under an accepted native authority were fashioned successfully in Tanganyika, so that a grouping like the Usukuma Federation of the north-west could be administered as a single unit.

Under Indirect Rule, native Administrations dealt with local law cases, controlled native treasuries, and operated medical dispensaries, and in some cases maintained roads and bridges, and supported agricultural enterprises—all under the wing of the District Officer. The principle of Indirect Rule has undoubtedly been of great value over the major part of the British territories in Africa. The best local traditions could be retained and tribal machinery brought to form an

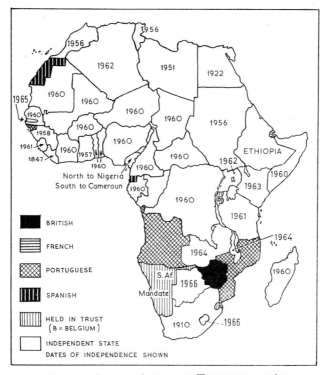

Fig. 95. Africa: States and Territories, 1964.

No fewer than twenty-eight States gained independence between 1956 and 1964 (compare with Figs. 93 and 94), and the United Nations formally took responsibility for South-West Africa, ending South Africa's mandate.

effective local government; otherwise there could only have been a loose control by European officials, in view of the limited number of officials available, the large and often widespread populations, and the poverty of communications. In addition, advanced tribal communities, under the guidance of the District Officer, have been enabled in this way to acquire a sense of responsibility and some experience in administration.

Sometimes, of course, it happened that, through a lack of perspective and in the name of tradition, native authorities sought to obstruct improvement schemes, and made it difficult for the District Officer to push through such projects against strong opposition. In parts of East Africa, for instance, it was found difficult to introduce agricultural reforms necessitating redistribution of land in areas where tribal law insists that any tree planted remains the property of its original owner.

In some districts without tribal organisation there were no traditional channels through which the administration might operate. Thus the existence of a polyglot population, or the disintegration of tribal civilisation, which has taken place in many parts of Africa, meant that Indirect Rule became very difficult to apply. The alternative has been *Direct Rule*, once more aimed at giving ultimate self-determination to the African communities. This was the case in the West Indies, where there is an extremely mixed population and a singular lack of tradition to bind the people into definite communities. Here a Federation briefly inherited the problems of dealing with mixed communities, problems now faced by the independent states.

French and Belgian Policies

In general, the French aimed at introducing French culture into their tropical colonies; and although administering Direct Rule, tended to foster the adoption of French customs among native ruling classes, rather than encourage the persistence of local observances. In this way an influential group could be established, with French education and a French way of life, regarding themselves as part of "France overseas" instead of mere representatives of a subject people. The presence of this bloc, intermediate between the European administrators and the bulk of the population, undoubtedly helped to prevent the creation of a rigid colour bar.

In the Belgian Congo there was for a long period remarkably little political unrest. The general policy was to ensure a reasonably high standard of living, and of native welfare, *before* sponsoring universal education on Western lines. This policy was much affected by geographical factors. The enormous mineral resources and a considerable agricultural output of the Belgian Congo provided the wealth with which these aims might have been achieved. But the diverse regions and difficult terrain of the Zaïre (Congo) Basin acted against the establishment of coordinated native political activity, and the scattered tribes received less organised education than the majority of those in the more compact territories of British (Equatorial) Africa. Higher education was, to some extent, reserved, along with membership of

Belgian society, as a reward for proved ability in local administration.

Under Belgian control, with officials, missionaries, doctors, agricultural experts, and other Europeans operating in this vast territory, a general overall stability was achieved. But with a rapid hand-over on independence, it became obvious that there were great differences in the standards of living and welfare between the main centres of population, the rich Haut Zaïre (Katanga) province, and the rest of the country. It was also obvious that the lack of general education throughout the country left great gaps in the man-power required for efficient administration and control. With the withdrawal of Belgian administrators and technicians many of the vacant positions could not be filled immediately. It was also evident that regional and tribal, rather than national, loyalties were the by-products of a policy which was in part successful, but which, at the time of hand-over, left too many ends untied.

Summary

Contacts between Europeans, Africans, and other peoples within the tropics have brought considerable advantages to all communities, while, at the same time, creating equally obvious difficulties and tensions. It is easy to point to the drawbacks without considering the advantages.

For most Africans, education must go hand in hand with any increases in material prosperity achieved under independence. Europeans, in places, alienated land, restricted native movement, and sometimes introduced diseases; but in other parts put an end to tribal warring, enabled roads and railways to be built, provided sources of national income, eradicated or controlled many indigenous diseases; and have given a voice to millions throughout the tropics.

CHAPTER XII

GLOBAL OUTLOOK

Geographical Position—A Relative Concept

The disposition of lands and seas has remained more or less stable during the period of human history. Yet, in a sense, the position of any place is a relative concept, and varies in significance to different observers and at different periods in history.

The Roman garrison must have regarded Britain as not only on the fringe of their mighty Empire but almost at the edge of the world.

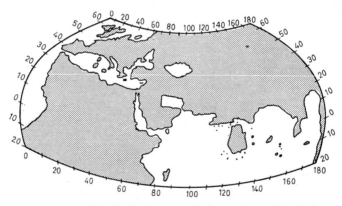

Fig. 96.   *A.D. 160—The World as known to Ptolemy.   Men of the Mediterranean States regarded the British Isles as marginal lands.*

Up to the dawn of the sixteenth century the men of the great maritime powers of Portugal, Spain, Genoa, Venice, saw the British Isles as marginal lands, quite far enough away for ships which were built only to sail the enclosed waters of the Mediterranean and the coastal waters of the Atlantic. After 1492 and the great voyages of Columbus, Vasco de Gama, and Magellan, the Atlantic no longer set a limit to human movement, and thence forward, as European influences spread over the surface of the globe, the centre of gravity of Europe and her overseas possessions lay among the maritime powers of the north-west. Thus Britain, with ease of access to overseas markets and settlements, and free from the military disturbances on the Continent, was, by the

254

nineteenth century, regarded throughout the world as the leading representative of the European style of civilisation, then reaching out to so many distant parts of the earth.

Chapter XI has given ample illustration of the fact that relative accessibility varies with changing communications and forms of transport.

Fig. 97.   BEFORE 1492—THE WORLD KNOWN TO THE EUROPEAN NATIONS.

The interior of Africa, Greenland, and the Siberian north-east, were then unknown.   South-east Africa had not been reached by an all-sea route from Western Europe, although land trade routes had long existed, and sea journeys were made from ports in the Red Sea and the Persian Gulf.   (A Zenithal Equal Area Projection.)

Just as a given region may have latent possibilities in the shape of undeveloped natural resources, so, too, it may be an area of potential political and strategic importance, later to acquire a widespread significance by virtue of the behaviour of its occupants.   In 1939 the majority of Europeans regarded Germany as a springboard whence armed movement might be made in almost any direction; a few years later it had indeed become the centre of Nazi domination over much of continental Europe and beyond. But, since 1945, this same territory, although of strategic importance, is no longer looked on as being at the hub of European affairs, and its separate portions have become part of the peripheral zones of two great political groupings—the Western powers and the U.S.S.R. and its satellites; yet the physical features and natural resources remain virtually unaltered.

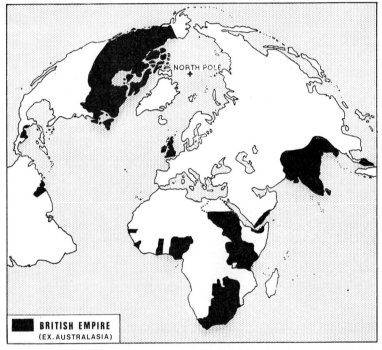

BRITISH EMPIRE
(EX. AUSTRALASIA)

Fig. 98. *By the late nineteenth century the British Isles lay at the hub of a great empire, and the seas carried shipping from the United Kingdom to all parts of the world.*

Thus, besides an appreciation of the *actual* geographical location of a place, there can be, in the minds of men, a conception of its position which is a *relative* one, and which may vary with changing circumstances.

The " Flat Map "

For centuries Mercator's projection has served to map the sailing routes along which the bulk of world trade has passed, and the relative position of the lands has become rooted in men's minds according to their location on this "flat map".

The coming of the steamship should have heralded the fact that the time had arrived for a more truly global outlook. For whereas the sailing vessels chiefly followed the prevailing winds, the more independent steam vessels could attempt to travel along direct routes. Mercator's projection enables a true course to be followed but does not show the most direct route as a straight line, except where it

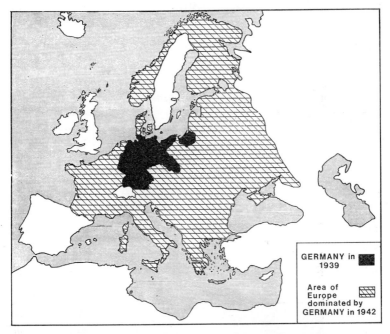

Fig. 99. *Germany at the hub of European affairs: during the years* 1939-42 *Germany occupied a central position, of great strategic value to a powerful state.*

follows the great circles of the meridians or the equator. It has also the disadvantage of large distortions in area towards the poles.

The development of air travel has emphasised the necessity of regarding the world from a global point of view; and as a large globe is inconvenient to study, men now use suitable map projections. As the navigator turns to a gnomonic plot to find the shortest route, so the student geographer should turn to appropriate projections of the land masses, in order to obtain a clear picture of their relative positions. A suitably-centred zenithal projection can help to remove

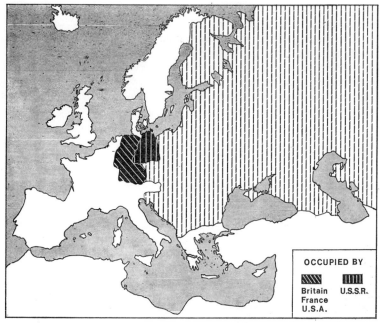

Fig. 100. *Germany in 1946, divided by the zones of occupation, and lying at the frontier between contrasting political systems.*

many of the false ideas of location which are given by a cylindrical projection such as Mercator's.

World War II brought to light an outstanding example of a public misconception of the relative position of Japan and the U.S.A.

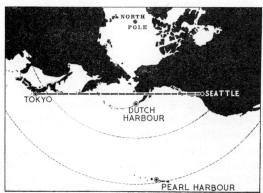

Fig. 101. *Great Circle Route—Seattle to Tokyo. Notice the location of Pearl Harbour.*

Atlases, consulted by millions, gave the impression that the direct route from San Francisco to Honshu passes close to Hawaii and the base of Pearl Harbour, whereas in fact a direct course would take the vessel nearer to the Aleutians, rather than the Hawaiian Islands; in fact the great circle route from Seattle to Tokyo passes through the Aleutians (but compare this with an apparently direct route on a Mercator's projection). As a result the public were not conscious of the menace of a Japanese movement through the Aleutians until after the hasty fortification of Dutch Harbour by American troops.

A zenithal equidistant map centred at the North Pole can be a revelation to those who have studied the disposition of the continents in these latitudes from maps centred on the equator. Consider, for example, a route from Churchill, on Hudson Bay, to the mouth of the

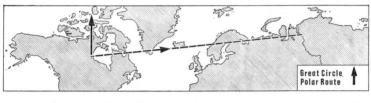

Fig. 102. *The Apparent Choice of Routes from Churchill to the Mouth of the Yenesei River allowed by Mercator's Projection.*

Yenesei River in Siberia. The Mercator map would offer a choice of the following flights: across Canada and Alaska, and from the Bering Straits across vast stretches of Soviet territory; or by a journey from Canada across the Atlantic, through Norway, Sweden, Finland, and north-western Russia. The zenithal map on the other hand, shows a shorter route from Canadian territory passing close to the Pole, and thence direct to northern Siberia.

GLOBAL POSITION AND MILITARY STRATEGY

In recent years great developments have been made in the use of polar air routes. Although a successful air-line operates most profitably along a chain of commercial airports, each of which may contribute or receive passengers or goods, the saving of time by these fast, long-range aircraft with a full pay-load makes the shorter polar crossing attractive to certain passengers and for sending special types of cargo; so commercial air-lines operate long-distance passenger services across this part of the world.

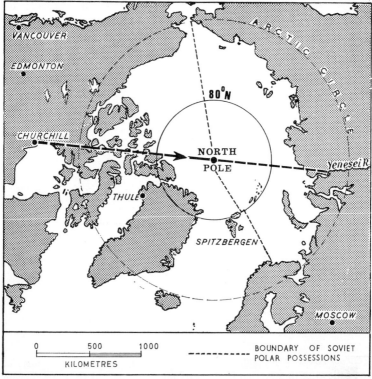

Fig. 103.   POLAR ROUTE—A ZENITHAL PROJECTION CENTRED ON THE
NORTH POLE.

Compare this polar route from Churchill to the mouth of the Yenesei River with the routes shown in Fig. 102. Notice the strategic position of Thule, an Arctic air base of the U.S.A., lying as it does between North America, northern Europe, and northern Asia.

Mackinder's Heartland

Today, the great powers maintain Arctic air bases, like that at Thule in western Greenland, which guard against warplanes and guided missiles directed to take advantage of the shorter polar crossing between Asia and the Americas. Rings of observer posts aim to detect planes and missiles crossing the polar regions.   Figs. 103 and 104

Fig. 104. MACKINDER'S "HEARTLAND" AND THE STRATEGIC POLAR AREAS OF TODAY.

Mackinder's Inner and Outer Zones, relative to his original concept of a "Heartland", are compared with the "Inner Polar Areas" which have become strategically important now that the nations of Western Europe, North America, China, and the U.S.S.R. can employ fast, long-range aircraft and guided missiles.

show that territories immediately bordering on the Arctic Ocean are in the interior of the land hemisphere, and consequently have great strategic significance.

Long before the full dawn of the air-age, Mackinder proclaimed the significance of the interior lands of Euro-Asia. He defined a "heartland", inaccessible to naval power, which could be controlled by land forces, and from which a large military force could dominate the marginal lands. In 1943 he re-defined the area as: ". . . the northern part and the interior of Euro-Asia. It extends from the Arctic coast to the central deserts, and westward to the broad isthmus between the Baltic and Black seas". Today the territory of the U.S.S.R. is almost equivalent to the heartland, except for the land east of the Yenesei.

To emphasise the strategic value of the heartland, Mackinder wrote in 1919:—

"Who rules east Europe commands the heartland.

Who rules the heartland commands the world island.

Who rules the world island commands the world."

Since that time Soviet Russia, from her base in eastern Europe, has made great progress in colonising this territory, and has begun to exploit its considerable potentialities. Russia thus occupies at the least a strong defensive position, and commands land areas which, by their very extent, allow her freedom of withdrawal and dispersal, and enable her to stretch the lines of communication of an invading force to the maximum, while removing at least some essential industries into the interior, tactics which were employed against the German invaders in 1942.

However, the climate over most of the heartland is one of extremes of temperature, with long spells of severe cold, and large areas with low precipitation; agricultural possibilities are limited, and it is not surprising that even now it is relatively sparsely peopled. Essential control, and power, is still in eastern Europe.

The majority of the inhabitants of the "world island" live in the marginal lands—China and India, south-east Asia, and west and central Europe, and considerably outnumber the inhabitants of the interior. But, despite the enormous reservoir of man-power of the marginal lands, the heartland is unified, while the marginal areas are divided. Should the power which controls the heartland succeed, by whatever means, in dominating *one* of the main marginal regions the total resources and man-power would make the combination most formidable. In this respect the relations between the U.S.S.R. and China, and the U.S.S.R. and western Europe, have great significance.

Whereas the original appreciation of the significance of the heartland was related to the Euro-Asia land mass, a global outlook must bring the Americas and their large and growing population into the picture. Since the publication of Mackinder's original thesis, air travel has brought North America ever closer to Europe in time, and also brought the realisation that the American continent faces the heartland across the polar ice-cap. The importance of this new outlook is illustrated by the fact that as long ago as 1947 Canada's Air Defence Command shifted from the old east and west bases of Halifax and Vancouver to two central positions—Edmonton, and Trenton, Alberta, with outer bases in the Canadian far north linked strategically with those of the U.S.A. in Alaska and Greenland.

"*Eastern*" *and* "*Western*" *Hemispheres—* *Some Misconceptions*

It is obvious, then, that a correct appreciation of geographical position is essential to both geographer and politician, and both must beware lest "Mercator-mindedness" leads to false conclusions. This is illustrated by the widespread misconceptions about the positions of Brazil and the Argentine relative to ports in Europe and the U.S.A. Because it has long been accepted that the Atlantic divides a western from an eastern hemisphere, it is understandable that most people expect the U.S.A. and Latin America to have many affinities, and are surprised when they do not behave and act as "natural partners"; at the same time they may regard American interest in the defence of western Europe with misgiving. Yet western European ports are considerably nearer the east coast bases of the U.S.A. than are those of the Argentine or Uruguay, and Suez is no more remote than Buenos Aires; to the man in Chicago all the European capitals, except Athens, are closer than the Argentinian capital. It is also instructive to observe that Gibraltar is closer by sea to the entire South Atlantic coast of South America than is the nearest point of the United States— Miami.

Changes in the Relative Situation of the "*Middle East*"

The frequent use of other general descriptive terms, such as "the Middle East", also tends to distort our view of the true location of the area concerned. The vague terms "Middle East" and "Near East" commonly used to describe the arid and semi-arid lands of the Arabian Peninsula, the Arabic-speaking lands of north-east Africa (from Egypt to Tripolitania), those bordering the eastern Mediterranean (Anatolia, Syria, Lebanon, Israel, and Jordan), and Iraq and Iran, imply that these areas separate western Europe from a "Far East".

Western Europeans have regarded these lands in this particular way (as a "middle zone") for many centuries; and rightly so, for in eastern and south-eastern Asia lay the sources of many desirable

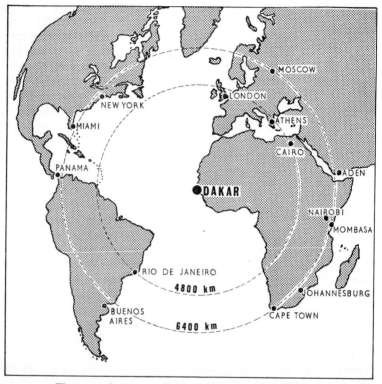

Fig. 105.   Azimuthal Projection Centred on Dakar.

This projection, centred on Dakar, shows that the custom of studying the continents as separate land areas may give a false impression of distance between places on the globe.   Dakar, for instance, is nearer to Moscow, in Eastern Europe, than to Johannesburg, in Africa, nearer to New York than to Cape Town or Mombasa, and as close to Rio de Janeiro as to Cairo.

Such a projection also helps to dispel the idea of a rigid division of the world into "Eastern" and "Western" Hemispheres, and emphasises that, in the days of rapid sea and air communication, the Atlantic now joins rather than divides, the continents of Africa, Europe, and the Americas.

commodities, and the produce of the Far Eastern lands travelled to the markets of Europe along the trade routes of central Asia, and through the Persian Gulf or the Red Sea, passing through the hands of merchants at "half-way houses" in trading cities such as Aleppo, Damascus, and the Levantine ports.

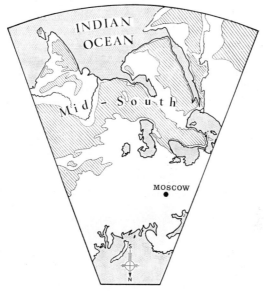

Fig. 106. The "Mid-South"—from the U.S.S.R.

Control of these Middle Lands, from Tibet to Libya, would mean access to the Indian Ocean and command of the East-West route via the Mediterranean.

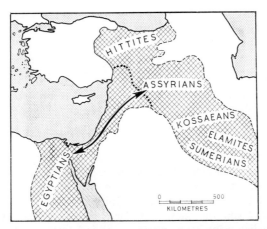

Fig. 107. Settlement in b.c. 1450, East of the Mediterranean.

These arid territories include a zone of tribal settlements and of constant struggles (marked by the double arrow) which lies along the axis of the route between Egypt and Mesopotamia, via the coastal lands and the Fertile Crescent.

However, this conception of a "Middle East" is valid only if we are thinking in terms of western Europe and eastern Asia. Although great mountain barriers lie to the north of Iraq and Iran, and although the desert lands stretch southwards into Africa, air travel has reduced the effectiveness of these barriers, and brings home the fact that these territories are also a "Middle South" in relation to the U.S.S.R. The "Far South" from the Russian viewpoint is the great continent of Africa, with its possibilities of economic development, and with

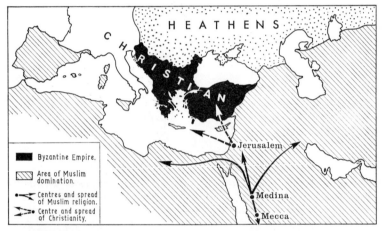

Fig. 108. MUSLIM DOMINATION IN THE EIGHTH CENTURY A.D.

During the following centuries the lands to the east of the Mediterranean became:—

(*a*) *The home of two great religions.*

(*b*) *An area dominated by separate Muslim Dynasties—though containing many non-Muslims.*

(*c*) *The setting in which developed many Muslim centres of learning (Baghdad, Cairo, Aleppo, Cordoba, for example)—in contrast to the lack of scholastic centres in Northern Europe.*

rather unstable relations between African and European; it is also India and Pakistan, and south-east Asia. The "Arab lands" as the "Mid-South", thus occupy a most important strategic position from a north-south as well as an east-west point of view.

Figs. 107 and 108 show that these lands have not always been an intermediate zone between strong political groups, but have themselves contained powerful states, which at various periods of history have had profound effects upon surrounding lands in Europe and Asia. From very early times strong tribes lived in the river valleys and more fertile coastal regions, frequently clashing as they sought ascendancy over one another, but together forming a belt of population numerically greater, and containing a greater potential of power, than existed in any of the surrounding lands.

Later, two great religions spread outward from the heart of these lands; Christianity taking hold on the northern Mediterranean shores,

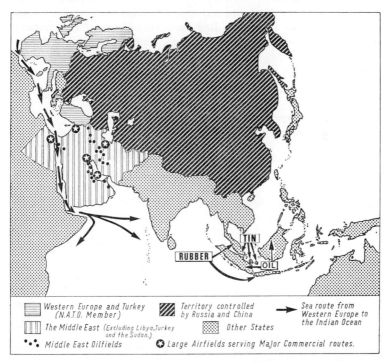

Fig. 109. THE MIDDLE EAST IN 1970.

(*a*) *It lies across vital sea and air routes between Europe and the East.*
(*b*) *It acts as a land link between the "Heartlands" of Asia and Africa.*
(*c*) *It contains a number of separate states, whose peoples are mainly Muslim.*
(*d*) *It contains many large oilfields and oil refineries.*

and eventually spreading, via Rome and Byzantium to the remainder of Europe; and the Muslim religion, rooted in the Middle East itself, which was carried westward through North Africa to Spain, and eastward to the heart of Asia and to the lands bordering the Indian Ocean.

These are but two periods of history in which power has been centred in the lands of the "Middle East". Today other powerful states, or groups of nations, seek to control or influence national policies within this area; not only to gain strategic advantages, but also because of the huge deposits of mineral oil which are known to lie beneath these lands.

Europe's former trade with the East in silks and spices, and other luxury commodities, has been replaced in priority by trade in the necessities of modern industry. The western European nations urgently required rubber, tin, and vegetable oils from south-east Asia, and their freedom to use the Red Sea—Suez Canal—Mediterranean route, and their ability to exercise proper control over their economic interests further east, depend to a large extent upon the stability of their relations with the countries of the "Middle East".

The Influence upon Politics of Minerals and Power Resources

In the last few chapters the discussion of relative global positions, boundary problems, and world population, touches on a few related parts of a most dynamic subject—sometimes termed "geopolitics". This term may be used to describe the relationships of political processes to geographical facts; and among such geographical facts are the distribution and estimated reserves of minerals and potential power resources, which have an immediate bearing upon political action.

Great reserves of the minerals required by modern industry are known to exist throughout the world, but in their workable form they are normally concentrated in fairly small regions; with the result that certain nations possess large quantities of them, while others have little; facts which do not make for political stability.

The knowledge of where to find, and how to use, minerals came slowly to mankind, but those who could make use of the stronger materials for cutting tools, for hoes or ploughs, and for weapons, had an immense advantage over their fellows. Thus, from the earliest times, minerals have had a strong influence on the course of human actions.

Various communities replaced their early tools of stone, bone, or ivory, with flints or other hard minerals chosen for the convenient shape produced when fractured. The adoption of bronze was a great step forward, and involved some form of commerce, for tin and copper occur together only in a few places, such as Cornwall. Although bronze was gradually displaced by iron, enclaves of stone-age culture have persisted until the twentieth century. At all stages of history there have been marked cultural differences between those who were skilled in the uses of metals, and had sufficient resources available, and those unable to make use of them.

Because of its widespread use in manufacturing, transport, and construction, iron is foremost among the resources of the modern world, and the distribution of its ores of special significance, not only in their actual quantity, but also in quality and accessibility. But the ore is valueless unless it can be smelted and processed, and therefore the location and availability of coal and other sources of power in relation to iron ore fields, or docks importing iron ore, is of economic concern, and an area rich in both ore and power resources is likely to be of prime importance.

An enumeration of the properties, uses, and distribution of the many other minerals, including petroleum, which are needed by modern industry, must be left to economic geography. Their exploitation, however, is very much a part of human geography (as far as it can be separated from the purely economic aspect). This is underlined by the lengths to which individuals and nations will go to secure them; by the disruption of a region through mining enterprises and the train of associated dwellings and communications; and by the more apparent results of their employment, in creating complex technologically "developed" areas—with all their advantages and disadvantages.

Some minerals may not appear to be of vital importance to man, and yet the threat of shortage emphasises their role in modern industry. The relative scarcity of sulphur, which is directly used in the production of sulphuric acid, and consequently an essential in many chemical manufactures, including fertilisers and explosives, is a reminder that minerals are acquired by destructive exploitation. With the increasing pace of industrialisation, and the havoc and waste of modern warfare, there is the possibility of serious world shortages of certain minerals; and although iron is the basis of engineering, in these days of high-speed tools, many other metals are alloyed with iron and steel to increase durability; so that shortages of chromium, manganese, nickel, tungsten, or vanadium, would be keenly felt by a manufacturing nation, whether due to world scarcity or boycott.

Today, as always, the possession of mineral wealth makes for power; power to make use of it oneself, and power to make it available, or to deny its use, to others. Unfortunately, the minerals so urgently needed by modern industries, and the sources of mechanical power—coal, oil, natural gas, hydro-electricity, uranium—are not uniformly distributed over the earth; and the same applies to certain vital plant products, rubber, for instance.

The unequal distribution of economic raw materials, and of capital to exploit them, means that nations that "have not" come under the domination of, or enter into a bloc with, one or other of the more powerful states, or associations of states, such as the U.S.A., U.S.S.R., and the E.E.C. group, each backed by huge material resources. Smaller associations and poorly endowed states tend to become economically or politically attached to whichever has the most to offer, materially, strategically, or ideologically. This is bound to lead to tension, and to attempts by the big powers to win the sympathies of certain key areas. Only a truly global outlook, and a really effective form of world organisation, can ensure a reasonably fair distribution of world resources. This is an ideal which is far from realisation, but is, nevertheless, a fundamental fact of geopolitics; the world is a single system and the problem of the peoples is how to live together and make the fullest use of all that the earth has to offer.

PART III

CHAPTER XIII

A REGIONAL APPROACH

Most geographers begin to learn about the earth and its peoples by reading what are termed "regional geographies" which describe the physical characteristics and the type of people found in the various political units which we call "countries". But the boundaries of a country, being man-made, are liable to be changed at any time so that, for instance, textbooks written in 1939 and 1950 when referring to "Germany" described different parts of the earth's surface. Also, all countries contain different types of relief, soils, local climates, and natural vegetation, so that the forms of human settlement and occupation vary from one part of the state to another. This must detract from the value of any "regional geography" which, for lack of space, generalises about the human settlement and activities within a country.

Geographers and planners frequently investigate areas considerably smaller than a nation state, concentrating on what may be described as "geographical regions". British geographers have defined a *region* as: "An area of the earth's surface differentiated from an adjoining area by one or more features which give it a *measure of unity*".

If, we consider an area throughout which there is some degree of uniformity among the various geographical elements, it is much easier to appreciate the ways in which men respond to and effect this particular environment.

A region may owe its most prominent characteristics either to natural phenomena, such as its relief, types of soil, or local climatic conditions, or else to the actions of man within this natural environment. Man may produce a recognisable pattern of agriculture or settlement which may come to be regarded as typical of a particular region. We may, therefore, consider two main types of region: the *"natural region"*, and the occupied or *"geographical region"*.

Natural Regions

First a word of warning. Not all geographers use the term "natural region" with the same meaning. A region may be called "natural" in the sense of being well defined, and in this context include man and the facts of his occupation, in the way that textbooks refer to the Vale of Kashmir as a natural region. Or, as in this book, "natural region" may be used to describe an area which is virtually unaffected by man's occupation, and therefore exists in the natural state.

Any region owes its special character to the interrelation of a great number of separate elements. We have already seen that even small variations in climate, rock types, or relief, may cause considerable modification of the plant and animal life, and so produce a characteristic flora and fauna. No two areas, therefore, are likely to possess similar features so exactly related to each other that they are in fact identical regions.

By making a classification of natural regions of the world it becomes possible to compare areas which have close natural affinity with one another. Such regions are usually similar in latitude, altitude, and continental or maritime location, and, therefore, have similar types of climate. But, however clearly they may be defined on a distribution map, there is usually a gradual transition between one region and the next, and the exact limits of a region are rarely apparent on the ground.

Geographical Regions

A complete geographical study of a region must include the human activities within it. But as soon as man's works are considered, in all their variety of form and continual change, it becomes even more difficult to define the limits of the region. Man may so alter the face of the land he occupies that it becomes almost impossible to discover a truly natural feature. While this is obviously true as far as the features of our towns and their suburbs are concerned, it may appear to be an exaggeration to those who observe the beauty of a rural countryside. But in a land such as Britain, renowned for its rural beauty, very few, if any, tracts of countryside are to be found in their natural state, for the axe, the plough, and man's domestic animals, have been at work for a very long time.

The fact that many of man's interests and occupations extend into surrounding areas, means that the limits of a region, which may be difficult enough to define in its natural state, become even more flexible in the geographical region. The result is that, as we shall see below, an occupied area can be divided into a number of quite different geographical regions, depending on what facts or conditions are looked on as providing the required "measure of unity".

The geographer seeks to identify regions in which facts, such as the relief, climate, and vegetation, combine to produce characteristic forms of agriculture or settlement. But geography as a subject has many facets, so that he may decide to use, or perhaps be biased towards, one particular feature, say the relief, as the basis of his classification. Thus, while he, personally, may pay great attention to the surface geology when defining his regions, another geographer may place emphasis on the climatological differences within the area. Therefore, because different geographers may use different characteristics on

Fig. 110. A Broad Classification of the Geographical Regions of England and Wales.

which to base their definition of the extent of a region, the ways in which they divide any area into regions are likely to differ considerably.

Planning Regions

Consider the many ways in which, for one reason or another, various authorities divide Britain into separate regions.

Many administrative bodies define regions or "zones" which are based on an appreciation of both social and geographical conditions:

examples of these are the Post Office regions, and those of the Electricity and Milk Marketing Boards.

In 1971 the various proposals resulting from the Redcliffe-Maud Commission were published, and envisaged setting up new metropolitan areas and administrative counties to replace a larger number of counties and county boroughs, with appropriate second-tier district councils as subdivisions. The differences in outlook between various authorities when "regional" definitions are to be made are underlined by the attitudes of certain individuals and groups to these proposals.

Many had hoped that the new administrative structure would "fit the facts of contemporary social geography", and felt that the desire to respect ancient county boundaries hampered this. With four out of every five Englishmen living in an urban area, it was hoped that more "city regions" might be established; instead of which, it seemed that in the proposals cities were too often divorced from their "commuter fields", where a numerically smaller, different social class would have too great a say in the organisation of a large part of the countryside. We are not concerned here with the rights and wrongs of these particular proposed regional divisions, but should appreciate that there are many different, highly subjective viewpoints to be considered when a closely settled country is to be divided into a pattern of regions for administrative or planning purposes.

During the 'sixties, England was divided into eight economic planning regions. This aimed at allowing successive governments to attempt to deploy social and economic resources to the best advantage of the economy as a whole. Among other things, this meant recognising some regions as special development areas—a "northern region", for instance, where the former dependence on coalmining, shipbuilding, and heavy industries was declining. But conditions are not, of course, uniform within the region; so in the late 'sixties special development areas were designated in the northern region (e.g., the Tees and Tyne-Wear growth areas), where particular incentives to manufactures were to be provided, roads improved, and new towns created. Hence, in a sense, there came to be recognition of regions within a region—and once more a strong connection with urbanisation, necessitating planning for a conurbation or a city-region as a whole.

Regional Consciousness

In many parts of the earth men feel that they belong to a certain geographical area, which they can roughly define, and to which they give their loyalty. Such an area does not necessarily coincide with a political unit, for the development of a regional consciousness in man, and the local traditions and customs which he observes, are usually

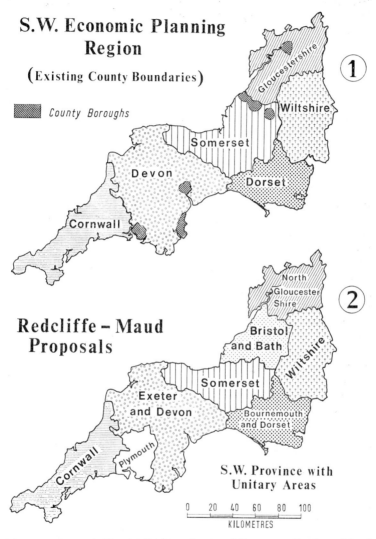

S.W. Economic Planning Region

(Existing County Boundaries)

▨ *County Boroughs*

①

Gloucestershire

Wiltshire

Somerset

Devon

Dorset

Cornwall

Redcliffe – Maud Proposals

②

North Gloucester Shire

Bristol and Bath

Wiltshire

Somerset

Exeter and Devon

Bournemouth and Dorset

Cornwall

Plymouth

S.W. Province with Unitary Areas

0   20   40   60   80   100
KILOMETRES

Fig. 111.   *Economic Planning Region and proposed Government Province of South West England.   The latter includes new areas of unitary authority, responsible for all local government services; whose chief characteristics are, "coherence" and "self-containment".   Among the evidence required to establish their limits were statistics on journey-to-work movements, of public transport services, and of newspaper circulation: while the spatial structure of professional and business organisations were considered.   (For a clear picture of the Redcliffe-Maud proposals and the background to the report, see "New Regions for Old" P. Haggett, Geog. Mag. 42 [3] p. 210.)*

responses to climate, relief, and to other geographical features which combine to give the region in which he lives a particular character, all of its own.

Geographical regions must not simply be regarded as artificial creations, deliberately drawn up by the geographer to help his studies or to aid administrative planning, but also as parts of the earth which have each a distinct character, partly natural and partly due to its human occupants, who are usually aware of a distinction between their own territory and the adjoining areas.

In Spain, for instance, the contrasts between the north-west maritime region, the Pyrenees, the north-east coastal area, the barrenness of the central Meseta, and the broad valleys of Andalusia, have produced strong regional loyalties, at the expense, in many cases, of a feeling of national unity. The Galiegos, Basques, Catalans, Castilians, and Andalusians, each have a separate and distinct geographical environment, in which they have developed a culture and traditions of their own. Even in recent years there have been movements towards separation from the Spanish state, especially in Catalonia and among the Basques.

Regional loyalties need not cause disunity, but can, on the contrary, give strength to the country as a whole. Administration carried out through regional centres which have the spontaneous loyalty of the surrounding countryside, often appears to the local population to be more sympathetic to their own interests, and modifications introduced to suit regional interests can help to enlist the support of the more remote areas for measures which are designed to benefit the country as a whole.

The strength of regional attachments within the United Kingdom is often underestimated, yet the fact that people tend to identify themselves with a broad region is indicated by the great popularity of the "family serials" which are produced by the B.B.C. on a regional basis, and which portray, for instance, details of the life of a "typical West Country family".

The Regional Capital

There is usually a central town or city, the focus of communications, in which are concentrated the headquarters of a great number of occupations or organisations which exist throughout the region, and to which the rural community turns—Norwich, for instance (page 132). The study of the site and the development of such a regional capital can be an important step towards the appreciation of the region as a whole. This was emphasised by the French geographers who laid the foundations for the advance of regional studies, and their regions were, in fact, defined as far as possible in terms of the "sphere of influence of the natural capital".

Similar Natural Regions Exploited in Different Ways

Although physical similarities may produce similar types of natural regions, they do not necessarily lead to the creation of similar social conditions. The way in which geographical regions are occupied and exploited depends, among other things, on the cultural background, the capabilities, and the historical legacies of their occupants.

This is emphasised by the different forms of human occupation in the "Mediterranean lands" of the world. In California, for instance, those commercial crops which are characteristic of the Mediterranean climatic regions have been established in the "railway age", and the development of this region was initiated, and accelerated, by the creation of good modern communications. Twentieth century commercial exploitation of the conveniently large Central Valley has been aided by huge irrigation schemes, and by the use of Mexican, Filipino, and other seasonal labour forces. Much of the landscape shows the regular patterns of highly organised "factory farms".

By way of contrast, in the region surrounding the Mediterranean Sea much of the agricultural land has been occupied continuously for thousands of years. Holdings are often, of necessity, small, and methods of cultivation traditional; while lack of capital makes it difficult to extend the area of cultivation or improve existing arable land. Plantations are few, and crops are usually cultivated in zones which have evolved about old nucleated settlements. Thus, despite the similarities of latitude, position, and therefore climate, the overall pattern of human occupation of the two regions is dissimilar.

The classification of geographical, as opposed to natural, regions is apt to be a difficult, and often unprofitable, exercise. Even a comparison of forms of land-use may be misleading, for though similar climatic conditions favour the growth of certain crops, the actual crops cultivated may vary with changing economic conditions. Methods employed in cultivation also provide little firm ground for direct comparisons. Because of their rubber plantations, Malaysia and Indonesia are often shaded on distribution maps as "regions" of plantation type of agriculture; yet over half their cash crops come from small holdings.

One cannot place geographical regions into any form of rigid classification, for, like human individuals, they have very different characters which are constantly changing and developing. In human geography we may study these changes, both human and regional, in their relations to each other.

CHAPTER XIV

LOCAL AND REGIONAL SURVEY

One of the most practical approaches to human geography is through a local survey. Some areas lend themselves to this type of study more obviously than others, but no geographical area can be absolutely unsuitable provided an objective is clearly defined, certainly not in a country such as England, where the landscape bears the impression of centuries of human occupation.

Three main types of countryside may be encountered: *natural* countryside, unmodified by man (unlikely to be met in a purely local survey); *rural* areas, which (besides arable, pastoral, or forested land) may include small hamlets and villages, and isolated quarrying or mining districts; and *urban* tracts, ranging from the small town, which may be surveyed as a single unit, to the large city, in which parishes, estates, factories, shopping centres, and various human activities may be investigated separately.

The choice is usually governed by the location of home or school, though it may be possible periodically to visit a distant area of some particular interest. If opportunity occurs, it is instructive to study two contrasting areas, one rural, one urban; one of the most interesting types of geographical area is found where urban and rural characteristics intermingle, as on the fringe of a large city.

Teamwork

Though such a survey may be undertaken by an individual, he will need to limit his objective carefully, and perhaps to acquire a great deal of information from secondary sources, and by consulting reference books and other relevant works, attempt to cover such technical matter as he is unable to observe and record at first hand. Secondary sources are usually valuable in any survey, but should be subordinate to individual observations and field work.

It is much more satisfactory for individuals to work together, forming a small team, in which the various members may be able to contribute some form of specialised knowledge, however amateurishly. A team in which the work, hobbies, or leanings of the members embrace, say, botanical, geological, and historical interests, should be able to make a well-balanced appreciation of the region as a whole; skill in photography or sketching, or interest in forms of transport or the weather, can all be put to practical use. Even where a diversity of interests is not of particular advantage, numbers are likely to allow more thorough investigation.

The Limits of the Survey

In urban areas, because of the multitude of different human activities, probably the most practical way of making a useful survey, even with a small team, is to concentrate on one form of activity, and consider the geographical causes which have affected its growth and influenced its present form. This may be a shopping/marketing activity, form of public transport, recreational activity, or business or manufacturing occupation (in a small town or district). On the other hand, a team may investigate the different forms of land-use within an urban district—the central business district, for example—and their relationships to the urban area as a whole. Whatever the form of survey undertaken, however, there should be a clear objective, and a careful allocation of the tasks of collecting the relevant information within the time available—by observation, questionnaires, or from secondary sources.

It may be much more difficult to decide upon the nature of the survey in a rural area, and the range of transport available may make it necessary to carry out the survey within a given radius of a small village. In this case a village survey may be made—investigating its site, origins, communications, population, and occupations, relationships with neighbouring villages or towns, its houses, social life, sources of supplies, shops, inn, school, etc. On the other hand it may be possible to make a sample survey—a particular farm study or agricultural activity, typical of the broader region within which the area lies.

For instance, by taking as an objective ten square miles of countryside in the vicinity of St Neots, the team would be able to survey arable farming under conditions which are typical of much of the land from the Great Ouse Valley to the broad farmlands of East Anglia. On the other hand, in some parts of the country an area of ten square miles may embrace a small physical unit with unique human activities. If a survey be taken of such an area spread along the length of the valleys of the River Exe or its upper tributaries (say from its source to about the vicinity of Dulverton or Bampton), it will include rural activities which are characteristic of this particular local environment. Here the low water meadows and the plantations of willow are in contrast to the cleared pastures on the wooded slopes and to the rough moorland grazing above, while lumbering and quarrying of the red sandstone are special local industries. The upper valley is thus a small well-defined region, within the broad region of Exmoor, and one does not have to go far beyond the edge of the overhanging moorlands to be able to make a comprehensive regional study.

It is instructive to choose an area which includes marked differences in relief and soils, and to make a comparative study of the changes in settlement or agriculture which occur in these different places. But, remember that forms of land-use respond to economic factors—supply, demand, subsidies, quotas, and restrictions as well as to physical conditions.

Much will depend on the time available and whether or not the survey can be a progressive one, carried out over a number of seasons or in successive years. Rotations and changing forms of land-use may be recorded in successive years, and for these outline 1 : 10 000 maps are particularly useful.

Finally, it may be possible to investigate the effects of a specific event on rural settlement, habits, and forms of land-use. The closing of a branch railway line, or the creation of a by-pass motorway may each have a marked effect on small rural places. Interviews and questionnaires distributed in villages along the now closed Bedford-Cambridge branch railway, for instance, showed marked changes in the local shopping habits, the use of local shops, and of journeys to specific market central places. The investigation was part of a survey carried out by school geographers at various times during a year.

Questionnaires

Human choice is involved in most geographical surveys, and it is as well to investigate motives and choices which have led to a particular decision—to settle, to plant a particular crop, to use a certain form of transport, and so on.

Interviews of a satisfactory cross-section of the people concerned may produce such information. But such interviewing requires skill and tact, especially where opinions are surveyed, and questions have to be phrased in advance to limit the range of replies. Geographic facts are much easier to obtain and record than opinions. The answers to such questions as "Where do you shop for daily vegetables?" and "How many men do you employ full-time?" can be precisely recorded.

In many ways it is better for the inexperienced investigator to draw up a firm questionnaire to be distributed, filled in and returned, or to be filled in by himself at the time of interview. Such questionnaires must be very carefully constructed. First, there must be information about the location of the respondent, and the date, time, and place of interview. There should be questions seeking information about the respondent himself. Then information should be obtained about the actions of the respondent relevant to the survey—in connection with his work as, say, a farmer or storekeeper, depending on the nature of the survey.

It may then be necessary to record opinions on subjects relative to the survey, or reasons for particular actions. Here, open-ended questions may produce material which is difficult to analyse; and so it may be preferable to formulate direct questions with choice of replies—asking the respondent to mark that with which he agrees most; or he may be asked to rank a set of alternatives in order of preference. Attitudes may also be examined in this way: "Do you consider the alteration has made—things worse; no change; a slight improvement; a great improvement?". Direct questions of this kind greatly help recording and analysis.

Questions should be clear and concise, and if with a Yes/No answer, set out in easily distinguishable rows or columns; and, above all, should be strictly relevant to the matter under investigation, so that coding and analysis is easy and the result informative.

There are many possible forms of questionnaire, and all are difficult to construct, if one is to be sure of their relevance, unambiguity, and ease of analysis. In general, it is as well for several people to help in the construction, and for test cases to be investigated first, before the questionnaire is distributed.

Maps, Sketches, and Photographs

The value of good illustration, and of recording facts by means of maps, sketches, or photographs need hardly be stressed. Everyone should be able to make quick and accurate sketches, on which detail, which is difficult to record with a camera, can be inserted. Photographs, however, are valuable, and should aim to show the commonplace as well as the more spectacular features which may not be typical of the whole region.

Maps are essential for the preliminary study, for identification of elements of the landscape, and as a means of recording information obtained. Plans produced as a result of personal survey may be transferred to an enlargement or to a tracing of the existing map.

EXTRACTING INFORMATION FROM MAPS

THE SIGNIFICANCE OF PLACE NAMES

We have already seen how a succession of invading peoples can leave the marks of their occupation upon the countryside. In Britain there are tens of thousands of settlements whose names bear witness to the origin of their former inhabitants. Celts, Romans, Angles, Saxons, Danes, Scandinavians, and Normans, have all left ample evidence of their occupation in the form of the names they bestowed on the places where they settled. Fig. 112 shows areas in which

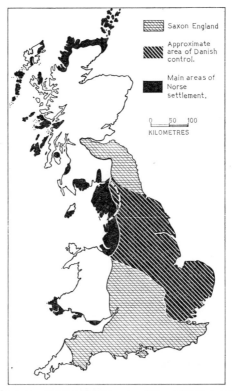

Fig. 112. SAXON, DANISH, AND NORSE SETTLEMENT.

The main Saxon occupation was in those areas shown by light cross-shading, and in places where relief and soils allowed agricultural settlement. (The broken line indicates the limits of Saxon settlement in the north-west.)

In the ninth century many Saxon settlements in the north and east of England were overrun by the Danes, who controlled a large part of the territory shown above. Norse settlement of the coastal "fringes" is shown in black.

Scandinavian peoples settled, and the extent of the Danish Empire under Knut, superimposed upon the divisions of Saxon England, and throws light upon the broad distribution of place names as illustrated by Fig. 113.

Groups Found in England

Celtic Origin. These are found mainly in the west of England and Wales, as well as in Ireland and Scotland. Most of the early inhabitants withdrew westwards, under pressure from later invaders. The following are of frequent occurrence in Cornwall and the West Country:—

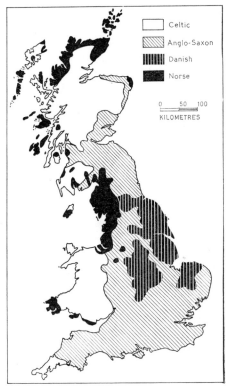

Fig. 113. ORIGINS OF THE PLACE NAMES OF BRITAIN.

The diagram shows those areas of Britain where certain forms of place name are common, though not necessarily predominant.

Bod, Bos—house or abode (*Bodmin*—a monk's house).

Combe—a valley [*Withycombe*—of mixed origin—a valley with copses (Anglo-Saxon)].

Gweath, Gwith—trees (*Trengweath*—a village among the trees).

Les, Lis—court or palace (*Liskeard* and *Lizard*—high court).

Pen—head or peak (*Penzance*—holy head).

Scawen—elder tree (*Boscawen*—house by the elder tree).

Tor—high rock (used to describe the feature rather than settlement).

Tre, Tref—village (*Tregear*—village by the castle).

Roman Names. The Romans had very little influence on the development of the smaller settlements, but the word "castra", indicating a camp, is found in many forms in towns which were formerly military cantonments, e.g. *Chester, Lancaster, Bicester.*

Anglo-Saxon Origin. The first settlements were in the south and south-east of England, and here such names are particularly common. But gradually the peoples spread out over the lowlands of England, and the names became widely distributed throughout the country.

Many of their place names which have survived were used to describe the countryside as they found it, and show the use the people were making of the land.

Borough, Burgh, Bury—a fortified place (common; though many names ending in "borough" have been corrupted from "berg"—a hill).

Bridge—modern meaning (*Tonbridge*—bridgehead settlement).

Dale—a valley [*Wooldale*, Yorks—wolves' valley (how easy to assume a connection with the Yorkshire woollen industry!)].

Fold—enclosure (*Cowfold*, Sussex).

Ford—modern meaning (*Wallingford*—Briton's fording place).

Ham—farm or enclosure [*Streatham*—farm near Roman Road (Street)].

Hoe—a spur of land (*Plymouth Hoe*).

Hurst—a wood (*Hawkhurst*).

Lea, Ley—a pasture, or clearing (*Studley*—horse meadow).

Ing—dwelling, or a field (*Tooting*—where Tota's family lived).

Stow—meeting place (*Plaistow*—place for plays).

Ton, Tun (from *tun* a homestead or enclosure, or from *dun*—a hill).

Wal—a foreigner, used when denoting British settlements (*Walworth*—a Briton's home).

Wich, Wick—place or farm (*Chiswick*—farm specialising in cheese-making).

With, withy—wooded (*Withycombe*—see above).

Worth—home [*Selworthy*—home by the willows (sallows)].

Danish and Scandinavian Origin. The Danes held power chiefly over the eastern part of England, while the Scandinavians followed an outer path via the north of Scotland to the north-west of England, Ireland, Wales, and even into the Bristol Channel.

By—homestead or hamlet (*Grimsby*—Grimm's homestead).

Holme—island (*Steepholm*—island in the Bristol Channel).

Kirk—church [*Skewkirk, Yorks*—church in the wood (skorg)].

Thorpe—village (*Scunthorpe*—Skuna's settlement).

Toft—field (*Lowestoft*—Hlover's field).

Normans and their Influence on Place Names. While the Normans introduced a certain number of French names, a few descriptive (like Malpas, Cheshire—a "bad pass" into Wales), and quite a number of family names, as in Okeford *Fitzpaine* (below), their greatest effect was the alteration of the spelling of older names, especially those with which they were unfamiliar. The name Searobryg, which described a Saxon settlement in Wiltshire, proved too much for the Norman clerks, who recorded it as Salbryg, which eventually became Salisbury.

The very fact that so many names have been altered in this way means that, before a name is taken at its face value, there should be as careful investigation as possible into its origin. The same care must be taken when deciding who were the former inhabitants of a place, for, although the name may have, say, a Celtic origin, it may well have been used as, or incorporated into, a descriptive phrase by the Anglo-Saxons; and, as we have seen, any former place name may have suffered corruption in Norman times or in the centuries which followed. Nevertheless, if one is prudent, place names can help to conjure up a picture of past settlement and activities, and can bring the facts and figures of the printed map to life.

RURAL PAST AND PRESENT FROM THE MAP

Besides describing the physical features, most Ordnance Survey maps can tell us a great deal of the human activities within their limits. A wealth of information can be obtained from the 1 : 63 360 map of any area; for purposes of discussion, consider sheet 178 of the One-Inch O.S., showing a rural area in Dorset near Cranborne Chase.

The Location

We could roughly deduce the location of this area, even if we did not know that it is in fact part of north-east Dorset. The place names indicate that it is part of the British Isles, and the nature of the ancient

remains bears this out.   The type of surface rocks (see below) and the
reference to Wiltshire (9217) further suggest that this describes part
of southern England.   However, these are but pointers, not in themselves conclusive, but demonstrating that a map can often tell its own
story in a surprisingly comprehensive way, from the broad setting
down to small details in the life of ancient peoples, as we shall see below.

The Topography

The outstanding physical features are the north-south scarp, and
the obvious contrast between the high ground to the east and north-east
and the lowland of the Stour Valley to the west.

There seems little doubt that the high ground is of chalk, for there
is little surface water, many dry valleys along the scarp and near
Tarrant Gunville, and frequent reference to downland—Gunville
Down, Bareden Down, Fontmell Down.   The consequent lack of
available surface water is underlined by specific references to places
where water can be found—Well Bottom, Well House, Washers Pit,
and by the wind pump (888123).

The lowland, by contrast, has numerous surface streams draining
to the Stour, and the names Marsh Farm, Marsh Common, and
Margaret Marsh would seem to refer to the presence of water upon
land which, lying beneath the chalk, is probably of clay.

Distribution of Settlement

Villages and hamlets are typically dispersed over the lowlands, and
are served by the small market town of Sturminster Newton—which
lies a mile or so to the west of this area.   Secondary roads are little
hampered by physical obstacles and run hither and thither over the
vale; only in the south-west is there an indication of regularity, where
the roads run parallel to the river (Stour), with few transverse links.

Further east there is a much closer connection between relief and
the alignment of roads and villages.   There is a marked line of settlement along the north-south road which takes advantage of the first
slopes of the chalk and avoids crossing the many streams which drain
westward.   Minor roads and trackways lead down to the small villages,
which are located where broad valleys open on to the lowland
(*e.g.* Compton or Coombe-town—a township in a hollow).   Most
of these tracks, like the one to Iwerne Minster from the east, follow the
more gentle slope along and across a spur (see Plate XXIV).

Hill farms are scattered upon the chalk, with indications of wells
nearby.   The two small villages are of very different form: Ashmore,
being a true hill village, is compact, with roads or tracks running down

in all directions, while Tarrant Gunville is extended along the dry upper valley of a small river, just to be seen in square 9212 (the Tarrant).

Early Occupation

The map gives a vivid picture of the history of this area, and traces for us, here and there with details, the long sequence of occupation.

The Ancient Britons must have travelled along the relatively easy pathways provided by the chalk ridge, and almost certainly followed the line of the road, 8810-8820. In early times the whole countryside would have been forested, and the lowland was undoubtedly more closely covered and certainly marshier than the upland chalk, on which large areas of relatively open forest land remain today. (The western extremity of the great Cranborne Chase, one of the few areas in England where there is truly ancient forest, is clearly marked on the map.)

There is much evidence that the men of the Stone Age, and the Celts and Germanic folk who followed, far from just passing through the area, made their homes, set up villages, farmed, created defences, and finally were laid to rest upon the downland. Their villages were usually situated on locally-prominent features, and, as in square 9110, protected by earthworks and ditches. Specially fortified camps were set up, and those of such prominence as Hod Hill and Hambledon Hill, which look out over the Stour Valley and along the line of the chalk, must have given a great sense of security to the people.

There would have had to be much clearing to obtain farmland, and the remains of "strip lynchets", a form of terracing (8716), show that the upper slopes were used for cultivation. More prominent are the burial mounds; the long barrows of the Stone Age folk and the early Celts, and the many tumuli of the Early Bronze Age people, who are thought to have introduced the round barrow, and of later peoples. This form of burial is known to have taken place up to the eighth century A.D., when Christian cemeteries were introduced.

The lowland shows less evidence of early occupation, though earthworks guard the river crossing (8212), and the endings of the place names Conygar (8112) and Binegar (8419) conceivably refer to early fortifications (Celtic).

The Romans also took advantage of the dominant position of Hod Hill, and under this military protection established villae above the level of the valley floor and where the soil, a mixture of chalk and clay, could be easily cleared and worked. The remains of such a villa lie to the south-west of Iwerne Minster.

The Saxons and Danes must, in their turn, have defended the heights of Hambledon, but whereas the latter have left little evidence

of their inroads, the majority of the place names are of Saxon origin
and tell of the long period of Anglo-Saxon occupation. Many of these
names were transformed by the Normans, who have also left a record
of the holdings of their great families, in somewhat disguised forms, in
the names of villages.

Place Names and Early Settlement

Celtic forms include the frequent references to "combes", or
valleys, and the descriptive words Pimperne (*pimp-pren*, five trees)
and Iwerne (*iw*, frequently found in river names, was also used to
denote the presence of yew trees). Iwerne Minster and Iwerne
Courtney take their name from the river, and indicate, respectively,
connection with the Church and with the family of de Curtenai.

Roman names would appear to be represented by Bedchester
(8517), but this is actually a corrupted form of Bedehurste; the
Domesday Book describes a "settlement at the wood which once
belonged to Baeda".

Saxon place names predominate, the majority of them describing
the place or its surroundings, such as El*bury* Hill, Child Oke*ford*,
Sut*ton*, Wood*ley*, and many others (see above). Here the endings
are stressed, but usually the whole word tells us a great deal about the
place. Child Okeford, for instance, not only indicates the setting
amid oaks near the fording place, but tells us that this was the stronghold of a little chieftain ("child"). The importance attached to this
crossing is shown by the protective earthworks set up nearby. [The
ending "keld" usually means the same thing, and a settlement of this
kind existed amid the willows (sal) near Salkeld Bridge, a few miles
west of Child Okeford.]

The Normans did little to interfere with the Saxon names, other
than making changes in their form, but we see the presence of Norman
families acknowledged by combining the surname with a descriptive
term of Saxon origin. Thus the village of Shillingstone was formerly
"Schilling's Town", belonging in Norman times to the family of the
Eschellings. There is the village of Hammoon (8114) which describes
the water meadow (*ham*) owned by a member of the Mohun (*moon*)
family; while a more obvious example is the village of Okeford
Fitzpaine (the Normans frequently used the word "Fitz" = fils,
son of) which lies just to the south-west of this area; and, again,
Tarrant *Gunville*.

All these names are descriptive in themselves, yet may have still
more to tell us if we observe their distribution. For instance, the
extent of the land owned by the Saxon and early English village is
indicated by the recurrence of the name of the village on the downland,

where the settlement lies near to the hill, and in the name of the common land belonging to the village of the vale; in each case the village had rights to the use of this land for pasture, and we find on the heights—Compton Down, Fontmell Down, Sutton Hill, Iwerne Hill, and in the vale—Sturminster Common, Okeford Common, Marsh Common.

The names tell also of the natural vegetation and of the animals which roamed the hills and lowlands. Modern words tell of oaks, ash, alders (though, oddly, not of beech), and woods, coppices, and bushes, while older forms indicate willows (*sallows*), yew trees, and woods on the slopes (*Waldron*). In the same way, besides *Hart*grove and *Fox*warren, there is *Everley*—the field of the wild boar (*ever*).

Later Settlement

There are many direct references to Manors and to Manor Farms throughout the area, and ecclesiastical holdings undoubtedly existed in the neighbourhood of Compton Abbas, Iwerne Minster, and Sturminster Newton.

Local events have added other names during the centuries, but from the map alone we can only speculate on the origin of such descriptions as Bussey Stool Woods, Cookwell Brook, or Gold Hill. But there is no doubt as to reason for the existence of Smuggler's Lane, for by the eighteenth century Cranborne Chase had become the hideout for smugglers, who brought illicit goods from near Poole and the coves of the south coast, and for ruffians of all kinds. Much of the forest was cleared in 1830 to lessen the menace of hidden cut-throats. The existence of a Gallows Corner more than hints at the lawlessness which must have affected this rural area. On the hills, the defiles of Stubhampton Bottom and Ashmore Bottom are wooded glens which must have been excellent rendezvous and hideouts.

Meanwhile the settled population continued their agricultural life, and no doubt kept busy the many mills along the Stour and its tributaries. The name Shepherd's Bottom emphasises that whereas the lowlands consist of pasture and arable land, grazing has long been the principal occupation on the downs (though it is just possible that "Shepherd", in this context is a surname). Orchards are represented by symbols, and the hamlets of East and West Orchard suggest that these are of long standing.

Finally, about the only features we can definitely ascribe to modern times are the railway, the road surfaces, and the golf course on Fontmell Down ... For anyone with imagination the map provides a wonderful panorama of human lives, from the drama of the Long Barrow to recreation on the fairways of a golf course.

Patterns of Rural Settlement

The relationships between size, ranking, and spacing of settlements discussed on pages 82-5 may also be investigated with the help of the 1 : 63 360 scale map. Lowland areas of ancient settlement on which towns firmly retained their market functions, at least until the nineteenth century, are likely to show patterns approximating to the Christaller $k = 3$ network. One may further note how more recent facts of settlement—the growth of manufacturing industries or the creation of trunk roads—have tended to distort this theoretical, hierarchical pattern of hamlets, villages, and towns.

Measurements may be made to enable more precise judgment to be made. The hamlets, villages, and small towns may be ranked in terms of the area each occupies on the map, or the facts of their population and ranking may be separately obtained and recorded. Straight-line measurement may then be made between each place and its nearest neighbour of the same or higher ranking, and average distances calculated for each class of settlement—average distance between hamlet and hamlet, hamlet and village, village and town, etc.—which may be examined and relationships analysed graphically.

On-the-spot surveys may then reveal the extent to which the patterns and spacings are relics of the medieval pattern of market central places, or whether they respond to the nature of the services offered by these places today.

In areas of strong relief, it is instructive to notice the influence of physical features on settlement patterns: one would expect the main market centres to occupy particularly advantageous positions—at valley confluence or highland/lowland junction—but still perhaps to show some regularity in spacing from one another and from other rural central places.

Features of Urban Settlement from the Map

Many British towns were quite small until the late eighteenth century, but have since expanded, in many cases in stages. Nineteenth century industrialisation and the coming of the railways tended to create industrial sectors beyond the compact medieval centre; the latter is still usually distinguishable on the map as a central focus of the major roads, with the old market square(s) and castle site, and a close street pattern with little obvious plan.

The nineteenth century growth saw planned patterns of straight regular streets, with a uniformity of design. Close rows of workers' villas were built near factories, which were often clustered near the railway station, goods yards and sidings. These usually stand out clearly on Ordnance Survey maps, particularly of 1 : 25 000 scale.

Even more obvious on maps of 1 : 63 360 scale and greater are the results of modern expansions beyond the Victorian-Edwardian limits of growth. Since the nineteen-thirties, and especially after World War II, many industries have been established on the outskirts of towns and along ring-roads. The accompanying industrial estates tend to show a regularity of planning which includes areas of housing and open spaces, both rectangular and radial in pattern, with a more open plan than those of the nineteenth century. Such peripheral estates are not necessarily linked with industries, of course; many have been established to house people moving from cleared deteriorating properties in the heart of the town, others as a conscious development of "desirable properties" on the rural-urban fringe.

A map study of the layout of a large town or city may, therefore, indicate quite clearly periods of historic growth and the nature of urban development.

Some indication of the economic importance of an urban centre may be given by direct observation of the associated features indicated on the map—features of power distribution, transport facilities, and direct references to factories, mills, or mines. Quantitatively, it is possible to measure the density of major routeways (A-class roads and motorways, or railways) within a specified radius of an urban centre— the length of road/rail per unit area, using the map grid to indicate area. Because of the close relationships between route density, traffic, and the presence of commercial and industrial enterprises, this may give some indication of the economic importance of an urban area; though a closer on-the-ground survey would be needed to establish the actual relationships.

A PLANNING SURVEY OF A RURAL COUNTY

The Aim

Local survey of the kind outlined above puts into perspective the varied facts of soil, climate, and human occupation, as they relate to a particular area; and may well be of some importance to those who plan for the future development of that area. For this reason, individuals, who can contribute a wide personal knowledge and experience, may be asked to combine to carry out research and survey on a larger scale as an aid to regional planning.

It is instructive, therefore, to observe the work of a team such as the West Midland Group in Post-War Reconstruction and Planning, whose principal aim has been "to provide a groundwork of facts upon which those responsible for planning in the county and the West Midland region may base their schemes". It is particularly enlightening to study their survey of the English county of Hereford; for here is an agricultural county, which is more or less a separate entity, with a fairly simple "make-up", and containing no large industrial area. Their method of approach is bound to be a great help to those attempting a local rural survey.

The survey considered the county from the points of view of the land, the peoples, the economic life, and the social environment and public services, before finally presenting a series of local, and general, recommendations. Though this survey relates particularly to Herefordshire, its further aim was "to describe a technique which may be usefully applied to a wider field", and it is equally obvious that the technique described is likely to be of useful application to our surveys at a lower level.

Splendid use is made of maps and diagrams, mostly in colour, and although there is not space here to include a broad selection of these, the table below shows a list of the subjects which are treated in diagrammatic form and helps to give an idea of the scope of a large-scale regional survey. In addition, over sixty tables provide further facts and figures which are not included in the diagrams.

THE MAPS AND DIAGRAMS OF A REGIONAL SURVEY

The Land

Location in the West Midlands.
Physiographic regions of the county.
Relation between geology and relief.
Areas with poor aspect and excessive elevation.
Photographs of sub-regions, each with an explanatory diagram.
Geological sections (south-west-north-east and west-east).
Rainfall distribution.
Solid geology (underlying rocks).
Physically difficult areas (showing average slopes).
Land classification (Grades I, II, III).
Landscape survey.
Inaccessibility (from main road plotting distances).
Physical factors (combining the features of the six maps above).

The People

Land-use zones.
Population distribution.

Settlement (agglomerated or dispersed).
Population changes over a number of years (*a*) sub-regions, (*b*) whole
   country.
The Parishes.

Economic Life

Industrial structure (per cent. employed in various occupations).
Agricultural labour: agricultural workers
                     casual labourers
                     employed workers
                     hop pickers (seasonal).
Holdings: small-holdings, small farms, large farms.
Grassland types.
Cattle density—distribution.
Sheep   „   „
Pigs   „   „
Cattle/Sheep ratio.
Utilisation of arable land (related to West Midlands and to whole country).
Land devoted to crops (details given) and livestock.
Distribution (map each) of: wheat, oats, barley, swedes, sugar beet, potatoes,
   market-garden crops, hops, and many varieties of top fruit and small
   fruit.
Forestry Commission holdings.

Social Environment and Public Services

Classification of houses (graded for replacement) for seven urban areas.
Piped water-supply and piped sewerage.
Suggested water-supply scheme.
Gas supplies.
Electricity supplies.
Railway communications with west and south of England.
Main road and rail communications.
Road traffic census.
Daily bus service.
Market day bus service (for four areas).
Public telephones (distance from 'phone).
Land classification and development (near Hereford and six other centres).
Village centres.
Market towns.
Hospital services.
Areas tributary to Secondary Schools.
Reorganisation of Infant and Junior Schools.
Library services.
Women's Institutes and Village Halls.

The following summary of the different sections of the report
emphasises that in every aspect of the survey the relationships between
man and the geography of the region have been carefully considered.

The Land

The Physical Setting. A detailed knowledge of the geographical
background is essential if the facts of human occupation are to be fully
appreciated, and, with this in mind, the Group considered various
aspects of the physical make-up of the county.

The county is remarkably compact, with Hereford at the centre; the greater part being included within a 25 km radius from the city. Its heart is a gently undulating lowland, but bordering it to the south-west and north-west is "bleak and elevated hill country": territory which, through a glimpse of its human occupation in the past, emphasises that the geography and history of any region are closely interwoven; for Border Herefordshire, which contrasts with the remainder in relief, climate, landscape, agriculture, and settlement,

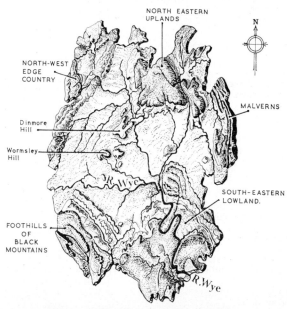

Fig. 114.   THE RELIEF OF HEREFORDSHIRE.

*Compare this with Fig. 115, which shows the surface geology of the county.
(After "English County", by permission of the West Midland Group on Post-War Reconstruction and Planning.)*

stood apart during the Middle Ages and contained semi-independent Marcher Lordships. The physical contrasts between this and the other parts of the county also influence, of course, the modern forms of land-use.

Figs. 114 and 115 clearly show the close relationships between geology and relief. Within the broad division of the lowland areas differences in the underlying rocks result in different soil types, so that, for instance, the economically important central lowland is floored with red marls, giving a heavy and close-textured loam, while the south-eastern lowlands are covered with a lighter sandy soil. We cannot examine the sub-regions in any detail, but there are, naturally, a considerable number with minor contrasts in topography which are none-the-less of singular importance from an agricultural point of view. Thus the twin uplands of Dinmore and Wormsley divide the central

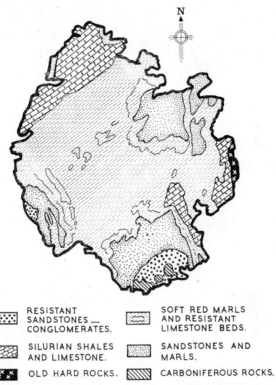

RESISTANT SANDSTONES — CONGLOMERATES.

SILURIAN SHALES AND LIMESTONE.

OLD HARD ROCKS.

SOFT RED MARLS AND RESISTANT LIMESTONE BEDS.

SANDSTONES AND MARLS.

CARBONIFEROUS ROCKS.

Fig. 115.   THE SURFACE GEOLOGY OF HEREFORDSHIRE.
(*After "English County", by permission of the West Midland Group on Post-War Reconstruction and Planning.*)

lowlands into two main sub-regions—the plains of Hereford and Leominster—each showing notable differences in land-use.

Over much of the lowland, glacial drift covers the red marls and includes gravels which are, in places, important both to agriculture and to water-supply. The Wye and its tributaries meander over the lowland, and serve as routeways, as sources of water-supply, and as attractions to fishermen and holiday-makers.

Climate. The county lies in the rain shadow of the Welsh uplands, so that only in the higher west does the rainfall exceed 750 mm (Fig. 116), an isohyet which divides the county into two major regions: a drier, sunnier, eastern region producing wheat, barley, and sugar beet; and a damper western region where the range of crops is restricted, and oats is the principal cereal.

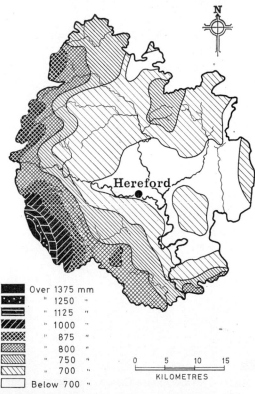

Over 1375 mm
" 1250 "
" 1125 "
" 1000 "
" 875 "
" 800 "
" 750 "
" 700 "
Below 700 "

0   5   10   15
KILOMETRES

Fig. 116. THE ANNUAL RAINFALL—HEREFORDSHIRE.

(*After "English County", by permission of the West Midland Group on Post-War Reconstruction and Planning.*)

The uplands have a markedly shorter growing season than the plains, but have more snow, whose duration is of importance to upland farming. The sunshine in deep valleys is from 15-20 per cent. less than on the plains, and the lack of insolation during winter on many north-facing slopes of the Black Mountains means that settlement is more common on the south-facing slopes.

The distribution of likely "frost pockets", which occur here and there, is of much significance in the fruit-growing districts.

Relief and its Connections with Future Development. The Group considered the following to be of outstanding importance in view of their likely effect upon future land-use:—

(*a*) low-lying positions, liable to flood;

(*b*) degree of elevation;

(*c*) excessive slope; . . . all of which act against development.

Living conditions tend to become arduous above 250 metres, and about 8 per cent. of the county is adjudged unsuitable for settlement on these grounds, together with a further 21 per cent. where the slope is greater than 1 : 10. Maps are presented to show the location of such areas.

Land Resources. In a rural area planning must aim to preserve for agriculture as much high-grade land as possible. With this objective the existing agricultural land was surveyed and divided into three broad categories:—

    I   Good quality—highly productive;

    II   Medium quality—medium productivity;

    III Poor quality—low productivity;

with the subsequent recommendation that land placed in the first two categories be retained for agriculture as far as possible.

Hereford possesses a high proportion of first-class land, so that it is probable that the greatest benefit to the county, and to the country as a whole, will come from "an adequate utilisation of this asset".

The scenic beauty of the countryside must also be safeguarded whenever large-scale development is planned. With this in mind the Group drew up zones from which industries should be excluded, or where only certain specified forms of light industry should be permitted. In fact, it was found that, "on scenic and amenity grounds", development should be controlled over 59 per cent. of the county's surface.

Areas where development would be difficult or undesirable, for one reason or another, were then "sieved out". It was finally decided that there are, in fact, no areas eminently suited to serve as a site for new settlement of any size, and that any necessary development "should take place around existing towns, and especially the smaller centres".

The People

Herefordshire has a population of about 140 000, of whom no less than 54 per cent. live in rural areas, though almost a third are concentrated in the county town. The rural population is spread fairly uniformly over the county, with the most extensive area of close settlement focusing on Hereford, and with a second area of relatively high density in the arable parts of the south-eastern lowlands.

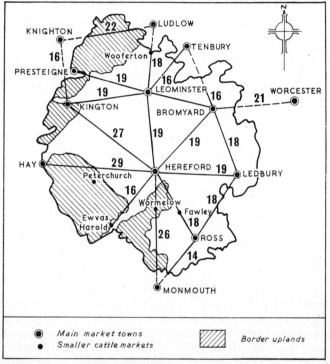

Fig. 117. THE SPACING OF HEREFORDSHIRE MARKET TOWNS.
Numbers indicate the distance between the towns in kilometres.

(After " English County", by permission of the West Midland Group on Post-War Reconstruction and Planning.)

Types of Rural Settlement. The pattern of settlement is disseminated, with small market towns lying some 16-20 kilometres from the county town and from one another (Fig. 117). In the uplands the dispersed settlement is characteristic of the pastoral economy. The only parts devoid of habitations are the higher slopes of the uplands, flood areas, and woodlands.

Local supplies of surface water or spring water are available in almost all parts of the county, thus allowing the scatter of individual farmsteads or cottages, which is typical of much of the Herefordshire countryside. Only locally are supplies sufficient for any large cluster of habitations, so that it is only where river terrace, or glacial gravel provides a dry site, together with adequate water, that the clustered village becomes the characteristic form of settlement. The villages are all clustered, rather than nucleated, settlements, and the exact location of each has been determined by various local facts, such as river or route crossing points.

Where settlement is dispersed or semi-dispersed, planning for the provision of services becomes a difficult matter. One example, typical of the western highlands, is the distribution of sixteen houses over some thousand hectares, making it difficult to provide adequate school, library, or recreational facilities. With such dispersal the market towns play an important part in the lives of the rural community, and their comparatively regular spacing is significant.

Population Changes. In common with many rural areas of England and Wales the county population has decreased, declining 13 per cent. between 1871 and 1951, with the greatest losses from the western uplands. At the same time the city population increased by 50 per cent. Since 1951 increasing farm mechanisation and new urban industrial developments have led to further rural depopulation within the county itself.

Economic Life

Industry. At the time of the survey only about 6 per cent. of the employed population were engaged in manufacturing and mining industries, compared with about 32 per cent. for England and Wales. The county town is pre-eminent as a transport and public utility centre, and all the towns contain distributive trades, building firms, commercial and financial concerns, and professional and entertainment services. There are few minerals, but the rich agricultural resources have given rise to works in the food (jam and fruit preserving), drink (cider making), and leather and skin, orders of industries. Bricks and tiles are made in several parts of the county, and many workers are employed in small branches of agricultural engineering.

The survey found two main reasons why further industries should be set up in the county. Firstly, Herefordshire should play its part in national plans for the dispersion of industry from congested urban areas; secondly, its population, with a low proportion of wage-earners per family, would benefit from chances of further employment. The

Group therefore recommended that carefully selected industries be set up in areas indicated as suitable for industrial development and that these include more agricultural engineering and food processing plants, and factories which need not be located near their source of raw materials, as in the light metal and plastic industries. Since then, a large metal-alloy concern, employing several thousand, has come to Hereford, and other, smaller, factories have opened in Hereford, Leominster, Ross, and Ledbury.

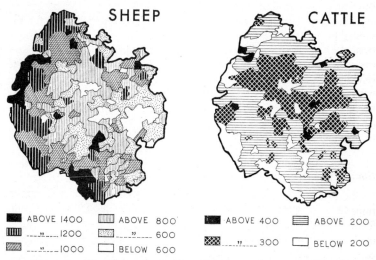

SHEEP   CATTLE

	ABOVE 1400		ABOVE 800
	....."....1200		....."...... 600
	....."....1000		BELOW 600

	ABOVE 400		ABOVE 200
	....."..... 300		BELOW 200

Fig. 118.   The Density and Distribution of Sheep and Cattle in Herefordshire.

(*The figures show the numbers of livestock per thousand acres.*)
Notice the relation between these distributions and the relief of the county (Fig. 114.)

(*After "English County", by permission of the West Midland Group on Post-War Reconstruction and Planning.*)

Agriculture.   Permanent pasture occupies about two-thirds of the agricultural land, and arable farming less than a third.

Cattle are concentrated on the central lowland and have a low density upon the upland districts, whereas the chief areas of sheep-rearing are the poorer hill grasslands of the western and north-eastern parts of the county.   Fig. 118 shows the summer distribution of sheep, and it is worth noting that the winter distribution is different, for many of the sheep are moved to the lowland areas.   The possibility of seasonal changes of this kind should always be borne in mind when making distribution maps.

The survey recorded that much of the grassland, besides the rough upland grazing, was of poor quality, and, although Hereford cattle are hardy and thrive on a relatively poor diet, recommended an extension of a husbandry based upon root crops and improved pastures.

On the arable land wheat and barley are grown chiefly on the lowlands and in the south-east, while oats is typical of the damper and cooler regions, mainly in the western and north-western parts of the county. Roots are already widely grown for livestock. There is no space to reproduce distribution maps for the individual fruit crops, but orchards, chiefly apples, occupy about a sixth of the arable acreage, and hops a thirtieth. The influence of soil types and conditions upon crop distribution is emphasised throughout; hops, for instance, are best suited by the deep, rich, loamy, and close-grained soil of the eastern districts, to which parts they are chiefly confined. The location of the types of apple (cider, dessert, and cooking) also varies with the soil, and the distribution of small fruit (strawberries and blackcurrants) is even more localised. In this connection the investigation into the incidence of "frost pockets" led to the recommendation of change of location for some orchards.

Social Environment and Public Services

The table on pages 292-3 gives some idea of the numerous investigations of a sociological nature which were carried out. Each separate feature, water-supply, communications, social centres, was examined in the light of the geographical elements which are part of the region concerned.

Finally, let a quotation from this survey of an English county emphasise the value of this form of combined geographical and sociological research:—

"The various elements in the physical background of any region exercise a vital influence on man's life and work within that region. Surface relief, character, and arrangement of the underlying rocks, climate and soils, mineral deposits, and water-supply have played, and will continue to play, an important part in determining the operation of human activities. The successful integration, within any region, of human needs and economic and social potentialities must, therefore, be based on full knowledge of the geographical background."

Just as a regional survey of this kind helps to put the facts of geography and of human occupation into perspective for all who are concerned with the future of that region, so may a local survey help the individual geographer to a better appreciation of the relationships between man and his surroundings which are the whole fabric of human geography.

DIFFERENT APPROACHES TO THE STUDY OF

HUMAN GEOGRAPHY

Controversial Viewpoints

The student geographer who has reached the stage where he can attempt to broaden his outlook by individual study, is apt to find a perplexing difference in style between his earlier regional textbooks and the more advanced treatises. Many school libraries include the works of those distinguished geographers who have contributed to the rise, in less than a century, of a definite human geography; but there is often an initial lack of understanding on the part of the student, of the ways in which the authors of the more advanced works may approach the subject. Some attempt should, therefore, be made to give the student an outline of the broad philosophies and methods of approach of different schools of geographers. Once he is able to discriminate between, say, the cruder forms of deterministic approach and the writings of those who accept a "possibilist" view of the relations between man and his environment, there will be less danger of confusion during the early stages of private study. Later he should find these differences stimulating rather than otherwise.

For this reason there is included here an outline of the main points of controversy concerning the extent of the influence of environment upon man's actions. This is presented apart from the main chapters so that it may be used either by way of introduction, or left until the question of the extent of environmental influence is raised in discussion at a later stage.

Reasons for using Quantitative Techniques

Another approach which a student may view with some misgiving is through the collection of quantified data, which enables more precise methods of measurement and analysis to be applied to the problems of human geography and, at least, supplements the verbal descriptions, which must necessarily be subjective.

The danger here is that teachers anxious to inculcate new techniques for processing and presenting data may appear to be offering these as "geographical achievements" per se. The student, justifiably proud of acquiring skill in the application of these techniques, must take care that he keeps his perspective, and remembers that these are simply valuable aids towards understanding the facts and problems of human geography, which still require individual investigations into the relationships between men and their environment—backed by observations and description.

The Main Points of Controversy

The relations between man and his environment and the role played by man himself as part of the whole environment, are the essentials of any study of human geography. There are two principal ways of regarding these relationships, and which we choose to accept depends largely on the answers we find to two basic problems:—

(*a*) Are man's activities invariably controlled by his environment?

(*b*) Is man's own will, his apparent freedom to choose between alternative courses of action, a dominant factor in deciding how and where he will live?

If the truth be a compromise, depending on the circumstances, we must consider to what extent man's free-will (assuming such to exist) liberates him from the influences of his natural surroundings.

Naturally, there is much controversy about the extent of this relationship; but, this being an introduction to human geography, it is perhaps as well to ignore many of the shades of opinion, and simply present the two major contrasting points of view—as black and white.

Determinism

Broadly, one school of thought favours the view that the environment determines the pattern of man's behaviour, so that all his actions, his settlement, his mode of life, are conditioned, however indirectly, by his surroundings.

The scientific developments at the beginning of the eighteenth century were followed by Darwin's theories concerning the origin of man, which, coming together, focused the attention of many geographers upon the relations between man and nature. There are many obvious connections between climate, relief, and soil, and man's houses, communications, and agriculture, and these caused some of the earlier geographers to generalise on such relationships, and later to adopt rather extreme forms of determinism. Their observations caused them to conclude that man's immediate surroundings have a decisive effect not only on his occupations, his dwellings, and the materials he uses in everyday life, but also on his personal traits, his general character, and his religious beliefs; but while in some cases this may be true, their assumptions were often based on incomplete evidence. For example, the apparent slant of the eyes of Mongoloid peoples were attributed to their lengthy occupation of the wide plain-lands of central Asia, where a lifetime spent scanning the horizon, with eyes puckered against the keen, dusty winds was deemed to have wrought permanent change in their features. Modern physiology does not bear this out.

Other conclusions about less tangible human characteristics were superficially more reasonable: such was the environmentalist explanation of the power of the religious orders in Italy, Spain, and Portugal. Here, the fear inspired by natural catastrophes, earthquakes, and volcanoes, was held to have established in man an awe which led to superstition, and thus to have fostered the growth of a class which flourished on local superstitions—the clergy.

Broad generalisations were also made concerning the effects of environment upon the character of men engaged in certain occupations. Some geographers concluded, for instance, that men farming the rich soil of the river valleys are destined to become unambitious and restricted in their outlook—in marked contrast to the inhabitants of the steppe-lands. Pastoral occupations on the broad plateaux allow man time, it was alleged, to contemplate distant horizons, whose limits he then feels urged to explore. In this way he is led to wander, and finally, aided by his own mobility, to attempt "imperial conquests".

The chief faults in the assumptions of the extreme environmentalists lay in over-simplification. Man *is* undoubtedly profoundly affected by physical conditions. Environment *does* strongly affect the nomad, and has almost certainly contributed to the nature of the religious beliefs of such peoples. But assertions of the kind quoted above are too sweeping, and were not, in the main, backed by the careful investigation that modern environmentalists employ in their search for a sequence of events which must lead directly from cause to effect. The examples given above represent the more extreme opinions of a school of determinism which has few followers today, and which went beyond the ideas of the early exponents of environmental control. Nevertheless, these views in themselves, radical as they were when put forward, helped to focus the attention of the systematic geographers, and of the general public, on the ever-present influences of nature on the affairs of man.

Consider two separate areas with approximately the same natural conditions and occupied by peoples of similar cultural development. If environment is all-important we should expect the two landscapes to bear a considerable resemblance to each other. In many parts of the earth, particularly in similar climatic regions, local adaptations in the form of buildings, and in agricultural practices, do, in fact, produce striking resemblances in the appearance of quite separate regions. The small, parched, stony fields surrounding the box-like adobe dwellings in many a north Mexican valley, and the fields which lie about the low squarish houses of sun-baked mud in the dry upper-river basins of north-west Pakistan, form part of landscapes which are far,

far, apart, and yet remarkably similar to each other. Similarly, the pattern of settlement of peoples as far removed from each other as the estuarine Malays and the lowland Indians of northern Colombia, gives a very similar visual impression. The homelands both of these Malays (the Orang Laut, for instance), and of the Colombian Indians, contain riverside villages, with palm-thatched houses built on piles, while their clearings in the forest show the apparent chaos of a mixed peasant agriculture.

The determinist is thus provided with a wealth of materials on which to base a case for rigid environmental control, and such obvious resemblances act as an inducement to the geographer to seek those natural features which will account for such similarities. But the value of comparative studies of this kind depends on the care with which the evidence is examined and the influence of each single geographical element probed, and this procedure can be full of pit-falls. It was such studies which led many of the early determinists to over-emphasise the influence of certain natural features (as in the attempt to account for the form of Mongoloid features).

Whereas some of the early environmentalists were apt to make unsound generalisations, modern determinists are more careful to seek and record, wherever possible, a true sequence from cause to effect. They are aware that man may be subjected to many surrounding influences that are not purely geographical ones. Sometimes geographical influences are not strong, nor their effects obvious, but to the environmentalist these geographical influences are always present as part of the general environment which determines man's course of action. Where the modern determinists differ most radically from the "possibilists" (see below) is in their view of the nature of human "choice". They do not allow that man has complete freedom to choose, but rather that he narrows down alternative courses of action in his mind, and, in selecting one alternative rather than another, is, perhaps subconsciously, influenced by some part of his general environment.

Though we admit that environment has a strong influence on man's behaviour, it is usually very difficult to decide the extent to which any one element is responsible. The following observation, from a description of the peoples of central Borneo, illustrates this point:—

"The hill way of life tends to make people more energetic and virile; thus during the war they proved outstandingly bold as guerillas. On the whole I found these peoples more logical and sensible than any others I know—of course there are many individual exceptions." (Tom Harrisson, D.S.O., "Explorations in Central Borneo", *Geogr. Journ.*, vol. CXIV, p. 129.)

The hills are the outstanding features of the natural environment. But does the hill life in fact *make* the people energetic and virile? It can be argued that the relatively harsh surroundings have brought out latent abilities in those who have striven to overcome them, and that a livelihood exists in the hills for those possessing sufficient energy and alertness to make the most of it. Thus, although environment undoubtedly calls forth a response from these people, it is not necessarily deterministic in the sense of moulding the hill-folk to a definite pattern—and even here there are "many individual exceptions".

After reading the following section, consider this same observation from the "possibilist" point of view.

Possibilism

All geographers would agree that the nature of man's responses to a given environment depends to a large extent on his particular state of cultural advancement, and that man can exploit his natural surroundings only to the extent to which he is mentally and technically equipped. But many geographers, whose views may be termed "possibilist", would add that man's natural surroundings hold inherent possibilities, which some may deliberately choose to develop, and others to ignore; also, because man can make apparently unpredictable decisions, only the most general conclusions can be applied when assessing the probable effect of any particular environment upon mankind.

Possibilism does not deny the influences of environment, but at the same time allows man a selective power, within certain limits, which may vary with the prevailing conditions. Thus, when natural conditions are favourable and offer man many possible ways of exploiting a region, man's choice of, say, a site for settlement may be based upon little more than a whim. But where natural conditions are severe, as in the case of the mountain folk of Borneo, the choice may be between an effort to overcome local hardships or acquiescence and migration.

In areas where natural conditions are not in his favour man's choice of action may be limited, and it is here that environmental elements exert their strongest force. If, for instance, a man is ignorant of the more technical achievements of civilisation, such as the construction of irrigation canals, settlement in a desert area may be possible only in the neighbourhood of oases. In such regions even those with scientific knowledge must fight their hardest against the environment. The effort made must be great, and may succeed or may fail; but, in the case of failure, in view of the continuing progress in all branches of scientific development, the triumph of environment is not likely to be permanent if the incentive to occupy the area is sufficiently strong.

Thus, gold drew the white Australian to Kalgoorlie, but it is his ability to triumph over the climatic features of his environment, by piping water from Mundaring, three hundred miles away, which maintains him there. On the other hand, in Tanzania, the attempt, begun in 1948, to grow groundnuts on a large scale, though backed by many of the most recent developments in agricultural machinery, was baulked by nature. Failure to appreciate the disruptive power of a combination of adverse climatic and soil conditions resulted in acquiescence by man, temporary though it may prove to be.

The belief is that every region possesses a combination of environmental features which offer a number of opportunities, of which man may, or may not, take advantage. It is usually the lack of "know-how" which prevents people from fully exploiting the possibilities of any region. For example, the soils of the northern territories of Ghana have been little utilised as yet, though many areas are basically fertile, and even though there is over-population in Ashanti, to the south. It has taken the modern disc plough and the advice of soil scientists to open up the possibilities of considerable settlement for the native peoples, and allow them to obtain a livelihood which can be based upon crops grown locally on these soils. Yet, in Denmark, the government deliberately altered the form of land-use, turning a grain-producing country, naturally suited to the production of wheat, into a land of highly-organised dairy production; their action, prompted by the competition of cheap grain from the New World, apparently indicating that they had *chosen* to adopt one of several *possible* ways of exploiting the land.

The "possibilist" may well ask how these examples, which are such obvious demonstrations of man's "free will", can owe everything to purely environmental causes. The determinist would probably reply that other causes have interfered with purely geographical ones, leading men to take such actions; and may add that the business of geographers is to concentrate on the examination of those *geographical* facts which can act as determinants of human activity.

A Methodological Approach

Whether philosophically a geographer veers towards a determinist or possibilist view, he must approach any problem in possession of as many relevant facts as possible. But the inter-relations of physical and human phenomena are so complex and the statistics available may be so numerous today, that a methodological approach is essential. The increasing use of quantitative techniques, and the advent of computers, now allows the relationships of large numbers of variables which are not strongly correlated to be put in their proper perspective. The student geographer must, therefore, be prepared to learn such techniques as will help his judgment concerning the interactions of environment and social behaviour.

SUBJECT INDEX

WAR: and road construction, 33; and agriculture, 72; and settlement, 87, 99; and Hong Kong, 144; and boundaries, 190, 196-7; effect on population numbers, 204; and regional plans, 229; strategic positions and, 255-67.

Water: **18-26**; as moat, 10; supply and settlement, 18-26, 88, 89, 98, 136, 139, 141-3, 144, 149, 159, 200-2, 288, 295, 299, 307; catchment, 19-20; ground, 19-21, 23-4, 98; run-off, 19-21, 144, 218, 220, 223, 226; and ranching, 70; pollution, 20, 55, 117; power, grindstones, 116 (see also: *Hydro-electricity*); transport (see: *Shipping*).

Well: 19, 24, 88, 98, 136, 286.

White Settlement, in the Tropics: 220, 235-45, **246-9**, 249-53.

Wind: **5-6**; and sailing, 42; and air transport, 44; and settlement, 89, 94, 96; Föhn, 96; typhoon, 145; Trade Winds, 242; and steppe dwellers, 303.

Wind-break: 217, 223, **224**, 233-4.

Wind Erosion: **217-9**, 223-4, 233-4.

World: population, 197; cultivable area, **203**, 204-9, 210.

ZONES: rural land-use, 60-2; urban land-use, 119-24.

PLACE NAME INDEX